Black Power,
Jewish Politics

Brandeis Series in American Jewish History, Culture, and Life

JONATHAN D. SARNA, Editor
SYLVIA BARACK FISHMAN, Associate Editor

For a complete list of books that are available in the series,
visit www.upne.com

Black Power, Jewish Politics

REINVENTING
THE ALLIANCE IN
THE 1960S

MARC DOLLINGER

Brandeis University Press | *Waltham, Massachusetts*

Brandeis University Press
An imprint of University Press of New England
www.upne.com
© 2018 Brandeis University
All rights reserved
Manufactured in the United States of America
Designed by Eric M. Brooks
Typeset in Merope by Passumpsic Publishing
The Merope fonts are Charles Ellertson's modifications
of the open-source version of the Alegreya fonts designed
by Juan Pablo del Peral.

For permission to reproduce any of the material in this book,
contact Permissions, University Press of New England, One Court
Street, Suite 250, Lebanon NH 03766; or visit www.upne.com

Library of Congress Cataloging-in-Publication Data
NAMES: Dollinger, Marc, 1964– author.
TITLE: Black power, Jewish politics: reinventing the alliance in
    the 1960s / Marc Dollinger.
DESCRIPTION: Waltham, Massachusetts: Brandeis University Press,
    [2018] | Series: Brandeis Series in American Jewish History,
    Culture, and Life. | Includes bibliographical references and index.
IDENTIFIERS: LCCN 2017043057 (print) | LCCN 2017043441 (ebook) |
    ISBN 9781512602586 (epub, mobi, & pdf) | ISBN 9781512602562
    (cloth: alk. paper) | ISBN 9781512602579 (pbk.: alk. paper)
SUBJECTS: LCSH: African Americans—Relations with Jews. | Jews—
    United States—History—20th century. | African Americans—
    History—20th century. | Black power—United States. |
    United States—Race relations—History—20th century. |
    United States—Ethnic relations.
CLASSIFICATION: LCC E184.36.A34 (ebook) | LCC E184.36.A34 D65
    2018 (print) | DDC 305.800973—dc23
LC record available at https://lccn.loc.gov/2017043057

5 4 3 2 1

This book is dedicated to my parents,

DRS. MALIN AND LENORE DOLLINGER,

who instilled a social conscience in the suburbs,

spoke some truth at a Globetrotters game,

and delivered me to Berkeley,

where this project began.

This book grows from my own development as a student of Jewish social justice. Raised during the 1970s in a Los Angeles suburb that counted few Jews and even fewer African Americans, I learned to idolize Dr. Martin Luther King Jr. as a modern-day prophet. Stories of Jim Crow segregation with "whites only" drinking fountains countered by the tireless efforts of civil rights workers taught me the most basic lesson in right and wrong. Racists, I learned in my elementary-school years, judged blacks because of the color of their skin, turned fire hoses on protestors, and supported the renewed version of the Ku Klux Klan. Social justice activists watched the film clips of police brutality with horror, supported African American organizations dedicated to racial equality, and self-reflected on the disproportionate role played by American Jews in the struggle.

My interest in civil rights, race relations, and the black-Jewish alliance focused as well during my early religious-school education. Each Sunday morning, my mom loaded up the station wagon and drove her four young children to Temple Beth El, located in a majority Latino neighborhood of San Pedro, California. Our teachers, in an approach typical of the decade, tended to focus on three curricular subjects: the Jewish holidays, the Holocaust, and the State of Israel. To be a good Jew demanded that we live according to the Jewish calendar, remember the Six Million, and, after inserting ten quarters into the Jewish National Fund cardboard "Tree in Israel" cutout, dream about making pilgrimage to the Promised Land. (What a heartbreaking day when I walked into the synagogue office to find my Israel tree certificate in the secretary's typewriter. My tree dedication, it turned out, did not arrive from the Promised Land. It happened just down the hall. Only much later in life did I learn it would take the donation of a 10,000-tree forest to get an acknowledgment from Israel.)

Especially in middle school, prophetic Judaism, the Reform movement's emphasis on the centrality of social justice to our religious expression, guided the curriculum. Old enough to trade Sunday mornings for Tuesday evenings, we learned how so many Jews risked their lives to protest segregation and how, in the shadow of the Holocaust especially, each of us needed to do our part to ensure that no one faced persecution again, Never Again! Jewish pride centered an affective approach to Jewish education: as long as we *felt* good about our Jewishness, then the rest would take care of itself. And we felt very good about the partisans who resisted the Nazis during the Holocaust, the early pioneers who realized a Jewish homeland in the State of Israel, and the Jewish civil rights workers (and even a few martyrs) who understood that it was a Jew's obligation to reach across the racial divide to help other oppressed groups.

In those years, I knew nothing of the South or the African Americans who lived there. Tucked away in suburbia, I remained insulated as well from the growing conflicts between blacks and Jews in the urban North and the ways race and racism played out in extra-legal ways. The concept of institutional racism and the powerful yet subtle ways it maintained racial privilege for whites proved too elusive to know or understand in a political culture that distinguished racists from reformers in a simple ethical binary. Never did I hear or learn about the limits of liberalism or the ways it too contributed to the racial status quo.

The early 1970s emerged as a time of great social unrest. The optimism of the protest movements of the 1950s and early 1960s faded into a radicalized political culture that encouraged some to folks to turn on, tune in, and drop out. Others followed a path to violence. For my parents and their friends, the assassinations of Dr. King and Bobby Kennedy signaled the end of an era. From their perspectives, the hope that framed an earlier decade faded away with urban rioting, ethnic splintering, and the rise of the silent majority's neo-Conservatism. My eight-year-old mind only knew the political culture of the 1970s. The pivotal events of 1968 seemed to me a distant part of history.

With this as prelude, I arrived on the campus of UC Berkeley to begin my undergraduate studies in the fall of 1982. The home of the Free Speech Movement, Cal-Berkeley boasted Upper Sproul Plaza, site of Mario Savio's most impassioned speeches and, in the years that followed, the campus center of political activism. Along its famed walkway, various student groups "tabled," distributing flyers and other information for interested classmates. My first stop: the Jewish Student Board, where opportunities abounded for Jewish ethnic and religious identity. Soviet Jewry activists promised they would rally in front of the Soviet Embassy on Green Street in San Francisco. The Israel Action Committee pressed for a progressive form of Zionism that defended the Jewish state even as it winced at Israel's recent invasion of Lebanon. Dina Levine, of blessed memory, a member of the Jewish co-op "Berkeley Bayit," invited new students to one of its regular "Open Shabbat" potluck dinner experiences at its Julia Morgan–designed home.

And all around, student groups of every sort appealed for new members, including the Black Student Union, which, in the culture of Berkeley, called itself the African Student Union (ASU), even though almost every one of its members proved U.S. born. Eager to synthesize the moral imperative of the civil rights movement, the impressive work of my fellow Jews in the struggle, and my own burgeoning identity as an activist Jew, I walked over to the ASU table and introduced myself to my African American counterpart.

"Let's start a black-Jewish dialogue," I proclaimed, offering to partner in an education effort between our two persecuted minorities.

He burst out laughing.

And kept laughing . . .

Until, I have to believe, he saw the shock, horror, and embarrassment on my face . . . and, with compassion, did all he could to control himself.

In an attempt to ease a really awkward moment, he smiled and let me know, "Hey, I'm from Harlem," assuming I would know what that meant.

On one level, I did know.

While I certainly understood Harlem as an African American neighborhood in New York City, I first learned of that locale from the famed Harlem Globetrotters basketball team. Each year, they played games at Inglewood, California's "Fabulous Forum," home to Wilt Chamberlain and Jerry West's NBA-champion L.A. Lakers. How exciting to venture with my family to witness the basketball and showmanship magic of the world-famous and (almost) never-losing team. The skill and antics of Meadowlark Lemon and Fred "Curly" Neal offered me an early course direction for life. With excited focus after the game, I proclaimed to my mom: "When I grow up, I'm going to be a Harlem Globetrotter." And, in my first experience of race rejection, my mom told me I couldn't. Only black people can be Harlem Globetrotters, she explained. At that point, at least, I understood that the Globetrotters were black, I was white, and the difference meant something.

Later, I learned of the Harlem Renaissance, of the development of jazz, and the race-tinged lyrics "high brows from down the levee, all misfits" in Irving Berlin's original version of "Puttin' on the Ritz." I studied the cultural import of the Apollo theater as a center of African American expression and the pained memories of Washington Height's Audubon Ballroom, the site of Malcolm X's assassination. In Professor Waldo Emerson Martin's UC Berkeley seminar on black culture and consciousness, I expanded my interest in African American history beyond New York City by joining a dozen classmates on a journey through the civil rights movement with one of its historical actors, the former student body president of James B. Dudley High School in Greensboro, North Carolina, where the FBI infiltrated campus elections.

Of course, the ASU student's reference to his Manhattan neighborhood meant more than simple geography. It communicated and reflected two generations of black-Jewish divide that followed passage of the Civil Rights Act, the Voting Rights Act, and the death of Dr. King. It focused a fundamental difference in upbringing between urban New York City and suburban Los Angeles, between African American youth and American Jewish teenagers. Blacks from New York, I understood quickly, did not see the social justice world through the same lens as white Jewish liberals.

In a gesture of kindness, my Harlem interlocutor offered to pitch my request for a black-Jewish dialogue to his club members, even as he let me know that he didn't think anyone would be interested.

"Thanks for the offer," I answered, "but there's no need."

And that ended the UC Berkeley black-Jewish dialogue.

This book responds to that moment.

It seeks to reframe the history of black-Jewish relations in a new generational context, seeking the views of those too young to have known King or his famed rabbinic partner, Abraham Joshua Heschel. It demands a reinterpretation of the black-Jewish civil rights alliance from the perspective of those raised in its wake. In a 1970s generation defined by residential and associational divide, few Jews engaged with African Americans as part of their primary friendship networks. In those years, the warm memories of the famed black-Jewish alliance of the Martin Luther King Jr. years did not endure as much in the African American community as they did within the confines of my religious school classrooms.

Rather than looking forward to a vision of interracial understanding, this project reflects back on a coalition that splintered. It reconsiders even the early postwar era with knowledge that the racial differences between blacks and Jews that split the coalition in the mid-1960s existed from the very start of the movement. In this account, the classic story of blacks and Jews marching together to forge a just nation reframes to a narrative of different groups with often-conflicting experiences of America. The coalition's splintering, rather than a sad end to a hopeful moment, reemerges as an inevitable, if necessary, development as each social justice–minded partner journeyed through the rough and tumble of American politics in the 1960s.

Historiography, at its essence, reflects competing generational approaches to an historic moment. I offer this personal recollection to locate myself in the historian's ever-developing understanding of postwar Jewish social reform efforts. Or, as my dissertation chair Regina Morantz-Sanchez reflected to me in my early work, scholars tend to write as self-discovery. This book follows that observation, focusing on Jewish social justice activism through the lens of those too young to have participated in the movements. By definition, then, it avoids the conflicted perspectives of authors who can remember the historical events or, in some cases, even participated in them. Yet, by the same token, my generational understanding creates its own limitations, waiting to be challenged yet again when the next group of scholars takes a fresh look at the subject.

The research and initial writing of this book was made possible by Princeton University's Center for the Study of Religion, where director Robert Wuthnow and associate director Marie Griffith extended a remarkable offer to spend a year in residence as a research fellow. Joined by six colleagues investigating different aspects of American religion, I enjoyed weekly seminars, invaluable feedback, and close proximity to the impressive archival holdings of the American Jewish Historical Society located at the Center for Jewish History in New York City. My time in residence at Princeton gave initial form to this book just as it, in a much larger sense, transformed my academic career.

Professor Marc Lee Raphael invited me to share this book's thesis at a consultation on the campus of William and Mary College. With the critical comments of colleagues gathered around a table once used by Thomas Jefferson himself, I sharpened my argument, learned about valuable new primary and secondary sources, and joined a community of scholars passionate about how American Jews interacted with other ethno-religious groups. That overview, "'Is It Good for the Jews?' Liberalism and the Challenges of the 1960s," later appeared as part of his edited volume, *Jewishness and the World of "Difference" in the United States*.[1]

Barry Glassner and Hilary Taub Lachoff published "'Until You Can Fight as Generals': American Jews and Black Nationalism, 1958–1964," which developed into chapter 1 of this book, as part of *The Jewish Role in American Life: An Annual Review*, volume 3. An earlier version of the Great Society chapter enjoyed publication in *American Jewish History* as "The Other War: American Jews, Lyndon Johnson, and the Great Society." Research for chapter 4 also contributed to "From Berkeley to the Beit Midrash: Jews and the California Counterculture" as part of *California Jews*, which I co-edited with Ava Kahn.[2]

Research funds made possible by the Richard and Rhoda Goldman Chair in Jewish Studies and Social Responsibility at San Francisco State University limited my teaching load and guaranteed the research dollars necessary to complete the manuscript. The university's administration supported my sabbatical leave and Jewish Studies department chair Professor Fred Astren crafted a professional work schedule that encouraged scholarship.

The professional staff of San Francisco's Jewish Community Library, a project of Jewish LearningWorks and located on the campus of the Jewish Community High School of the Bay, opened early, closed late, and offered unending support through the writing process. Thank you especially to library director Howard Freedman, reader services librarian Rose Katz, as well as JCHS librarians Adele Dorison and Robin Gluck. Thank you as well to the professionals of the American Jewish Archives in Cincinnati, especially senior archivist Kevin Proffitt, and the staff of the American Jewish Historical Society and the YIVO Institute at New York City's Center for Jewish History.

Professor Bruce Schulman remains my gold standard for scholarship, education, and the life of a public intellectual. Professor Milton Brown opened my eyes to Malcolm X and his generation. Ilana Kaufman helped me understand contemporary race relations, especially among Jews of color. Phyllis Deutsch of Brandeis University Press has guided my thinking and writing through three projects now. She seems to know exactly when to exert pressure . . . and when to offer an encouraging word at the most challenging moment. Thank you for knowing the difference. Shaul

Magid, whose work I have always admired, offered incisive comments on the manuscript, as did the anonymous reader from Brandeis University Press. Howard Simon, a scholar of Jewish history, social ethics, and, of course, grammar, pushed a fine-tooth comb through the manuscript several times over. Just for teaching me the difference between "less" and "fewer," I am grateful (as are my students, who no longer make the same mistake).

Marci Levine Dollinger, an English major from Brandeis University and an elementary-school teacher who gets to teach her students how to read, offered empathy, encouragement, and, when this project reached publication stage, joyous celebration. Our daughters, Rivi and Shayna, grew up with this book and, I hope, reflect its social justice lessons in their own lives.

Of course, I thank an anonymous but influential former member of UC Berkeley's African Student Union.

Black Power,
Jewish Politics

Is It Good
for the Jews?
Black Power
and the 1960s

n a February 1972 contribution to *Commentary* magazine, editor and leading Jewish neoconservative thinker Norman Podhoretz posed the question "Is it good for the Jews?" as the frame for an analysis of contemporary American Jewish life. To Podhoretz, the query seemed "as old, in all probability, as the Jewish Diaspora itself." Indeed, this well-known phrase established, and continues to animate, a baseline for Jews to navigate their relationships with the larger cultures that have surrounded them. Over the last three and a half centuries of American Jewish history, the question has provided a basic and vital litmus test for the political candidates, government programs, and social trends developing around the country. Jews could rest more comfortably knowing a benevolent government understood its obligation to its religious minorities.[1]

Yet, the significance of Podhoretz's article relies less on the self-interested question he posed and more on his decision to write about it in the pages of a widely read Jewish periodical. Even as he may not have been aware of the point, Podhoretz reflected a fundamental shift in American Jewish political culture: the transformation of Jewish self-interest and advocacy from the private sphere to the public square. Although "is it good for the Jews?" may have resonated since the Second Temple's destruction, the question typically was asked only within limited Jewish spaces. When Jews gathered together in their synagogues, around their dinner tables, or at social occasions, they certainly bantered back and forth about how larger developments resonated with them as Jews. Self-interest, though, demanded a level of discretion.[2]

For much of their history, Jews navigated a civic existence dependent upon the policies of government leaders who most often pushed the Jewish population to the margins of society. The closed corporate communities of medieval Europe, for example, relegated Jews to a second-tier status based solely upon their group identity. The creation of ghettos, the imposition of onerous "Jew taxes," and broad limitations on Jewish education and professional life reflected a political structure that refused to recognize individual rights. Similarly, Europe's eighteenth-century Enlightenment promised civil equality in a Christian-dominated society only to backtrack when government leaders mandated Jewish conversion to Christianity as a prerequisite for emancipation.[3]

Even in the United States, where American Jewish historians often claim an exceptionalist experience, Jews still tended to keep the politics of their ethno-religious heritage discreet. The natural rights provision in the Declaration of Independence and the church-state separation edicts of the U.S. Constitution gave Jews a platform for religious freedom that encouraged their continuing assimilation into American life. For generations, American Jews grew up learning that the category "Jewish" meant one's religious identification, while one's nationalist loyalties, for example, belonged to the U.S. government. Anything different risked charges of dual loyalty. As a result, Jews relegated themselves to minority status, accommodating their own sense of American Jewish identity to the church-state divide. When they needed religious protection, they claimed legal cover. But when their particularist needs as Jews demanded greater activism, they balked, unable to advance Jewish interests without apology or compromise.

In the postwar era that most directly informed Podhoretz's observation, the nation rallied behind a liberal anti-Communist consensus that touted the impressive economic expansion powered by the capitalist system. Democrats and Republicans alike shared fears of Soviet expansionism and a triumphalist embrace of American democracy as a social panacea for other nations to emulate. When Jim Crow–style racism threatened to besmirch the image of America as a safe haven for the dispossessed, the dominant political ideology of the 1950s helped nationalize the civil rights movement. If U.S. officials, and the public at large, charged Soviet authorities with civil rights abuses in the Eastern Bloc, then the entire nation needed to mobilize in defense of African Americans who offered an easy opportunity for Russian propagandists to undermine American democracy, capitalism, and exceptionalism. The rise of the civil rights movement testified to American democracy's ability to identify its shortcomings and solve them. Unlike the Soviet Union and its allies, Cold War–era patriots explained, the United States offered a nation that promoted free expression, limited the abusive power of government, and drew its citizens together for the common good.

American Jews celebrated this postwar consensus, keeping any sense of ethnic activism private. If Jews were to integrate into their new suburban surroundings, they needed to find common ties with their new neighbors. To that end, rabbis joined Christian clergy in National Brotherhood Week. Jewish religious leaders cited Will Herberg's classic 1955 volume *Protestant, Catholic, Jew* to press the case for Jewish religious conformity. Even though Jews represented only some 3 percent of the overall population, the rising popularity of phrases such as the "Judeo-Christian ethic" solidified their privileged status as one-third of the nation's religious triad. Among parents, resisting efforts of public Jewish expression sometimes put them in conflict with classical interpretations of church-state separation. When Jewish self-defense agencies protested public school demands that Jewish children participate in Christmas observances, some Jewish parents pushed back, demanding that their children join as an affirmation of their new American status.[4]

In the North, the well-known Jewish liberal support for the civil rights movement also reflected a focusing of Jewish political activism toward more universalist goals. By joining hands with African American leaders such as Dr. Martin Luther King Jr., Jews modeled a definition of ethno-religious identity that situated "is it good for the Jews" within a larger context of consensus-based social justice activism. While Jews certainly claimed distinctive religious imperatives as their rationale for engagement, they entered political activism with a public affirmation that what was good for America was by definition good for the Jews. Support for civil rights meant that Jews understood what it meant to be American. Their obligation as Jews demanded they focus their political activism on the "other" rather than themselves.[5]

On the international scene as well, American Jews shied away from strong public Judeo-centered positions. When Jewish defense groups wanted to press for better treatment of Jews around the world, they tended to frame their public appeals in the language of universal human rights rather than the particular threats of antisemitism. As Jewish communal leaders helped fashion the United Nations charter, for example, they lobbied for a document that ensured American-style protections of democratic government, religious freedom, and equal protection under the law. With those overarching guarantees, the rights and privileges of Jewish communities around the world would enjoy the protections they needed. The strength of Cold War anti-Communism encouraged Jewish leaders to leverage the power of the nation's dominant political ideology to advance, in more subtle and tacit ways, priorities that would prove "good for the Jews."[6]

Early academic work on postwar Jewish political life, written in many cases by participants in the era's various social protest movements, tended to emphasize the symmetry between Cold War–era American democracy and the ethical imperatives of the Jewish people. Murray Friedman's *What Went Wrong?*, for example, noted the disproportionate influence exerted by American Jews in grassroots liberal activism, philanthropy, and electoral politics, celebrating "the Jewish phase of the civil rights revolution." Friedman and others touted an exceptionalist thesis, lauding Jews for sacrificing their time, money, and in a few well-known cases, their lives, in order to guarantee the equal treatment of African Americans. These books reaffirmed the idealistic image of America as a land of opportunity and the Jewish community's central responsibility in helping to achieve it.[7]

Despite such self-congratulations, even in the 1950s the political behavior of American Jews failed that prophetic standard. Southern Jews, for example, embraced Dixie more than they did any sort of northern-based Jewish political exceptionalism. Although scholars such as Mark Bauman and Berkeley Kalin have noted the import of "quiet voices" seeking social change in the South, the overarching public silence of southern Jews on the civil rights question challenges self-serving theses that equate Judaism with the social justice imperative. Northern Jews faced their own political challenges as well. Although the overwhelming majority of northern Jews boasted of their support of civil rights, most experienced that movement from the safety and comfort of their living rooms, where they read about the direct-action protests in the newspaper or watched images on their televisions. As southern Jews already knew, it was one thing to offer verbal support for civil rights and quite another to engage it in your own backyard, with one's livelihood, and perhaps safety, at risk.[8]

Podhoretz could not have titled his article "Is It Good for the Jews?" in the immediate postwar years. Its explicit acknowledgment of Jewish-centered public activism collided with the larger accomodationist desire for American Jews to assimilate into the larger Cold War consensus. As late as 1960, respondents to an American Jewish Committee (AJC) request to define "who is a Jew" offered the universalist qualities of "ethical behavior, general humanitarianism and keen civic spirit." At a time when instances of antisemitism plummeted, once restrictive suburban housing covenants eased, and American Jews enjoyed an unprecedented opportunity to join the nation's mainstream, few contemplated an activist stance that would shine the spotlight on Jewish particularism. If American Jews wondered whether a political issue proved "good for the Jews," they most likely limited those discussions to their coreligionists.[9]

Within just a decade, though, "Is it good for the Jews?" morphed from a private conversation among Jews to a public proclamation of ethnic and religious identity. Against a backdrop of radical social change, the consensus-based political alliances of the 1950s and early 1960s gave way to the rise of identity politics. Group-based status emerged as political currency when African American activists pressed their communal agenda into the public square without compromise or apology. Latino students formed Mecha as an activist expression of Chicano student empowerment. The American Indian Movement (AIM) claimed its historic rights to ancient lands while the group Indians of All Tribes succeeded in a nineteen-month takeover of Alcatraz Island in San Francisco Bay. The gay rights movement emerged after the 1969 Stonewall riots, while feminism enjoyed a resurgence in the early 1970s with the creation of the National Organization for Women.

Among American Jews, the rise of group-based identity politics upset an historic affinity for consensus-based liberalism that forged an alliance between African Americans and Jews in the civil rights movement. With the rise of black militancy in the mid-1960s, the interracial effort splintered among reciprocal charges of black antisemitism and Jewish racism. American Jews, the nation's most liberal white ethnic group, flinched when a new generation of civil rights reformers embraced Black

Power, a separatist ideology that demanded African American leadership, distrusted white liberals, and held special contempt for Jews, who were sometimes accused of aligning themselves with blacks for the sole purpose of improving their own social standing. White purges from historic civil rights organizations alienated Jewish activists who lamented the end of Dr. King's vision of interracial cooperation.[10]

Across the organizational spectrum, American Jewish leaders reflected on the demise of consensus-based movements and the rise of identity politics. Although a third of Chicago's suburban Jews polled in the 1950s considered liberalism "essential" to the definition of a "good Jew," a national survey of Reform Jews conducted twenty years later revealed a far different story: a majority told pollsters that one's liberal orientation "makes no difference," while those who considered liberalism "essential" numbered only 15 percent. Conservative movement rabbi Harold Schulweis, a progressive theologian who used his Oakland, California, pulpit to condemn recalcitrant Jewish slumlords in the late 1960s, reassessed his coreligionists' historic affinity for political cooperation across racial lines. "Pulpits and pews in the '70s resonate to messages different from those of the '50s and '60s," Schulweis observed. "The voice of the liberal is muted." For Schulweis, the embrace of identity politics announced the demise of classic liberal individualism: "The Enlightenment vision of a constantly progressing universal society calling for Jews to involve themselves in the battle for social justice," he lamented, "is now interpreted as suicidal."[11]

Leaders of the Reform movement, well known for their high-profile support of the civil rights movement, also took pause. In 1976, the movement's rabbinic organization, the Central Conference of American Rabbis (CCAR), noting the Jewish community's rapid economic ascent as well as the loss of Israel's "underdog status in the Middle East," lamented that "the community's selfish interests diverge significantly from the dictates of abstract universalism." With that shift came a reevaluation of the Reform movement's prophetic-driven impulse for social reform activism. "Until the recent past," the rabbinic group explained, "our obligations to the Jewish people and to all humanity seemed congruent. At times now these two perspectives appear to conflict."[12]

In the Reform movement and the nation at large, Jews faced critical new challenges to their ethno-religious identity. For the first time in their experience on American shores, Jews wondered, as the CCAR did, whether they were "primarily members of a tribe, Americans, or 'citizens of the world.'" Jewish leftist writer, academic, and *Moment* magazine founder Leonard Fein put it in even starker terms: "The last decade of cacophony has effectively destroyed the simple, and somewhat simple-minded, liberal myth of the first half of this century." For Fein, the race-based tensions so prevalent in the late 1960s pointed to one of liberalism's major failures: its inability to solve racial inequality through the legislative process. "Among the many lessons we are now beginning to learn," Fein wrote, "is that even with the best of will and the most amply funded of government programs, group conflict persists." For many American Jews, it seemed, the transformation of 1960s American liberalism from images of blacks and Jews marching together to black antisemitism, urban riots, and government-sponsored quota programs failed the "Is it good for the Jews?" test.[13]

What started as nonviolent civil rights protests in the 1950s developed by the mid-1960s into the apparent balkanization of American life. The growth of identity politics splintered activists into well-defined ethno-racial factions distrustful of one another. As Earl Raab, director of San Francisco's Jewish Community Relations Council (JCRC), reflected, the role of Jews as social justice reformers "became increasingly fuzzy as the 1950s yielded to the 1960s." African Americans, he explained, needed to "detach themselves from the marching army" because their interests differed from their white allies. Ultimately, Raab concluded, a new generation of black leaders demanded "a different drummer" in their march to justice. By 1971, those divergent political paths led American Jews to place antisemitism, the security of Israel, and the fate of Soviet Jews as high priorities while black-Jewish relations and "conditions of other minority groups" rated a low level of concern.[14]

Despite the widespread belief that the black-Jewish alliance fractured in the mid-1960s, leading African Americans toward a nationalist political orientation and Jews back to their classic individual-based liberalism, I argue that the rise of Black Power forged a new, powerful, and transformative partnership between the two communities. American Jews borrowed pages from the Black Power handbook and reinvented themselves as a strong, focused advocacy group intent on challenging the American Jewish status quo and building stronger and deeper connections to Judaism and Jewish life. At its most fundamental level, the rise of black nationalist thinking opened the door for Jews, as well as other ethnic, racial, and gender groups, to embrace identity politics for their own communal benefit. Simply put, Jews could only ask "Is it good for the Jews?" in public spaces because black activists paved the road for them to do so. As a result, Jews embarked on an ethnic, religious, and cultural revival that carried them through the 1970s and beyond. If "black was beautiful," to quote the popular expression of the time, then so too was Jewish.[15]

Black Power buoyed Jews, who saw in it an unprecedented opportunity for Jewish-centered activism. While Jewish leaders in the early civil rights movement trumpeted the essential similarities between African Americans and American Jews, a new paradigm emerged in the wake of Black Power that acknowledged and even celebrated the differences between the two groups. Jewish leaders envisioned a better and stronger future for their own constituents if only they learned from the work of black militants. As Leonard Fein opined in a 1969 address to the Synagogue Council of America (SCA), Jews could benefit from "the new Negro assertiveness." Though Black Power activists did not intend to strengthen American Jewish life, Fein understood that if their call for greater autonomy proved successful, then Jews proved "likely to be among its unintended beneficiaries." The emerging black-Jewish relationship helped frame an approach to democratic pluralism that offered what Fein described as "more elbow room for Jewish assertiveness."[16]

Jewish religious and thought leaders backed Fein's analysis. In a 1971 High Holiday sermon, Rabbi Dov Peretz Elkins of Philadelphia's Har Zion congregation embraced Black Power thinking when he, too, lamented the historical passivity of his own religious community. "For almost a century," Elkins offered his congregants, "we Jews have asked America to let us be Jews, to let us have our share in shaping America and the world." Thanks to the activist political culture innovated by Black Power, Elkins reflected, Jews enjoyed new opportunities to press their own communal agenda. While Jews in the 1950s sought ways to assimilate into suburban America, Jews in the 1970s could, as Elkins pressed, "*demand* the right to be Jews, to be proud, loyal, and *active* Jews."[17]

In a variety of political movements and efforts, American Jews turned inward, borrowing from Black Power ideology, strategy, and tactics to advance their own particularist causes. As journalist Gil Beckerman explained, Black Power emerged as a catalyst for Jews who "were becoming much more assertive and proud" during a 1960s "turn inward." Even as many Jews rejected the separatism of black militancy, Beckerman noted that it inspired other Jews to emulate its approach. Throughout the country and across all denominational lines, a new generation of Jewish youth emerged with few of the inhibitions that inspired their parents to keep their Judaism private. On college campuses across the country, Jewish students stepped away from the free speech and civil rights movements in favor of grassroots efforts to strengthen Jewish education, even when doing so meant challenging the established Jewish leadership of their communities. As Jewish student leaders Bill Novak and Robert Goldman observed, "Those who previously had been fighting everybody else's battles started to pay attention to questions involving their own identities."[18]

The rise of Black Power sparked a Jewish religious revival as well. As blacks embraced African names, clothes, and hairstyles, young Jews pressed for their own return to tradition, creating a network of Jewish day schools, many from the once-assimilationist Reform movement. Synagogues revitalized their worship services with modern liturgy, guitar music, and even an occasional drum for added spiritual effect. With the rise of the modern feminist movement in the early 1970s, groups such as Ezrat Nashim challenged the male-dominated power structures of organized Judaism and eventually won ordination of women at the Jewish Theological Seminary (JTS), joining their sisters at the Reform movement's Hebrew Union College–Jewish Institute of Religion (HUC) and the Reconstructionist Rabbinical College. Even Orthodox Jews, historically absent from the public square of political activism, emerged in this period as an "ethnic pressure group, much the same in character as other ethnic groups."[19]

Black nationalism also encouraged Jews to rethink their relationship to Zionism, especially when news of Israel's dramatic victory in the 1967 Six-Day War reached an American Jewish youth purged from leadership in several important civil rights organizations. While American Zionism met historic resistance over dual-loyalty concerns, the rise of Black Power–inspired identity politics recast the nation's approach to pluralist democracy. By the late 1960s, Jews, thanks to black activists, could press for their own nationalist agendas without compromising their status as loyal Americans because Jewish affinity for the State of Israel aligned with the nation's emerging identity-centered political culture. In an ironic twist, Black Power's embrace of the Palestinian cause and turn against Zionism only strengthened an American Jewish support for Israel enabled by black nationalists themselves.[20]

In the wake of the Black Power purge of Jewish liberals, American Jews internationalized the civil rights movement to focus on the particular needs of Soviet Jews, pressing the Communist superpower to improve its record on human rights and antisemitism. As the generation of Jewish youth in the 1950s and early 1960s looked to the American South as the locus of their political activism, college-age Jews a decade later directed their political activism to the needs of their brethren in eastern Europe. When African American militants demanded control of their own civil rights organizations, Jewish activists followed suit, wondering which political cause made sense for them in the emerging identity-politics era. If African Americans proclaimed that the movement to guarantee racial equality in the United States belonged to blacks, then Jewish Americans responded with the assertion that the religious rights of Jews belonged to them. Because American Jews already enjoyed constitutionally protected religious freedom while Soviet Jews did not, they turned their attention to Moscow, Leningrad, and beyond.[21]

Even those American Jews who seemed to be on the opposite end of the political spectrum benefited from the rise of Black Power. Just as the rise of black nationalism inspired American Jews to strengthen their relationship to the State of Israel, it also emboldened nationalist proclivities of Jews in the United States. When the Jewish flight to the suburbs left working-class and elderly Jews behind in America's economically depressed and largely African American urban centers, the Jewish Defense League (JDL) organized as a right-wing, grassroots, identity-centered organization determined to assert the particular rights of marginalized Jews in the same fashion as did black activists in the African American community.

The JDL led the call to free Soviet Jews, accusing mainstream national Jewish organizations of timidity for their less-confrontational approaches to the Soviet Union and took to the streets to protect poor urban Jews otherwise abandoned by their more affluent, suburban-dwelling coreligionists. While the JDL opposed almost every policy position of black nationalists, it celebrated ethno-centrism and considered itself a Jewish version of Black Power. In its opposition to group status based social programs that excluded Jews, support for law and order as a remedy for continued civil rights protests, and calls for recognition of white ethnicity, JDL members as well as other Jewish conservatives simply reconfigured the contours of Black Power for their own purposes.[22]

The American Jewish turn inward moved Podhoretz's question to center stage. Reflecting the newfound acceptability of Black Power–inspired ethnic advocacy, American Jews demanded that their activism focus without apology on what proved "good for the Jews." Thanks to the work of black revolutionaries, Earl Raab argued in 1969, American Jews enjoyed the opportunity to "ask seriously a question which has only been asked jokingly for a number of decades: 'Is it good for the Jews?'" In a 1972 *Midstream* article, Fein asked whether the era's Jewish political activism proved "good for the Jews." Schulweis wondered in a 1975 article for *Moment* whether right-leaning politics proved "good for the Jews." The American Jewish Congress (AJCongress) added a Yiddish twist when it asked, "Is it gut far Yidden?" in a 1970 newsletter.[23]

An instructor in Berkeley, California's community-based Free Jewish University opted to recruit students for a course on contemporary issues in American politics with the title "Is affirmative action good for the Jews?" In 1969, the Orthodox press played both sides of the query when it paraphrased Charles Wilson, a former CEO of General Motors who also served as secretary of defense under President Dwight D. Eisenhower, in its assertion that "what is good for America is good for the Jews and what is bad for America is twice as bad for the Jews." As Podhoretz predicted back in 1972, "Is it good for the Jews?" had "not quite reached the end of its ancient career as a useful guide to thought."[24]

Black Power, Jewish Politics: Reinventing the Alliance in the 1960s charts the transformation of American Jewish political culture from the Cold War liberal consensus of the early postwar years to the rise and influence of Black Power–inspired ethnic nationalism in the decades that followed. It challenges much of the historiography describing the motivations for and limits of Jewish involvement in various social protest movements and accepted wisdom on the origins and nature of the Jewish turn inward. This study argues that a new political consensus emerged at a moment of great intergroup conflict, drawing blacks and Jews under their own identity politics banner as their Dr. King–inspired civil rights movement alliance fractured. In the process, this study challenges commonly held beliefs about the nature of the black-Jewish alliance, the course of American Jewish liberalism in postwar America, and the ways in which this story about Jews informs our understandings of politics, race relations, and the larger cultural transformations of the era.

Historiography

In both contemporary journalistic accounts and the scholarly work that followed, the rise of Black Power in the 1960s has been characterized as an abandonment of the high-minded consensus-based approach of Dr. King and his allies. Black nationalists faced charges that they had undermined the very foundation of pluralist democracy, seeking separation and division rather than coalition building and consensus. According to this theory, the purge of Jews from leadership in civil rights organizations and the identification of Jews as privileged whites combined to ruin a cooperative effort that, in part, achieved the most far-reaching federal civil rights legislation since Reconstruction. The rise of black antisemitism, opposition to Zionism (especially in the years after the 1967 Six-Day War), and the balkanization of individualist liberalism into group-based identity politics seemed to evidence a fundamental breakdown in a once-historic interracial alliance. These stories end poorly, with a fractured nation and an unappreciated and unrecognized Jewish community.[25]

In a wide-ranging analysis he titled "Black Power, Jewish Power," Eric J. Sundquist surveyed the historical, sociological, and political underpinnings of 1960s America, weaving a complex mosaic of overlapping and at times competing impulses in the relationship between blacks and Jews in the late 1960s. While he acknowledged similarities between Black Power and the emergence of Jewish power, Sundquist argued, "the ideological shift and its debilitating consequences for the black-Jewish question in both political and cultural terms is beyond dispute." His interpretation limited the number of Jewish Black Power supporters to just a small group of leftist radicals who also turned against Zionism, especially after the 1967 Six-Day War. Instead, Sundquist believed, Jews as well as blacks retreated. Both groups "withdrew the hand of brotherhood, sought to protect their own communal interests, and reverted at times to ugly stereotypes." By 1970, he concluded, the notion that Jews might still react with favor to Black Power was "bound to seem perverse."[26]

In *Blacks in the Jewish Mind: A Crisis of Jewish Liberalism*, Seth Forman devoted a third of his book to the question of Jews and Black Power. Forman described the rise of Black Power as "perhaps the most unsettling development for American Jews" that "was caused by the deterioration of relations between Jewish and Black Americans." Although Forman acknowledged the argument that draws Black Power into parallel relationships with expressions of heightened Jewish identity, he concluded that such comparisons reflect a basic misunderstanding of the historical facts. Black and Jews, in this analysis, "were so obviously at cross purposes." Forman blamed Black Power for racializing the civil rights movement, effectively marginalizing Jews whom blacks considered incapable of truly understanding or advocating for racial justice. While Friedman blamed the rise of black militancy for the end of the "Golden Age" of the civil rights movement, Forman took the metaphor a step further, arguing that the Black Power movement "hastened an end to the 'Golden Age' of American Jewry" itself.[27]

Cheryl Lynn Greenberg's *Troubling the Waters: Black-Jewish Relations in the American Century* recalled how the rise of Black Power brought Jewish activists together with "their more moderate parents." Committed and passionate in their quest for social justice, Jewish liberals across generational lines were pained when black militants purged them from their leadership positions. "Black militancy and separatism," Greenberg explained, "confirmed their sense that African Americans were moving away from the political vision they had shared." Yet, Greenberg also understood the nuance as American Jews embraced their own form of ethnic activism. She noted a renewed interest in both the State of Israel on the international scene as well as organized Jewish life at home. Jewish opponents of Black Power, then, forged the mistaken conclusion that "they and African Americans were moving in completely different and incompatible directions." Still, Greenberg concluded that the support offered Black Power by a few American Jewish leaders still paled in comparison to "most Jewish leaders" who "strongly disagreed." Black Power, it seemed, emerged as "a direct threat both to civil rights advances dear to Jewish hearts and to Jews more directly."[28]

From African American historiography, sociologist William M. Phillips Jr. offered an analysis of American Jews and the Black Power movement as part of his larger volume covering a century of black-Jewish relations,

An Unillustrious Alliance: The African American and Jewish American Communities. By the mid-1960s, Phillips argued, "contradictions that may have always existed between the disparate as well as mutual interests of the African and Jewish American communities, and which had tended heretofore always to be muted, now became problematic." In an analysis similar to both Friedman's and Forman's, Phillips located in Black Power the end of the historic alliance between blacks and Jews. In the early postwar years, Phillips believed, the common experience of marginality meant that blacks and Jews "needed each other." By 1965, though, "the objective character of the societal situations of the two minority communities had been radically modified." Instead of marching arm in arm for racial justice, blacks and Jews experienced "passionate hostility and bitter resentment." Despite what Phillips acknowledged as "political and emotional similarities between Zionism and nationalistic ideologies indigenous to the African American community," the rise of Black Power, he believed, brought "organizational chaos" and marked the end of the black-Jewish alliance.[29]

Waldo E. Martin Jr., in an essay, "Nation Time!," included in a larger anthology on black-Jewish relations, argued that "innumerable Jews viewed the growth of Black militancy and Black nationalism, especially in its antisemitic elements, as deeply troubling." He described the relationship as "unraveling" as a consequence, in part, of black America's identification with the Third World and Jewish America's affinity for Israel and its allies in the First World. In fact, Martin reflected, the increasing popularity of Zionism among American Jews, especially after Israel's victory in the 1967 Six-Day War, forced "the perennial question 'Is it good for the Jews?'" to rub "up against the increasingly insistent question, 'Is it good for the Blacks?'" The State of Israel's close ties with the apartheid regime of South Africa only further distanced the two communities. Clayborne Carson, editor of the Martin Luther King Jr. papers, focused his analysis largely on Jewish activists working under the auspices of established civil rights organizations, rather than as members or leaders of Jewish agencies. Carson identified early points of tension between blacks and Jews, arguing that "the increasing militancy of the civil rights movement exposed tensions that existed between African Americans and Jews regarding the usefulness of interracial political strategies."[30]

At the most basic level, this book challenges the popular belief that

Black Power activists bore primary responsibility for the breakup of the black-Jewish coalition in the mid-1960s. In this classic American Jewish historiographic rendering, Dr. King and others leveraged pluralist visions of American democracy to unite northern white liberals with southern blacks in a common fight for universal rights, while black militants destroyed that legacy by pressing for separatism. A close examination of the primary sources tells a very different story. With antecedents reaching back to the Progressive era, Jewish leaders understood the limits of Jewish liberal support for civil rights and the inevitability of a black-Jewish split. Even during the heyday of interracial cooperation in the 1950s, national Jewish self-defense officials understood the limits of their partnership with blacks. In published sources as well as private memos, they described a tentative, fractious, and complex relationship between a socially ascending American Jewish populace and an African American one still stagnated by the impact of racism.

With that as a foundation, major national Jewish organizations predicted the rise of black nationalism and approved of its key tenets. Amidst a flurry of popular attention to black anti-Zionism, purges of Jews from civil rights organizations, and a spike in black antisemitism, Jewish leaders took pause, urging their constituents to empathize with African American upset over white liberal gradualism. They defined an historical timeline that necessitated black separatism and demanded that their coreligionists back off their knee-jerk rejection of black empowerment. Blacks and Jews did not split in the mid-1960s. Instead, they continued down an unsurprising and entirely predictable path toward group-based identity politics.

Black Power, Jewish Politics also upends the common narrative describing African American militancy as antithetical to American Jewish interests. As an American religious and ethnic minority that followed a more assimilationist path in the 1950s and early 1960s, Jews imagined their own communal possibilities with the rise of Black Power and its embrace of identity politics. Even though a series of Jewish ethnic, religious, and political revivals bore no superficial resemblance to black nationalism, each owed its genesis to the work of a new generation of African American leaders intent on placing their own group interest first. By watching Black Power advocates press for greater African American empowerment, Jews learned how to reinvigorate their own ethno-religious community.

Whether in a religious revival that brought the children of consensus-minded suburban parents back to tradition, the rise of American Zionism after 1967, or the reinvention of civil rights activism in the growing movement to save Soviet Jews, Black Power proved "good for the Jews."

This new understanding of American Jewish support for Black Power dramatizes the import of constructed memory in the creation of historical narratives. *Black Power, Jewish Politics* reveals a set of primary sources at odds with the ways most journalistic and even scholarly accounts described black-Jewish relations in the 1960s. In my early research, I anticipated finding a treasure trove of speeches, resolutions, memos, and letters echoing the prevailing historiographic argument that African American militants ended the black-Jewish alliance as part of their own desire for greater autonomy. Instead, and to my surprise, the primary sources revealed strong, public, and wide-ranging Jewish communal statements that anticipated the split and supported it as a tool to inspire greater Jewish activism.

Even a casual reader of published Jewish sources in the mid-1960s would have read of broad support for black militancy. Yet, those sympathetic writings all but disappeared in the secondary sources. Why didn't these documents get voice? Why did contemporary observers and later the scholars reflecting on them construct narratives more attuned to filiopietism than historical accuracy? Of course, historiography reflects a relationship between the era of the historian and the era under study. In this case, a narrative that championed Jewish civil rights activism emerged as a more popular telling than one that acknowledged Jewish understanding, if not complicity, in the alliance's end. In a way, this "rediscovery" of countervailing primary sources becomes an important historiographic point on its own. The construction of historical narratives themselves tell an important story about the American Jewish past (and present).

The prevailing narratives tend to credit American Jews for turning back the clock and rediscovering their ethnic and religious heritage. Seen this way, the Jewish "turn inward," would evidence a communal embrace of more particularist thinking. Viewed in generational terms, the identity politics–immersed youth of the 1960s rejected their suburban parents for compromising their Jewish identities in the name of cultural conformity. Yet, both groups of American Jews followed a strategy of accommodation because each generation followed the mores of its time and place. In the early Cold War years, Jews embraced the larger American political culture of the time: assimilation as part of a larger consensus. By the mid-1960s, a new consensus emerged on the American scene: identity politics, in which a wide variety of ethnic groups in America found their individual voices and coalesced around the idea of self-advocacy.

Although Jews may have perceived themselves as becoming more Jewish, their activism actually reflected a new identity-based *Americanist* credo. In what seems an ironic twist, Jews became more American by acting more Jewish. Only in the United States and only in the identity politics of the 1960s could this population of Jews stake such strong and public claim to their own ethnic identity. In both the 1950s and the 1960s, Jews followed the dominant political culture even if they manifested themselves in seemingly opposite ways. Whether as civil rights marchers in the 1950s or Soviet Jewry activists a decade later, American Jews followed the larger political currents of the day. Instead of breaking from the American Jewish tradition of consensus-based politics, Jewish activists simply reinvented it for a new political age. Taken a step further, because the Americanist embrace of ethnic differentiation grew from the pioneering work of Black Power activists, a new generation of American Jews owed its very definition of Jewishness to African American nationalist constructions. At a moment when Jews claimed a stronger, if more authentic, Jewishness, their ethno-religious expression actually proved a reflection of blackness as well.[31]

The proliferation of Black Power–inspired ethnic activism in 1960s America extended as well to other ethnic, racial, and gender groups. Black Power encouraged interested American constituent groups to explore their own heritages and strengthen their sense of themselves as part of a distinctive history. The story outlined in these pages offers just one of many examples that redefined American political and social culture writ large. Examined with a comparative lens, the Black Power movement inspired many revivalist movements, redefining American pluralism in a way that celebrated difference. Just as Jews internalized the lessons of black empowerment, so too did Chicano students with the creation of their organization, Mecha. The nation's indigenous peoples leveraged this new political platform to bring public attention to claims of historic injustices against them. Even white ethnics rallied as Irish Americans and others rediscovered their heritage. In each case, one's group-based status enjoyed renewed gravitas as a rallying cry for heightened awareness. Although scholars have examined some of these movements, much more work remains to be done.[32]

The story of American Jewish support for Black Power also undermines the argument in both history and political science that liberalism imploded in the mid-1960s, replaced by the rise of Nixon's "silent majority." Allen Matusow, for example, titled his history of liberalism in the 1960s *The Unraveling of America* while political scientist Theodore Lowi called his seminal work *The End of Liberalism*. Bruce J. Schulman's *Lyndon B. Johnson and American Liberalism* echoes the prevailing belief that by the time Richard Nixon took the presidential oath of office in January 1969, the New Deal liberal coalition dissolved with a neoconservative backlash. Robert Self's *All in the Family* held that the demise of liberalism "ran through the politicized American family." According to this interpretation, American liberalism declined because it suffered severe blows from both sides of the political aisle. From the left, militant African Americans, dissatisfied with the ideology and tactics of Martin Luther King Jr., rejected nonviolent integrationist protests in favor of Black Power and the politics of cultural nationalism. New Left activists on college campuses across the nation condemned the liberalism of their parents' generation as well as a U.S. domestic and foreign policy governed, in their minds, by imperialist objectives. From the right, urban northern white ethnics, once the backbone of the New Deal coalition, soured on the war on poverty, abandoned the Democratic party, and worried especially about maintaining law and order.[33]

Reinventing the Alliance of the 1960s

Instead, I argue that the Black Power–inspired growth of identity politics across the ethno-racial landscape energized liberalism into a powerful and dynamic force uniting left-of-center constituent groups around a common approach to social change. What seemed a rapid retreat from liberalism was in fact an embrace of the era's new self-directed credo. Despite the election of a Republican president and Democratic losses in Congress, liberal activists, especially at the grassroots level, leveraged identity politics to further progressive causes among multiple constituent groups. In addition to groups such as Mecha and AIM, activism from various Asian

American communities as well as the emergence of the second-wave feminist movement in the early 1970s testified to an expansion of progressive activism beyond the classic black-white racial binary that defined social justice in the civil rights movement years.[34]

While not the focus of this study, the emerging identity-politics consensus played in both directions. Leadership from the Black Power movement, on occasion, referenced Jews, Zionism, or Jewish history in their own advocacy work. Two thousand years of diaspora living, resilience in the face of discrimination, and eventual victories in the creation of the State of Israel and the realization of middle-class social status in the United States offered black nationalists an example of ethnic power against tough odds, even as the day-to-day relations between the two communities deteriorated. Stokely Carmichael, for example, boasted a close relationship with Jewish leftists and often urged his colleagues to consider Jews "a group to be emulated rather than one to be resented." During one speech, he invoked Hillel's famed quote, "If I am not for myself, who will be for me? If I am only for myself, who am I? If not now, when?," as his favorite.[35]

This study engages a question that has become a hot-button political issue: the role of white allies in the civil rights struggle. Over a sixty-year historical arc, African American attitudes about the wisdom, dedication, and effectiveness of white allies in racial justice movements have run the gamut. In the early postwar years, the notion of an interracial alliance that welcomed white liberals anchored the strategies of most major national civil rights organizations. Black leaders from groups such as the National Association for the Advancement of Colored People (NAACP), Student Nonviolent Coordinating Committee (SNCC), and the Southern Christian Leadership Conference (SCLC) sought a pluralist vision of their work that encouraged their diverse activists to learn and work together. By encouraging cultural exchange, civil rights leaders envisioned a democracy that integrated all Americans, regardless of group status. In this pluralist approach, liberal activists enjoyed interracial education and socialization in the hopes of building a more inclusive nation.

After the rise of Black Power, alliances with whites continued, though within a new set of parameters. White Jews could emulate the strategy and tactics of black nationalism, though with the stipulation that each group operate within its own ethnic sphere. As this book demonstrates,

Jews borrowed from political approaches innovated by African American leaders while Black Power advocates offered appreciation for Jewish activism, even as neither group interacted directly with the other. When asked, for example, "what a sincere white person can do," Malcolm X told an aspiring civil rights activist that she should go back to her own community and fight racism there.[36]

The very definition of Jewish community sets the contours of this study and helps determine the conclusions it makes. In a population of roughly 5.5 million Jews in 1960, no single definition of community can capture the complex and often competing political impulses of those who claim Jewish heritage. Because Jewishness does not demand a faith-based imperative, individuals who call themselves Jewish can identify as secular or cultural Jews. Jewish leftists can reject organized religion even as they ascribe their political beliefs to Jewish values. Even those who believe in religious Judaism can span the denominational spectrum or, in many cases, maintain a spiritual connection to their faith without any organized affiliation. Finally, many Jews know that they are Jewish yet do not identify as such in any public way.

Designing a study about Jewish politics requires some decision making around this question. Social historians, for example, can cast a wide net by examining voting records in Jewish neighborhoods. This grassroots approach to political history captures a wide swath of Jews. It gives a more populist view of Jewish political preferences by counting most every Jewish voter. Political historians, in another approach, can focus their studies on the positions of established Jewish leaders, whether they guided organizations in the Jewish world or the larger secular one. This approach draws a tighter connection between Jewish identity and historical change, though, by definition, it omits the vast majority of American Jews.

For this study, I have decided to focus on the organized Jewish community, its leaders and members. While there are limitations to this approach, it presents Jewish politics from the perspective of those who made Jewishness the causal factor in their decision making and activism. This population acted with Jewish intention, however they defined it, as they made the case for their various political stances. In their work, identified Jews navigated a path that distilled secular, cultural, ethnic, and religious impulses from both the larger political culture as well as particular Jewish interests. The critique that this definition of Jewish community proves too limited and embraces a top-down pattern is mitigated in part by the broad array of Jewish organizations as well as by unaffiliated Jews whose voices can be captured in their opposition to the establishment status quo.

Among Jewish religious organizations alone, scholars can glean complex and nuanced understandings of how political activism intersects with various interpretations of Judaism. A quick survey of Reform, Conservative, Reconstructionist, and a variety of Orthodox perspectives reveals contested notions of Judaism's social justice mandates as well as contradictory policy positions and tactics that followed. If, as House Speaker Tip O'Neill once declared, all politics is local, then an organization-based study illuminates the profound political differences between northern Jews and those in the Deep South, between urban dwellers in places such as Los Angeles and those who live in small Midwestern towns. Even among the more secular national Jewish agencies, policy debates over the many political questions they faced offer rich, complex, and diverse perspectives.

Primary sources from the organized Jewish world also reflect the attitudes of unaffiliated Jews. Periodicals boasted readerships across Jewish America. Jewish leaders, in their efforts to reach a broader audience, spoke to and about rank-and-file Jews. Controversial decisions made by Jewish leaders sometimes inspired grassroots Jewish protest, giving insights into a broader Jewish constituency. During the era of this study, the organized Jewish leadership faced serious and far-reaching challenges to its authority from a younger generation of political activists who criticized the Jewish establishment for its anachronistic approaches to Jewish life. In these cases, Jewish newspapers offered a lens into American Jewish political behavior that, by definition, differed from that of leadership. By engaging the dialogue between Jewish communal insiders and outsiders, this study casts a much wider net. Finally, I have included results of public opinion surveys throughout the study to give added context and perspective to the arguments of organized leadership.

Changing the Equation

Black Power, Jewish Politics: Reinventing the Alliance in the 1960s offers six chapters that trace Jewish communal responses to the development of black nationalism from the early Cold War years through the 1970s, as well as an epilogue that offers a perspective on the more contemporary period. The first chapter, "Jews and Black Nationalism in the 1950s," challenges the filiopietistic accounts of black-Jewish cooperation in the 1950s. It explores otherwise unexamined moments of interaction between Jewish communal leaders and black nationalists. While most of the era's historiography touts a strong interracial alliance, this deeper exploration of the sources uncovers Jewish leaders who predicted the rise of Black Power, understood its rationale, and pressed American Jews to support its efforts. Even a cursory review of published sources reveals that Jewish organizations supported black militancy throughout the 1950s, offering far-reaching empathy for African American leaders who, just a decade later, would be recast as antisemitic villains. Based on both private communications and public pronouncements, the eventual political split between blacks and Jews surprised few. Rather than periodizing black-Jewish relations as early postwar cooperation followed by a Black Power–inspired split in the mid-1960s, this chapter reframes the era in ways that anticipates, if not predicts, the alliance's eventual breakdown.

The second chapter, "Jews, Group Status, and the Great Society," explores Jewish communal responses to the development of group-based programs in President Lyndon Johnson's social reform effort. During the heyday of the civil rights movement, American Jews rooted their liberalism in an individual-based approach to public policy. A color-blind society, as it were, demanded equal protection for all Americans because the U.S. Constitution and the larger legal system guaranteed the same rights to all citizens. By the time Lyndon Johnson offered his vision of a more just nation, though, one's group status had moved to center stage. Communities of color, in large measure, endured greater levels of discrimination because of their membership in marginalized groups. Johnson responded with a series of reforms that recognized the racial double standard and focused specific programs to ameliorate its negative effect.

For Jews, the abandonment of a color-blind public policy evinced mixed reactions. Jewish leaders understood the need for more aggressive measures but also lamented the end of a more optimistic stage in American liberal politics. Debates over the Great Society's recognition of institutional racism and exclusion of Jews as a designated minority focused Jewish communal leaders on some of the most important presumptions of the Black Power movement. The Great Society called out white Jewish liberal paternalism, pressing for maximum feasible participation of local urban and African American communities. It pressed for affirmative action and at times quotas as a means to remedy racial injustice. Through the lens of the Great Society, Jews confronted a Black Power–informed perspective of American society and offered strong empathy and support.

Chapter 3, "American Jews and the Rise of Black Power," chronicles the organized Jewish community's responses to the emerging Black Power movement. With the rise of group-based consciousness and northern white liberal understanding of institutional racism, American Jews increasingly backed African American calls for greater autonomy in historic civil rights organizations. Leading national Jewish leaders as well as regional and local officers agreed with black nationalist critiques of American society and shared African American concerns over the limits of Jewish liberal civil rights activism in the urban North. Even as most contemporary and historical accounts interpreted the rise of black militancy through the lens of Dr. Martin Luther King Jr.'s interracial nonviolent approach to civil rights reform, Jewish leaders offered support for Black Power's message and goals.

At the same time leading black nationalists espoused anti-Zionist and even antisemitic tropes, national Jewish leaders took pause, reflecting on the deeper meaning and implications of the rise of Black Power. They argued that black antisemitism posed little threat to American Jews just as they understood the relevance and necessity of the new activism. Across the Jewish organizational landscape, leaders paralleled the rhetoric and posturing of black nationalists to the Jewish historical experience, cheering strategy and tactics within the African American community that paralleled Jews' own ethnic history. Looking to the future, Jewish leaders located in Black Power an opportunity for American Jews to advance their own communal agenda without fears of compromising their status as loyal and patriotic Americans.

Chapter 4, "Turning Inward: Black Power and Jewish Youth Movements," explores how, in the years after the rise of Black Power, American Jews turned inward, initiating a cultural revival modeled on black nationalists' embrace of their ethnic identity. On the college campus, Jewish students pressed for a more serious engagement of their ethno-religious heritage. Black Power's call for an Afrocentric approach to education encouraged Jews to press for the development of Jewish studies courses.

More and more Jewish students enrolled in courses that viewed the world through a Jewish lens while, off campus, they created, attended, and sometimes taught noncredit classes on subjects of Jewish interest. The campus Jewish organization Hillel faced critique from Jewish students demanding more innovative, and politically infused, expressions of Judaism. Across the country, Jewish undergraduates formed radical student groups and created their own Jewish newspapers as part of an ambitious Jewish ethnic, political, and religious revival.

Off campus, Jewish activists took aim at their community's organized leadership, whom they critiqued as too secular and too apologist in their Jewish outlook. Combining the tactics of the civil rights movement with their newfound enthusiasm for stronger Jewish education and religious expression, Jewish student groups launched a series of protests across the country. Whether advocating "pray-ins" at Jewish Community Federation buildings or protesting Jewish slumlords outside synagogues on the High Holidays, radical Jewish groups demanded that their leaders align their organizational priorities with the larger social justice imperatives of the day. Jewish day schools, once the exclusive purview of the Orthodox, grew in the Conservative and even the once-assimilationist Reform movement. Alternative prayer communities emerged as well, challenging the established synagogues for a claim on the souls of Jewish youth.

The fifth chapter, "Black Power, American Jews, and the Soviet Jewry Movement," details how American Jewish activists combined strategies and tactics from the civil rights movement with the Black Power mandate to focus on one's own ethnic community to rally on behalf of their brethren in eastern Europe. If Jewish liberals valued civil protection under the law and labored on behalf of southern blacks in a bid to end Jim Crow, then the purge of Jews from civil rights organizations posed a basic political question: how should Jewish activists redirect their civil rights energies? Because Jews already enjoyed the rights of citizenship, a coalition of Jewish activists from across the political and religious spectrum redesigned the civil rights movement for an international and Jewish stage. Instead of journeying south to register African Americans to vote, all Jewish activists traveled east to smuggle religious objects to oppressed "refuseniks." They staged massive protests at the Soviet embassy and consulates, marched in parades, and added Soviet Jewry content to the Jewish Passover seder, a holiday celebrating freedom for Jews.

And when Soviet Jewry activists needed to secure support from the nation's most powerful politicians, they switched gears, leveraging anti-Communist sentiment to convince national political leaders that what was good for the Jews was also good for America. In a creative amalgamation of early postwar political culture with the Black Power call for ethnic particularism, Jewish leaders succeeded in rallying their coreligionists to a Jewish cause while they simultaneously convinced the anti-Communist nation at large to back their movement. Although members of the United States Congress may not have prioritized the religious rights of Russian Jews, they certainly exploited an opportunity to point out Communism's failure. With the Soviet Jewry movement, Jewish activists burned the postwar consensus candle at both ends. Early postwar anti-Communism met the Black Power 1960s.

When the State of Israel achieved a remarkable military victory in the 1967 Six-Day War, American Jews responded with overwhelming support. Chapter 6, "Black Power and American Zionism," traces the history of American Zionism in the postwar period, focusing on how the growing popularity of black nationalism motivated Jews to rally for the State of Israel. Historically, the constitutional separation of church and state discouraged American Jews from embracing the Zionist movement. While American Jews benefited from protected religious expression, they feared charges of dual loyalty if they proclaimed their allegiance to another nation-state. As a result, Zionism remained a minority movement among American Jews throughout most of American Jewish history.

The rise of Black Power changed the equation. When black nationalists pressed for greater African American political autonomy and heightened respect for their African heritage, American Jews drew strong parallels to the modern Zionist movement. Just as many late-nineteenth and early-twentieth-century eastern European Jews, victimized by the group-based institutional discrimination of their governments, sought relief in an effort to secure political sovereignty, African Americans in the mid-1960s followed a similar path. Jews, more than any other American ethnic group, understood the African American nationalist impulse. When the State of Israel won the Six-Day War, American Jews responded with unprecedented support. Not even the strong anti-Zionist proclamations of Black Power activists dampened their renewed sense of black-Jewish solidarity.

In an ironic twist, the Jewish embrace of Black Power inverted a classic dispute between American Jews and their Israeli brethren. As part of the rise of the modern Zionist movement, Jewish nationalists often charged their American coreligionists with *galut* mentality, invoking the Hebrew word for "diaspora" in a harsh critique that argued Jews could realize their true potential as Jews only in a country with Jewish sovereignty. Diaspora Jews, the argument followed, mediated their Jewishness against the forces of assimilation. Jews couldn't be as Jewish in the diaspora because they needed to accommodate to the culture of the non-Jewish society around them.

Thanks to Black Power, American Jews countered the Israeli claim. Jews could for the first time in their American experience press their nationalist claims without fear of dual loyalty. They could express as public, unapologetic, and proud Jewish identities as they wished. By embracing the larger political culture of non-Jewish America, Jewish activists rejected the alleged link between *galut* thinking and Jewish apology. American Jews broke from *galut* thinking by embracing its very expression in Black Power America. Black Power proved quite good for the Jews.

Jews and
Black Nationalism
in the 1950s

orty years before Dr. Martin Luther King Jr. sought a political alliance with white liberals, Joel Spingarn, an American Jew and cofounder of the NAACP, offered an analysis of race relations that undermined many of the consensus-based assumptions that typified the postwar civil rights movement. In a 1914 address to an African American audience, Spingarn revealed that he was "tired of the philanthropy of rich white men toward your race." He acknowledged the limits of white liberalism, its gradualist approach to social change, and its reluctance to cede operational control of the civil rights agenda to African American leadership. For racial equality to be achieved, the Jewish NAACP founder understood, well-intentioned white leaders needed to step away from the paternalism that often defined middle-class white liberalism. African Americans, he explained to those assembled, need to "fight your own battles with your own leaders and your own money." In language that anticipated the rise of the Black Power movement in the 1960s, Spingarn announced, "We white men of whatever creed or faith cannot fight your battles for you." White liberals would certainly "stand shoulder to shoulder" with African Americans but only, as he concluded, "until you can fight as generals all by yourselves."[1]

Spingarn's analysis ran counter to the common postwar depiction of Jews as part of an interracial alliance linking white liberals with consensus-minded African American civil rights leaders. In the 1950s, this theory argues, three different reasons explained why Jewish liberals joined the civil rights struggle. First, blacks and Jews shared common historical experiences. African Americans suffered from 250 years of slavery on American shores while Jewish Americans recalled their slavery in Egypt as part of each year's Passover seder. Although the impact of these two slavery experiences could not have been more different in contemporary times, the Jewish mandate to remember slavery in Egypt created a sense of empathy for the African American struggle. Second, both blacks and Jews understood social marginalization. The histories of racism and antisemitism, the common sociological experience of "otherness," drew the two communities to another common bond. Finally, the prophetic impulse of Judaism, especially in the Reform movement, added a religious dimension to the coalition. In order to perfect the world, Judaism demanded that its adherents work toward justice in the societies around them.[2]

At first glance, Spingarn's more critical perspective did not seem to describe the postwar civil rights movement. By all outward appearances, the relationship between blacks and Jews in the mid-1950s could not have been better. Spingarn's NAACP worked within the American legal system and with strong Jewish legal and financial support to win victory in the landmark 1954 *Brown vs. Board of Education* case that desegregated schools. Jewish college students journeyed south to register voters, marched alongside Dr. Martin Luther King Jr., tested complicity with federal civil rights laws, and, in a few cases, endured imprisonment, injury, or death in pursuit of their social justice goals. Jewish organizations stood alongside the NAACP, the SCLC, and its youth wing, SNCC, to align their interpretations of prophetic Judaism with the struggle against Jim Crow.

Polling data from the late 1950s revealed that support for the civil rights movement outweighed even Zionism in the hearts of American Jews. About 40 percent of those Jews interviewed agreed that status as a "good Jew" demanded support for the "Negro struggle" while only half as many said the same for the State of Israel. While the Orthodox tended to refrain from civil rights activism, the well-respected Talmud scholar Rabbi Aaron Soloveichik linked support for African American racial equality with the requirements of Jewish law in a teaching at New York City's Young Israel. Rabbis from the Reform as well as the Conservative movements preached sermons on the civil rights movement. Some headed to rallies in Alabama, Mississippi, and Georgia to protest Jim Crow. In one of the most popular images of the era, Rabbi Abraham Joshua Heschel "prayed with his feet" as he marched alongside Dr. King during the famous Selma protest.[3]

Reinventing Black-Jewish Relations in the 1950s

A closer look at the primary sources, though, showed that early postwar Jewish leaders empathized with Spingarn's lament. In private communications and in published statements, they revealed a keen understanding of the tensions between blacks and Jews, the need for greater African American–centered leadership, and the limits of individual-based liberalism in an American society that engaged in deep group-based discrimination. In this sense, a new reading of the black-Jewish alliance in the 1950s anticipates Jewish support for the group-based programs of the Great Society as well as broad-based Jewish empathy for the eventual rise of Black Power. Since the early postwar period, popular images of black-Jewish cooperation built an American Jewish historical memory that ignored published accounts to the contrary. Jewish leaders demonstrated understanding and support for black separatism long before it became part of the public discourse.

Several exchanges between Jewish leaders and their African American counterparts animated American Jewish awareness of the black-Jewish alliance's fragility. In some, leaders from several national Jewish organizations acknowledged Jewish complicity in what Great Society reformers and Black Power activists would later label "institutional racism." In others, national Jewish organizations such as the AJC and the Anti-Defamation League (ADL) came to the defense of the black militant group, Nation of Islam. These interactions, occurring at a time of perceived black-Jewish consensus, complicate the prevailing narrative that tended to minimize differences between blacks and Jews. Instead, Jewish leaders understood the deep roots of American racism, acknowledged at least tacit Jewish complicity in the system that created it, and empathized with the African American leaders who pushed back against it.

In a 1958 article published in the NAACP's newsletter, *The Crisis*, the nation's leading civil rights organization charged American Jews with complicity in the country's system of racial oppression. "There is increased feeling of bitterness," its editors wrote, "over the fact that Jews in better neighborhoods and suburban areas are often as hostile as other whites when Negroes attempt to move into a community."[4] By the 1950s, American Jews enjoyed the privileges of inclusion in the white middle class. Even as they boasted a disproportionate presence in liberal reform, Jews had already separated themselves from blacks, both physically and sociologically. Restrictive housing covenants eased, encouraging Jewish families to buy homes in less crowded and predominately white suburban real estate developments. Quota restrictions in education imposed a generation earlier to limit Jewish access to undergraduate, graduate, and professional schools all but ended. By 1960, the opportunity to pursue higher education made college degrees a new cultural standard in American Jewish households.

With economic and educational success came social acceptance as well. Although intermarriage rates remained relatively low throughout the period, Jews developed close professional and personal relationships with their non-Jewish neighbors, who most often accepted them into their communities. In a 1950 example illustrative of the newfound friendliness between Jews and Christians, a group of Cleveland, Ohio, Jewish parents petitioned their local chapter of the JCRC to withdraw its challenge of public school officials who planned a dual observance of Christmas and Hanukkah. Even as Jewish self-defense leaders feared a violation of church-state separation, postwar suburban Jews welcomed the opportunity to draw closer to their Christian neighbors.[5]

Yet, realizing their dreams of upward mobility also demanded Jewish acceptance of continuing race-based discrimination. Even though American Jews enjoyed the right to purchase homes in the suburbs, racism still ensured blacks could not buy property in white (and Jewish) neighborhoods. Although northern cities and towns did not include Jim Crow-style racial restrictions in their local laws and codes, they did look the other way when private legal agreements, social customs, and informal understandings created a de facto segregationist web that approximated the racial segregation at the center of the southern civil rights movement.

By purchasing homes in whites-only neighborhoods and adopting exclusive bylaws in their own organizations, suburban Jews emerged complicit in a system of racist discrimination, undermining the consensus-based assumptions of the black-Jewish alliance. When Jews retreated from their apartments in urban America to homes in the suburbs, they also tended to hold on to their business interests in the cities, angering

African Americans who complained about price gouging, substandard apartment buildings, and the exodus of precious capital from their neighborhoods to the well-trimmed affluent neighborhoods of their landlords. For critics in the NAACP, Jewish liberal support for civil rights slowed north of the Mason-Dixon line.

The 1958 NAACP article alarmed AJC official Sydney Kellner, whose work in New York City often brought him into contact with local African American leaders. He reached out to James Pawley, the director of the Urban League in Essex County, New Jersey, to see whether the African American civil rights leader would sit and discuss the issues raised in the piece. Pawley responded in the affirmative, acknowledging Kellner for his willingness to engage challenging questions even as he let the AJC leader know that no other Jewish leader had ever reached out or shown a willingness to speak truthfully about their communities' differences.[6]

At the meeting, Pawley surveyed long-standing tensions between African Americans and Jews in urban America. He spoke of black disappointment in northern Jewish liberals, so enthusiastic about fighting segregation in the South but abandoning their passion for change when it hit close to home. As Pawley reminded Kellner, the issue grew so profound in his hometown of Newark, New Jersey, that African Americans developed a "blind resentment" of Jewish owners, even though they also knew the American Jewish community's overwhelming support for civil rights. The emerging class divisions between blacks and Jews, Pawley argued, led to conflict between a group of white, middle-class, privileged Jews on the one hand, and blacks on the other, the latter remaining on the margins of an expanding postwar economy. "Part of the resentment," he said, "comes from the impression that Jews draw their income from these areas but reinvest very little of the profit into the cultural life and community needs of the neighborhood." To make matters worse, Pawley lamented that few Jewish merchants responded to his own appeal for Urban League support and those who gave often made a minimal contribution.[7]

In the most poignant observation, Pawley recounted his own negative experience in the Newark rental apartment market. Just a few weeks prior to his meeting with Kellner, Pawley had tried to secure an apartment for his own use in a Jewish-owned apartment house. The building, he noted, had once been occupied by Jews but changed to African American renters when the Jewish residents fled. In the course of that transition, Pawley observed, the landlords raised rents but did not make needed improve-ments to the building. While Pawley was careful to note that he thought the conflict grew more from class differences than racial or religious ones, he urged Kellner to address the issues. Kellner, for his part, forwarded Pawley's concerns to the AJC's national leadership and pressed for more grassroots organizational work in American cities.[8]

Other prominent Jewish communal leaders showed similar aware-ness of a widening gulf between the optimistic consensus-based rhetoric of black-Jewish cooperation and the starker realities of an alliance that joined a community of white privileged Jews with African Americans suf-fering from institutional racism. In 1960, the same year that students in Greensboro started a wave of integration sit-ins, Judge Justine Wise Po-lier, a civil rights activist, leading voice in the AJCongress, and daughter of rabbi Stephen S. Wise, acknowledged in comments to the organization's executive committee that American Jews already had lost touch with the needs of the African American community. She warned her colleagues that they had "not come to grips with some of the critical problems facing Jews in the North and in the South" and urged them to devote more of their organization's efforts toward understanding and addressing the na-tion's growing racial divide and its particular impact on American Jews.[9]

Wise Polier challenged the popular Jewish assumption that blacks and Jews shared an essentially similar American experience. Much of the peri-od's political rhetoric trumpeted the common bonds between blacks and Jews: both suffered histories of discrimination, understood the meaning of persecution, and deserved equal constitutional protection in the United States. Cold War competition with the Soviet Union strengthened that historical interpretation by highlighting the essential similarities of all Americans, regardless of race or religion, and marginalizing the Commu-nist Eastern Bloc as the enemy of democracy, freedom, and human rights.

But the AJCongress leader understood that blacks and Jews experi-enced America in different ways. For Jews, the United States delivered on its image as a haven for the oppressed and a land of opportunity for new arrivals. Although antisemitism limited Jewish mobility in the early part of the twentieth century and spiked during the isolationist 1930s, unprec-edented economic and political opportunity in the postwar years thrust most American Jews into the middle class. African Americans, despite a century of emancipation, still suffered from Jim Crow segregation in the

South and extralegal institutional racism in the urban North. Each successive generation did not improve its social or economic condition, as was typical in the Jewish community.

Even though postwar optimism united white liberals under the civil rights banner for the first time since Reconstruction, racial equality remained elusive. Liberal ideals and political activism meant to bridge the racial divide offered important hope for social change but did not erase the black and Jewish communities' divergent historical experiences. Wise Polier admonished her colleagues not to paint too rosy a picture of the black-Jewish relationship and warned of growing intergroup tensions. According to Wise Polier, she and her coreligionists were "living in a period of American history where the relationships between minority groups . . . have become key questions" even as she noted an increase in black anti-semitism and greater anti-Jewish discrimination in white America. Although the AJCongress and other Jewish defense organizations achieved remarkable success in their outreach and coalition building efforts, Wise Polier cautioned the Jewish leadership not to ignore continuing signs of intergroup discord.[10]

Wise Polier's colleague in the AJCongress, governing council chair Nathan Edelstein, articulated similar views, but in even more dramatic terms. Five months after Wise Polier made her observations to that small group of key AJCongress leaders, Edelstein stood before representatives of almost every major national Jewish organization and acknowledged, in words reminiscent of Spingarn's 1914 address, a deteriorating relationship between blacks and Jews. Edelstein alerted his colleagues to several of the most important systemic issues confronting the interracial alliance, placing much of the blame for black-Jewish discord at the feet of his fellow Jewish liberals. Continuing Jewish communal calls for gradualism, he argued, failed to bring transformational change.

Instead, Jewish social justice activists, in the eyes of African American leaders at least, retreated to policies of tokenism that reflected a strong paternalistic attitude toward blacks. For the interracial alliance to blossom, Edelstein warned, Jews must ease their hierarchical approach to the black-Jewish coalition and recast their African American partners as equals "with full recognition of his new and proper status." Without a great deal of organizational autonomy, the two communities would cleave along racial fault lines well defined in American political culture.

Edelstein revealed a critical social transformation in American Jewry, one at odds with consensus-based assumptions of the black-Jewish alliance. "Jews," he affirmed, "are part of the white community." With that assertion, Edelstein reframed the interracial relationship in a profound new way, challenging the notion that Jews shared a sense of marginality with African Americans.[11]

Jewish Gradualism, Tokenism, and African American Critique

African American leaders offered similar assessments when they were invited to address Jewish leaders. In 1961, the AJC welcomed Whitney M. Young Jr., the new national head of the Urban League, to speak before their Human Relations Institute. In his remarks, Young offered frank critique that underscored the growing divisions between blacks and Jews. "Face the fact that your community does discriminate," he implored. Breaking with the idealistic vision of black-Jewish cooperation years before the rise of Black Power, the African American leader warned the AJC group that "words like gradualism and moderation are meaningless." To continue such a centrist social reform path, he warned, invited black militancy, an approach he considered "only natural in view of world changes."[12]

Throughout the 1950s, American Jews reacted to these critiques with ambivalence. Northern suburban Jews understood that antisemitic quotas had eased in housing, education, and employment. Jews entered middle-class white neighborhoods and businesses, watching African Americans continue to struggle for the most basic civil rights. And these new suburban Jews also knew that they differed in fundamental ways from their white Christian neighbors. As recently as the 1930s, domestic antisemitism spiked while World War II reminded American Jews that an attempted genocide occurred in what was considered an enlightened European nation. In the postwar world, American Jews assumed the mantle of world Jewish leadership with a keen understanding of Jewish vulnerability. African American claims against Jews pressed against overwhelming, disproportionate and particularist Jewish support for liberal political causes. American Jews, more than any other non–African American group, put their philanthropic support, electoral backing, and even physical safety on the line for the cause of racial justice.

Despite that uneasiness, postwar Jewish social mobility and the whitening of American Jews, even as it realized the dreams of so many, complicated the Jewish community's relationship to African Americans. Edelstein's proclamation, more than just an expression of Jewish social acceptance in the larger white society, carried with it strong sociological implications. White Americans, as part of the mainstream, enjoyed privilege. As Jews traversed the racial continuum from marginalized and nonwhite to part of America's white power structure, their American experiences moved farther away from those of most African Americans. The black-Jewish conflicts inherent in the whitening of Jewish America came to the fore when Jewish organizations constructed communal buildings in their new all-white communities. A 1951 ADL survey of Jewish Community Centers in forty-two American cities, for example, revealed that a third of those admitting non-Jews would not admit African Americans. When Jewish Community Centers began to accept non-Jews, St. Louis Jewish Federation director Herman Kaplow admitted, "they did so, in most instances, following the precept of the majority community-whites only."[13]

Edelstein's analysis challenged those who trumpeted the essential similarities between blacks and Jews. As Edelstein explained, "We need only remind ourselves that prominent Negroes have been excluded from predominately Jewish clubs and that the best known builder of 'whites only' suburban developments is William Levitt." In these situations, Edelstein argued, "Jews share much of the anti-Negro prejudice of the rest of the white community." The AJCongress leader empathized with black leaders whom he understood expected "that Jews, victims themselves, will refrain from discriminatory practices against other minorities." He understood the impact of white privilege on Jews and the tensions it created in black-Jewish relations. In Edelstein's estimation, the growing racial divide between blacks and Jews in the 1950s demanded an eventual split between the two communities. Informed by what Edelstein called a "long-standing distrust of white people," African Americans would respond with a "growing spirit of 'go-it-alone'" that would cause a reevaluation of the black-Jewish alliance, "a period of mutual irritation and misunderstanding" and, ultimately, "new and more active forms" of black antisemitism.[14]

The perspectives articulated by Wise Polier, Edelstein, and Pawley pointed to a much larger concern emerging within the Jewish communal world: postwar liberalism's inability to address the systemic problem of

American racial inequality and the organized Jewish community's failure to critically examine its own role in the stalemate. Much of the attention focused on liberal gradualism, the concept that racial equality can best be achieved through measured, and oftentimes slow, political maneuvering. To its supporters, gradualism offered the promise of uniting a diverse constituency behind a common platform. For Jewish civil rights activists, gradualism formed the basis of their alliance with black leaders eager to gain the influence of sympathetic whites in the struggle. Focused as it most often was on the legal process, gradualist political strategies appealed to whites who could frame their civil rights support in a universal embrace of the Constitution's call for equal protection under the law.

To its critics, gradualism translated into nothing more than a stall tactic meant to stifle social change. Some among a younger generation of African American civil rights leaders grew to distrust liberals, whom they perceived as nothing more than self-congratulatory proponents of the racial status quo. As MIT professor Harold R. Isaacs observed in a 1962 AJC *Commentary* article, "A reluctant or timid white liberalism clings to 'gradualism' in a situation where slowness has become failure." At a time of growing northern white liberal support for the civil rights movement, Jewish leaders understood its limits and predicted the tensions that would soon arise.[15]

The dissonance between the hopeful ideals of consensus-based Jewish liberalism and its underlying gradualist challenges came to the fore at the 1960 biennial meeting of the AJCongress. Rabbi Joachim Prinz, who would later deliver a speech at the famed 1963 March on Washington for Jobs and Freedom, lauded the black-Jewish alliance and issued his own "Declaration of Interdependence" to promote a universalist approach to social reform. Holding tight to the liberal ideals that brought Jews into the civil rights movement, Prinz condemned isolationism as "ghettoization" and a "form of intellectual and moral slavery." He would remain, throughout the tumultuous years of interracial discord, a stalwart defender of a consensus-based approach to American Jewish life.[16]

Biennial conference attendees, though, would hear a competing interpretation of black-Jewish relations from Kenneth B. Clark, a City College of New York professor invited by AJCongress leaders to offer a differing interpretation. Clark, an African American psychologist best known for his "doll test" experiments that confirmed a white racial preference among black children, played a significant role in building the legal case against segregation in *Brown vs. Board of Education*. Later, he became the first African American to head the American Psychological Association. Clark criticized Jews for their failure to meet African Americans on equal political grounds. Anticipating Black Power, he warned of the emergence of a new group of African American civil rights activists who could "best be characterized by a stolid, confident unwillingness to accept token progress for genuine progress in American race relations." Despite the celebrated achievements of the interracial alliance in the struggle for racial equality, African Americans, according to Clark, would "no longer accept patronage and condescension" and resented Jewish liberals for pressing political compromises at odds with their best interests.[17]

Liberal gradualism, Clark believed, led inevitably to paternalism. As blacks and Jews interacted in the civil rights movement, he argued, African Americans soon learned that their white liberal friends took it upon themselves to speak on behalf of blacks. In doing so, and with even the best of intentions, white liberals "oftentimes sought to alleviate his hunger by the crumbs of gradualism." Jews proved all too willing to compromise African American demands for equality when the larger political climate seemed to require it. With the advent of what Clark defined as "the present assertive pattern of the Negro," African Americans needed "a change in the role of his friends." The day's most important concern, he urged, "is the fact that [African Americans] assert in clear and controlled voices that they will not have others speak for them. They insist on speaking for themselves."[18]

Clark then moved the conversation from the Jim Crow South to the racism plaguing the urban North. Tensions would spike, Clark feared, when northern Jewish liberals confronted the racism in their own communities. More covert forms of racism, invisible to the law books but still effective in limiting equal opportunity for African Americans, plagued northern cities and inspired a growing number of black activists to expand the geographic reach of the civil rights movement. Without a fundamental reevaluation of Jewish communal strategy on the civil rights issue, the future looked bleak. Clark understood that it was difficult for people to adjust long-held social attitudes, not to mention abandon the rather benevolent self-perceptions they nourished. Still, he sounded the call. The potent combination of gradualism, paternalism, and entrenched liberal thinking threatened to implode the interracial political alliance. Unless Jewish leaders pressed for strategic changes in their approach to racial inequality, Clark predicted, a new generation of black leaders would emerge whose "goals will pose a very real threat to liberal whites and previously accepted Negro leaders." The consensus-driven coalition that brought like-minded blacks and Jews together would splinter in the face of an emerging black nationalism.[19]

Leaders from the AJC agreed. At its 1960 annual meeting, program director David Danzig acknowledged the more paternalistic approach of Jewish liberals when he warned his colleagues "these people are not looking for bread alone." African Americans, he stressed, "are not looking for jobs alone. They are looking for dignity." In a challenge that anticipated future black-Jewish tensions, Danzig asked his colleagues "to what extent is America ready to adapt itself to this new image which the Negro has of himself, and which he invites us to share with him?" In similar fashion, the AJC's publication, *Commentary*, carried two articles in 1961 alerting its readers of serious and growing discord between blacks and Jews. In the first, Julian Mayfield warned that the traditional African American leadership bloc, defined by centrist political views and a middle class orientation, "is in danger of losing its claim to speak for the masses of Negroes."[20]

Five months later, Tom Brooks criticized Jewish labor unions for opposing Brotherhood of Sleeping Car Porters Union head A. Philip Randolph's 1959 call for an all-black Negro American Labor Council. "One wonders if this growing antagonism between the Jewish and Negro labor camps," Brooks worried, "is a precursor of strained relations between the larger Jewish and Negro defense agencies and ultimately between the two minority communities in general." He blamed Jewish liberal gradualism, wondering whether "what white liberals often regard as 'progress,'" could better be defined as "tokenism." It all added up, in Brooks estimation, to "the further spread of the black nationalism bewailed by white and Negro civil rights spokesmen alike." In 1962, editors at *Commentary* published an article by MIT professor Harold Isaacs predicting the rise of Black Power as well. Sharing research that would shape his upcoming book, *The New World of Negro Americans*, Isaacs described "a newly militant, newly self-assertive Negro who will no longer submit to the humiliations of the past." While earlier generations of activist black leaders failed, the "New Negroes," Isaacs contended, "are appearing in a situation where for the first time the odds are with them; their newness, their militancy, and their self-assertion are bound at last to pay off."[21]

Even Jewish organizational opposition to African American nationalist thinking revealed a deeper understanding of the new political dynamics at play. In the same year as the Isaacs article, Charles Wittenstein, the southeastern regional director of the AJC, received a letter asking whether Jewish organizations should boycott a black separatist conference organized by SNCC. While Wittenstein supported a boycott with the stark directive "Damn the torpedoes, full speed ahead!," he understood the rise of black nationalist thinking, sharing his belief that a split between black militants and Jewish civil rights workers proved "inevitable."[22]

American Jews and the Nation of Islam

In a less-explored chapter of early postwar black-Jewish relations, leaders in national Jewish organizations defended the Nation of Islam (NOI). While Jewish leaders in the 1950s knew and understood its antisemitic and separatist orientation, they framed the black Muslim group in consensus terms, lobbying for their constitutional right to religious expression and minimizing the impact of its antisemitic rhetoric. At a time when the Dr. King Jr. approach to black-Jewish relations dominated the political culture, Jewish leaders sought to marginalize any groups that threatened its consensus message. The more platform afforded the NOI by Jewish leaders, the greater threat to the existing model of black-Jewish cooperation. The more marginal the NOI, the less of a danger it posed to the race relations status quo.

Founded in Detroit in 1930 by Wallace Fard Muhammad, the Nation of Islam sought to "teach the downtrodden and defenseless Black people a thorough knowledge of God and of themselves, and to put them on the road to self-independence with a superior culture and higher civilization than they had previously experienced." In 1934, Elijah Muhammad took control of the organization, heading it until his death in 1975. In the years of his leadership, the Nation of Islam sought strict racial separation; embraced anti-white, anti-Christian, as well as antisemitic attitudes; and called for a wholesale realignment of power relationships in American society. Malcolm X, its most charismatic leader, joined the group in 1952 and built its strength and influence until he broke with Elijah Muhammad in 1964, a year before Malcolm X's murder.[23]

The Nation of Islam's relationship to the organized Jewish community proved especially charged. As early as the 1950s, the black Muslim group rallied its supporters with a critique of American society filled with vitriolic antisemitism. Nation of Islam minister Jeremiah X, in rhetoric typical of his organization, argued, "Jews are the Negro's worst enemies among whites." Louis Farrakhan, who came to power in the late 1970s, earned national outrage when he referred to Judaism as a "gutter religion," called Jewish landlords "bloodsuckers," and praised Hitler as "a very great man." In 1991, the Nation of Islam's Historical Research Department published *The Secret Relationship between Blacks and Jews*, a 334-page document accusing "Jewish pilgrim fathers" of kidnapping African Americans "disproportionately more than any other ethnic or religious group in New World history."[24]

Most descriptions of the Nation of Islam in American Jewish historical scholarship recount this narrative of black Muslim antisemitism. Centering their analyses on the coalition between Jewish liberals and consensus-minded blacks, they portray the Nation of Islam as the common foe to both blacks and Jews. Murray Friedman, for example, described black Muslims as "a potent and divisive force in black-white relations," while Seth Forman considered them the era's "most conspicuous instance of Black anti-Semitism." Other surveys offer similar analyses that marginalize the Nation of Islam and characterize the black Muslim movement as a serious threat to Jews and to liberal social reform.[25]

But investigation of the early relationship between black Muslims and the organized Jewish community counters these conclusions. In August 1959, for example, AJC leader David Danzig asked his regional officers to report on the growth of black antisemitism in their local communities. Given what Danzig termed "rising tensions over desegregation and worsening slum conditions suffered by Negro communities in urban areas," AJC officials were invited to comment on the status of black antisemitism in general, and the growth of "Negro nationalist" organizations such as the Nation of Islam, in particular. While some officers, including southeastern area director Samuel Kaminsky, offered pessimistic appraisals of the Nation of Islam, most did not sense a threat from the black Muslim group. As the editor of *Jewish Currents* wrote, "I can understand the Black

Muslims' attitude and feeling, because I think it arises from the same frustration and fear."[26]

When *Time* magazine published an article in 1959 accusing the Nation of Islam of antisemitism, the ADL's Arnold Forster surveyed the charges and concluded that they lacked veracity. Concerned that the journalistic piece might raise unnecessary fear among America's Jews, Forster issued a confidential memo to his regional officers informing them of his conclusions and urging them to downplay the *Time* story in their local communities. "*Time* magazine notwithstanding," Forster wrote, "we have no documentable evidence of anti-Semitism on the part of the Temples of Islam movement or Elijah Muhammad." In fact, Forster pointed out, American Jews enjoyed a "friendly and cooperative association" with Arab-American officials. The greatest threat posed by black Muslims, Forster believed, centered on what he described as the "basically anti-white" orientation of the Nation of Islam. While Forster did acknowledge that Jews formed part of white America, he cautioned that the black separatist group was "not anti-Jewish per se." For the ADL leader, postwar accommodationism extended to black nationalist groups as well.[27]

The following year, Nathan Edelstein of the AJCongress framed his understanding of the Nation of Islam in similar terms. While he warned in his June 1960 speech to the National Community Relations Advisory Council (NCRAC) that the Arab nationalist component of the black Muslim movement tended to push the organization to an anti-Jewish position, the AJCongress leader still minimized the threat posed by the Nation of Islam. "We doubt whether the bulk of its followers," Edelstein argued in reference to black Muslims, "are presently committed to anti-Semitism." For Edelstein, the conflict between Jews and black Muslims paralleled the larger divisions emerging between Jewish liberals and black moderates. In language similar to Spingarn's, Edelstein warned, "The new militant Negro demands his rights" and "will not accept patronizing assurance of future action." He criticized his coreligionists for their failure to respond to the fast-changing race-relations scene. "Little thought and attention have been given to the relationship between the Negro and Jewish rank and file," he admonished, forcing Jews to focus on what he described as the "serious consequences" and "growing conflicts" between blacks and Jews.[28]

In 1961, AJCongress Commission on Law and Social Action founder and chairman Shad Polier, a defense attorney in the famed *Scottsboro* case and later executive committee member of the NAACP, adopted what would seem a surprising position toward the Nation of Islam. Polier received word that thirty-eight black Muslims incarcerated at the U.S. Reformatory in Lorton, Virginia, were "forbidden to wear medals symbolic of their faith, although that privilege is accorded to Catholics, Baptists, etc." Nation of Islam inmates, Polier also learned, had been denied their right to speak to religious advisors and could not recite daily prayers. In his analysis of the situation at Lorton, Polier made no mention of black antisemitism, the divisive rhetoric of the Nation of Islam, or the possible threat these inmates could pose to society. For him, the case revolved around the constitutional right to free religious expression: the black Muslim inmates had been treated unjustly. In a written appeal to the warden, Polier demanded that their religious rights enjoy protection.[29]

The AJC took a more cautious tack in its 1959 investigation of the Nation of Islam. AJC regional director Kaminsky learned of a mass rally and address planned by Nation leader Elijah Muhammad at the Mosque Theater in Newark, New Jersey. While Muhammad had delivered an address in Newark the previous December, his strength and popularity in the ensuing months caught the attention of the community's black leadership, local politicians, the media, and the AJC. Despite the Nation's political marginalization, AJC officials still feared its leader. His charismatic personality, willingness to confront racism in the most dramatic rhetorical terms, and ability to inspire even nonbelieving African American listeners concerned Jewish leaders. Elijah Muhammad, they feared, could earn the respect of his black audiences, even if they chose not to join his movement.[30]

In the weeks preceding Muhammad's scheduled Newark talk, the AJC's Samuel Kaminsky mobilized, urging local black leaders and elected city officials to renounce the Nation of Islam as a divisive splinter group. Kaminsky called the Urban League's Pawley, who downplayed the threat. While Pawley was "distressed about this racist group coming into Newark and very unhappy about it," he did not think the Nation posed a serious risk to intergroup relations. The black Muslim group, according to the Urban League director, amounted to nothing more than "a comparatively new group" that did not enjoy much visibility in the black community.[31]

Pawley's assessment was shared by local and state NAACP leader Sam Williams, who thought a high-profile campaign against the Nation of

Islam would backfire. Williams rebuffed Kaminsky's call for a public condemnation of the Nation because, as he explained to the AJC leader, the national office of the NAACP had already gone on record against the black Muslim group. As Kaminsky reported to his superiors, Williams thought that "it is one of those things that the less you do about it, the better." According to Williams, the Nation would "die a natural death if you let it alone" and warned that "if Muhammad is attacked and gets a great deal of publicity, unthinking Negroes will rally to his support."[32]

Local news coverage surrounding the Muhammad lecture reaffirmed Williams's position. An AJC-sponsored review of local African American and mainstream news media outlets revealed few areas of concern. Kaminsky reported that Newark's largest black newspaper, the *Afro-American*, "seems to have no concern or interest" in Muhammad's talk. In the issue circulating just a day prior to the Mosque Theater speech, the AJC reported "no mention or reference whatsoever to this meeting, to Muhammad or to the organization he heads." Only one newspaper, *The New Jersey Herald News*, published sympathetic stories on the Nation, encouraging readers to attend the event and reflect on the import of Muhammad's message. AJC leaders, though, proved unconcerned by the coverage. Kaminsky reassured his colleagues that "there are no references to Jews in the article" and was further buoyed by his personal friendship with Herbert H. Tate, the treasurer of the newspaper's board of directors. Tate, Kaminsky explained, was "very well disposed toward Jews" because he was quite active in several intergroup organizations and had just returned from a visit to Israel "with glowing reports" of the Jewish state.[33]

However, AJC officials still thought it important to monitor the event and appealed to the Newark chapter of the Urban League as well as the mayor's office for support. Both agreed to the AJC request. The Urban League's Pawley asked Arnette East, a human relations activist from the group's Essex County chapter, to "attend the Mohammad meeting and to give [the AJC] a complete report of what takes place and her impressions." The mayor sent Walter D. Chambers, the assistant director of the city's Commission on Group Relations, to offer his own undercover perspective of the evening.[34]

In his September 8, 1959, confidential report on the speech and rally, Chambers noted that the 1,500 to 2,000 attendees heard a lengthy, rambling, and disjointed speech that critiqued racism and offered Islam as a powerful alternative to Christianity, a religion, Muhammad charged, imposed upon blacks by whites during slavery. Although Chambers did hear a "cryptic statement" made by the Nation of Islam leader that "they killed Jesus and he was preaching good," neither Chambers nor the AJC officials who read the report reacted with concern. Instead, most of the analysis focused on the anti-white sentiments of the Nation of Islam and its refusal to admit light-skinned blacks to the event. The AJC, like the AJCongress and the ADL, did not perceive the Nation of Islam as a viable threat to Jewish interests.[35]

In the three years following Muhammad's 1959 lecture in Newark, the Nation of Islam grew in both size and prominence. Although the numbers are disputed, estimates of the Nation's membership range from a low of 100,000 to a high of 250,000. Nearly forty American cities hosted black Muslim houses of worship. Assessments of the Nation of Islam's influence, though, cannot easily be gleaned from membership numbers alone. By 1962, many African Americans turned a sympathetic ear to the Nation's message. Even as nearly three-quarters of black community leaders registered their disapproval of the black Muslim group in a Harris poll published by *Newsweek* magazine, rank-and-file African American respondents offered a much smaller 43 percent disapproval rating. When asked whether they supported the Nation of Islam, only 10 percent of the black leadership agreed. But when pollsters asked the same question to the African American community at large, nearly half (47 percent), responded that they were "unsure." The idea of a powerful black-centered organization willing to challenge the racial status quo offered at least some appeal to millions of African Americans without formal ties to the group.[36]

Yet American Jewish leaders continued to frame the black Muslim movement in sympathetic terms, even as the group's antisemitic rhetoric reached a crescendo with the rhetoric of Malcolm X in 1962 and 1963. When the Zionist quarterly *Midstream* decided to run a 1962 article on black Muslims by William Worthy, the foreign correspondent for the Baltimore *Afro-American* newspaper, it urged readers to empathize with Worthy's subjects. "One of the chief weaknesses of our society," the *Midstream* editors admonished, "is the fact that we are seldom aware of what the people on the other side of the street think or feel." In a biting critique of American Jews, they stressed that "this is particularly so in the case of the complete lack of empathy on the part of whites and Negroes." Black

Muslims, they concluded, "have become somewhat of a myth of whom nearly everyone has heard but whom hardly anyone really knows." When Elijah Muhammad allied himself with the notorious antisemite George Lincoln Rockwell in 1962, AJC leaders took special care to avoid public confrontation. Instead of launching their own campaign against Muhammad or the Nation of Islam, AJC staff was instructed to solicit the backing of local moderate black leaders who would, in ideal circumstances, lead the public charge against the black Muslim movement. Local AJC leaders were advised against taking action "which in any way would make it appear that the American Jewish Committee is instigating such reaction to the Black Muslims" and suggested that the AJC respond to the Nation of Islam's antisemitism by enlisting Jesse Owens as a possible narrator for a documentary film showing how Nazis persecuted blacks as well as Jews.[37]

The more antisemitic public profile of the Nation of Islam did not change Shad Polier's assessment of the group. When critics of the Nation charged that the black Muslims did not represent a legitimate religious group, the AJCongress leader recoiled, advising doubters to read *The Black Muslims in America*, a scholarly treatment of the Nation of Islam authored by C. Eric Lincoln, an African American Christian. In a full-page defense of the group's religious standing, Polier urged Jews not to let Muhammad's antisemitism sensationalize the black Muslim movement, which he considered "none the less essentially a religion."[38]

Two arguments explain this unusual response. During the consensus-oriented political climate of the early postwar years, Jewish leaders downplayed even the Nation of Islam's most objectionable rhetoric in order to minimize its negative impact and keep public attention focused on the cooperative work of blacks and Jews in the civil rights movement. This counterintuitive response demonstrated the organized Jewish leadership's abiding desire to project an image of America based on intergroup cooperation. In this tactical approach to liberal reform, not even the antisemitic rhetoric of Elijah Muhammad and his followers could challenge the consensus-based liberalism that united blacks and Jews. On a more practical level, Jewish leaders considered the Nation of Islam a small, marginal, and radicalized group. By placing it at the center of the Jewish political agenda, leaders would only offer it a stronger platform to advance its views. This posturing would contrast with strategies employed only a decade later when the black Muslim movement emerged in Jewish

communal politics as a symbolic nemesis to American democratic pluralism and Jewish communal self-interest.

The sentiments of Polier and his colleagues in organized Jewish leadership did not last much beyond the mid-1960s. The fiery antisemitic
rhetoric of an increasingly militant Nation of Islam combined with larger
tensions in the traditional black-Jewish alliance drove an insurmountable
wedge between Jewish leaders and a black Muslim group that, for a short
time, enjoyed the benefits of a consensus-minded Jewish leadership.
When those early postwar Jewish leaders offered their support for black
autonomy, they were constructing a new political model that would later
guide the American Jews through their own communal transformation.
The dissolution of the black-Jewish alliance and the embrace of group-
based liberalism in the mid-1960s did not emerge from divergent views on
American political reform: it matured from social dynamics well understood, predicted, and later emulated by a broad cross-section of American
Jewish leadership.

Jews, Group Status, and the Great Society

I n the early postwar years, civil rights organizations tended to focus their work on the premise that African Americans enjoy the same political rights as any other citizen. Rooted in the notion that each and every American enjoyed the same individual-based rights, black leaders demanded legal protection from the courts and eventually a federal civil rights law from Congress. Their strategic focus on individual rights contrasted with the Jim Crow system that categorized blacks as a group and deprived them of basic rights based upon that affiliation. Under the leadership of Dr. King and others, African American civil rights activists sought to undo centuries of group-based racism in favor of an individual-based legal equality that protected them from second-class treatment by white southern authorities.

For Jews who suffered centuries of group-based antisemitic discrimination prior to their arrival on American shores, the emphasis on individual rights in American law proved critical to their ability to live as free and equal U.S. citizens. The constitutional guarantees of free religious expression combined with a legal system that counted Jews equally with non-Jewish citizens fueled an impressive and relatively fast climb up the social mobility ladder. When Jews joined the civil rights struggle, they sought to extend the individual-rights protections of American law to African

America. In the early postwar years, civil rights activism meant an end to group status and an embrace of individual rights.

In the mid-1960s, the nation's political understanding of individual and group-based rights turned on its head. An emerging group of black nationalists pressed for greater and stronger group-based consciousness in the hopes that it could lead to a stronger, more identified African American community. They pushed back against the interracial platform of the early postwar years, pointing out the many ways racial discrimination wove into the very fabric of American society. Institutional racism, as this form of discrimination came to be known, energized young African Americans to press for a more ambitious and group-centered political agenda that focused liberal attention on the deep and profound social impact of a racism characterized, in part, by its very legal invisibility.

Black activists found a surprising political ally in President Lyndon Baines Johnson, whose desire to complete the unfinished work of his mentor Franklin D. Roosevelt's New Deal demanded federal government attention to the question of racial inequality. LBJ, unlike FDR, placed group status at the center of his social reform program. The Great Society recognized systemic racial inequality and designed government programs with that in mind. Whereas group status once meant marginalization, Johnson turned it on its head with programs that gave preferential treatment to designated minorities. Anything less, he and his policy advisors understood, would fuel a never-ending race-based cycle of poverty that would keep racial minorities at the margins of American society.

A critical study of Jewish organizational responses to the Great Society helps us better understand their evolving support for Black Power. While Johnson's social reform program ran contemporaneously with the rise of black nationalism, the Great Society provided an opportunity for Jewish leaders to wrestle with a fast-changing political climate. American Jews, otherwise averse to group-status recognition in the public sphere, embraced both black nationalist calls for group identity as well as the Johnson administration's desire to recognize institutional racism as an American scourge deserving federal government attention. They understood the deleterious impact of racism, joining government officials and civil rights leaders in their calls for a new approach to racial justice. Almost all Jewish leaders backed affirmative action efforts intended to redress historic discrimination. The rise of black militancy and Johnson's group-based social reform program, Jewish leaders understood, followed as the next logical step on the path to racial equality. Recognition of group status, once anathema to Jews, moved to the center of its new political strategy.

The Great Society also offered the nation's leading Jewish organizations a platform to wrestle with important issues internal to American Jews yet central to their ongoing role in the struggle for racial equality. Postwar social mobility complicated earlier claims of Jewish marginality as a rationale for bringing blacks and Jews together. Instead, the Jewish move into "whiteness" reframed the power dynamics at play and forced American Jews to rethink the terms of their alliance. When Great Society programs tested long-held Jewish communal opposition to funding private religious schools, Jewish leaders confronted constituents with competing notions of what it meant to be a loyal, patriotic American Jew, and, for the purposes of 1960s identity politics, a Jewish nationalist. In short, the Great Society operated as a political stage for Jews as they worked out a number of communal dynamics that led, eventually, to a sea change in their approaches to group-based liberalism, Black Power, and their own standing as American Jews.

The Great Society

In Washington, D.C., President Lyndon B. Johnson designed a social reform program, the Great Society, that brought a group-centered approach to federal policy. Its goals reflected many of the underlying assumptions informing the Black Power movement: that racism extended across regions and without regard to the presence of specific legal codes, and that equality of opportunity, a favored goal among white liberal gradualists, would never realize racial equality, and only through African American-led grassroots activism would change occur. Ultimately, the federal government would need to demand affirmative actions to ensure equal opportunity for designated minority groups who otherwise would never enjoy the full benefits of American citizenship.

Johnson's social reform efforts began within weeks of his elevation to the presidency following John F. Kennedy's assassination. During his 1964 State of the Union address, President Johnson declared an "unconditional war on poverty in America." He pressed Congress to expand its civil rights focus beyond Jim Crow and recognize the critical link between racial status and economic class. Rather than focusing federal efforts on relieving "the symptoms of poverty," LBJ sought a plan of action that identified poverty's underlying causes so that it could first be cured, and ultimately, prevented from reemerging in American society.

Johnson first employed the phrase "the Great Society" at the May 1964 Ohio University commencement. There, the president urged the graduates to "build a Great Society," which he defined as "a society where no child will go unfed, and no youngster will go unschooled." Two weeks later, LBJ expanded his thoughts at the University of Michigan's graduation ceremony. "We are going to assemble the best thought and broadest knowledge from all over the world," he implored, "to find these answers." Johnson announced plans to create "working groups" to address a list of race-based challenges that included deteriorating conditions in American cities and substandard public education in African American neighborhoods. Soon after the Michigan address, Johnson formed no fewer than fourteen different task forces, each charged with studying a separate social problem. The Great Society aligned the federal government with contemporary sociological research as well as African American grassroots activism that linked institutional racism to social, economic, and political inequality, writ large.[1]

In the months prior to the 1964 presidential election, Congress introduced, considered, and passed the Economic Opportunity Act of 1964, the inaugural legislative effort for LBJ's War on Poverty. The new law pressed for grassroots African American engagement by creating Community Action Programs, neighborhood youth corps, job corps, and VISTA (Volunteers in Service to America). These programs, and others, sought to achieve their goals by circumscribing established political infrastructure in favor of empowering local activists who had been historically disenfranchised.

When voters went to the polls in November 1964, they elected Johnson in a landslide. Garnering some 61 percent of the popular vote as well as 486 of the possible 528 electoral votes, LBJ also enjoyed an eighty-ninth Congress where the Democratic party counted a filibuster-proof two-thirds majority in both the House and the Senate. American Jews joined the Johnson victory party with 90 percent of their vote, a level unseen since Franklin D. Roosevelt's 1944 reelection. When the new Congress first met in January 1965, it debated the first of eighty-seven separate Great Society bills. By the end of that Congress, President Johnson signed no fewer than eighty-four bills into law.[2]

Johnson expanded on his legislative thinking when he addressed the historically black Howard University in June 1965. In a speech that would come to define LBJ's domestic priorities, the president called attention to the failures of the earlier rights-based approach to liberal reform. "You do not take a person who for years has been hobbled by chains and liberate him, bring him up to the starting line of a race and then say, 'you are free to compete with all the others,' and still justly believe that you have been completely fair." The president wanted the Howard University graduating class, and the nation at large, to know that equality of opportunity would not address systemic racism. More than just "freedom," LBJ urged, African Americans needed programs that brought "opportunity." In place of the historic reliance on political strategies that sought "equality as a right and a theory," Johnson wanted programs that brought "equality as a fact and equality as a result." Those words would serve as LBJ's controlling thesis for a host of Great Society program ideas.[3]

LBJ faced opposition from both sides of the political aisle. From the right, conservatives charged Johnson with undermining the individual rights-based approach of American democracy. They saw an abandonment of middle-class white America and feared that government intervention would remove incentives for individual initiative. A race-based society, many rightist critics argued, undermined a meritocratic system and gave unearned and undeserved rewards to people based on the color of their skin. From the center left, northern white urban ethnics, critical to FDR's New Deal coalition, considered LBJ's race-based policies too threatening. Satisfied with the legal protections won during the civil rights movement, many followed a path to political conservatism, voting for Republican candidates in both the 1966 congressional and 1968 presidential elections. Leftists criticized the president's willingness to compromise on what they considered the most important parts of his program. They faulted liberalism for its mediocrity, arguing that the Great Society amounted, in their minds, to nothing more than continued white liberal paternalism and accommodationism. With such broad-based political opposition, historian Allen J. Matusow observed, "the War on Poverty was destined to be one of the great failures of twentieth-century liberalism."[4]

Jewish Responses to the Great Society

The Great Society pressed American Jews into an awkward social and political position. At once, LBJ's social reform program affirmed historic Jewish affinity for liberal causes just as it demanded changes in the established narrative of black-Jewish cooperation. Jews flocked to Johnson as white America's leading supporters of his innovative approach to addressing racism. Yet, as a population experienced in antisemitism and conscious of itself as a marginal group, American Jews showed ambivalence when government policymakers' application of group status excluded poor Jews from government programs because they were considered part of privileged white America.

On an even deeper level, the group-based thinking that buttressed the Great Society offended American Jews sensitive to such an approach's discriminatory possibilities. When affirmative action programs led, in some cases, to the creation of numerical quotas to guarantee compliance with civil rights initiatives, most Jewish organizations balked, all too familiar with the use of antisemitic quotas from at least the 1920s through the 1950s. In early and mid-twentieth-century America, antisemites employed group-based thinking to corporatize Jews. Restrictive quotas limited Jewish matriculation at the nation's leading universities while housing covenants prevented Jews from settling in white suburban communities. Memories of popular antisemitic figures such as Charles Lindbergh and Father Charles Coughlin alarmed Jewish leaders who focused their communal political strategies on the protection of individual rights as the basis for social reform efforts.

Despite those concerns, American Jews across the communal spectrum backed Johnsonian liberalism. As African American leaders in a variety of civil rights organizations lobbied Johnson for greater grassroots participation, heightened focus on the needs of blacks, and federal legislation that embraced a group-based approach, Jewish communal leaders rallied their constituencies. As representatives of organized Jewish life, they recognized institutional racism as a grave threat to American democracy and, by and large, defended group-based programs such as affirmative action as a necessary step in the larger struggle for racial equality. When Great Society officials categorized Jews as "white," making them ineligible for programs designed for African American and other communities of color, Jewish communal leaders offered only limited objections, advocating support for poor Jews. Even as a minority of Jews would reject the Great Society, emerging in later years as leaders of the neoconservative backlash, most Jews aligned themselves with African American leaders dissatisfied with the limited goals of legal equality, at least as expressed by the Civil Rights Act of 1964 and the Voting Rights Act of 1965.

In national surveys, Jewish respondents supported administration calls for more aggressive liberal programs. In June 1964, the Gallup organization reported that 83 percent of its Jewish respondents approved of LBJ's job performance, compared to a national rate of 74 percent. Sixteen months later, Jewish backing of the Democratic president still hovered at 80 percent. When so many white urban northern ethnics jumped to the Republican Party during the 1966 midterm congressional elections, American Jews stayed within the Democratic fold. During the 1968 presidential election, Democrat Hubert Humphrey counted 81 percent of the American Jewish vote in his unsuccessful 1968 campaign against Richard Nixon. A 1968 poll revealed that Jews were almost twice as likely as white Protestants to consider "racial inequality" the most important major issue of the day. Over a third of Jewish respondents thought civil rights reform "too slow," again outpacing white Protestants. When asked to assess the importance of "law and order," a political slogan associated with opposition to continuing civil rights measures, fewer than one in ten Jews ranked it first compared to nearly a quarter of white Protestant respondents.[5]

Rabbis cited traditional Jewish text to recognize the needs of African Americans and support group-based Great Society programs. In sermons they delivered to their congregants as well as books and articles they published, Jewish religious leaders offered a Judaic rationale for Black Power as the logical consequence of a civil rights movement hindered by a federal government otherwise blind to extralegal racism. For them, the precepts of Judaism offered the building blocks necessary to construct a Jewish argument friendly to black militancy. Even as blacks and Jews took separate political paths, rabbis helped build a new black-Jewish consensus by linking Judaism's ethical obligations to the stepped-up demands of black activists. For these Jewish leaders, Johnson's social reform proposals aligned with rabbinic mandates to care for the poor, welcome the stranger, and remember what it was like to be a slave in Egypt.

In the Reform movement, Rabbi Richard Hirsch of the Religious Action

Center (RAC), based in Washington, D.C., drew parallels between LBJ's call to action and Judaism's impulse to take care of the poor. In a 130-page booklet, "There Shall Be No Poor," Hirsch differentiated the social justice approaches of American Jews from those of Protestant Christian denominations. Recalling the social Darwinist thinking that dominated government welfare policy in the late nineteenth and early twentieth centuries, Hirsch rejected "survival of the fittest" thinking. In a survey of Jewish textual references to poverty and its causes, the Reform rabbi affirmed that "our forefathers realized that an unrestricted pursuit of individual economic interest would result in massive concentrations of wealth for the few and oppressive poverty for the many. They sanctioned competition but they rejected 'rugged individualism.'" In Hirsch's view, Jewish tradition offered acknowledgment, and a plan of action, for the systemic race-based discrimination that led to African American impoverishment and the privileging of white Americans. Jews, informed by religious texts that do not place responsibility for poverty on the poor themselves, were obligated to recognize systemic inequality and care for each and every member of their community.[6]

Rabbi Henry Cohen, a participant in nonviolent direct-action civil rights protests, also drew parallels between the government's approach to the War on Poverty and traditional Jewish mandates to help the poor. In his 1968 book that took its title, *Justice, Justice*, from the Torah injunction to seek social reform, Cohen lauded Johnson for stepping away from Protestant-inspired notions that blamed individuals for their hardship and embracing the notion that systemic forces better explained the plight of the impoverished in America. Cohen taught his readers that it was New Deal Jewish social workers who first steered the federal government away from its habit of calling poor people lazy and blaming them for their own poverty, especially as the forces of a modern industrial economy wreaked havoc on Americans regardless of their willingness to work. Most of all, Rabbi Cohen pressed his coreligionists to wake up to the inherent weakness of the rights-based liberalism of yore. By focusing "less on equality before the law and more on social and economic equality, less on banning the discriminatory acts of individuals and more on attacking the basic causes of ignorance and poverty, less on the South as a region and more on America as a nation," Cohen linked his interpretation of Jewish tradition with the emerging group-based liberal approach of President Johnson.[7]

Within American Orthodoxy, Rabbi Jerry Hochbaum, a sociologist at Yeshiva University, opposed group-based programs in an address to the Rabbinical Council of America. For Hochbaum and other observant Jews, the Great Society posed two fundamental questions. First, is the Great Society even a Jewish matter? Because Johnson's social reform program grew from the civil authority, was focused on non-Jews, and did not specifically intersect with the needs of observant Jews, most Orthodox groups in the United States did not even engage the question. In their view, as Hochbaum summarized, "racial and urban unrest is not a Jewish concern." Some took the more strident position that Jewish support of the Great Society proved nothing more than the continuing civil rights work of "liberal extremists" from the non-Orthodox Jewish community.[8]

Second, did Great Society programs align with the communal needs of observant Jews? In Hochbaum's estimation, the Great Society failed to meet the needs of Jews because it backed "the switch from individual to group rights." While other Jewish denominational leaders led the call for broader understandings of cultural pluralism, and public programs that would support group-based identity, Hochbaum flinched. "Many Negro ideologues' conception of American pluralism," he argued in reference to the new group-based consciousness emerging in the African American community, challenged Jewish interests. Citing the American Jewish community's ability to scale the social mobility ladder without specific group-based privileges, Hochbaum argued that "it has been accepted as a principle that an individual's merit, rather than his family or group membership, must be the basis for his advancement and recognition."[9]

Outside of the religious sphere, leading national Jewish organizations connected their support for Johnson's War on Poverty with their backing of Black Power as well. In his signature Great Society program, LBJ understood the group-based and racist nature of wealth distribution. Poverty affected communities of color in disproportionate numbers, provoking black activists to press for more radical social reform programs. Jewish organizational leaders understood those race-based connections and pressed for a more aggressive federal posture in response. Echoing the religious arguments made by American rabbis, Jewish agency leaders also located their mission-drive support for black activism in the religious precepts of Judaism.

When the Council of Jewish Federations and Welfare Funds (CJFWF), the umbrella organization that united the main fundraising and grant-making bodies of local Jewish communities across the country, met for its 1964 General Assembly, it "commended the President and Congress for enacting the Economic Opportunity Act." Two years later the Council backed increased congressional appropriations for the War on Poverty, arguing, "our country has the resources to strengthen and expand these and other efforts to combat poverty." Officials from local chapters of the JCRC and its national parent group, the NCRAC, backed similar positions. At its 1967 meeting, the CJFWF pressed for "much stronger anti-poverty measures" and backed Johnson's strategy of grassroots activism to achieve success.[10]

The AJCongress stood squarely in Johnson's camp as well. At its April 1964 national convention, delegates passed a resolution that "warmly welcomes President Johnson's announced intention to wage a 'war on poverty'" and backed "federal legislation for such things as full employment, aid to public school education and the construction of needed housing." Even the AJC, positioned on the center-right of the American Jewish organizational spectrum, endorsed the War on Poverty, and embraced many of the sociological findings and public policy positions that would come to define both the Great Society and the emerging Black Power movement. In an April 1964 statement, the AJC affirmed, "The burdens of poverty fall heaviest on Negroes and members of other minority groups." It blamed this demographic reality on the pervasive impact of American racism.[11]

In a private 1968 memo to members of the AJC's executive board and urban affairs committee, the group's Washington, D.C., representative, Hyman Bookbinder, went so far as to invoke the controversial August 1964 Gulf of Tonkin resolution, passed by Congress to give President Johnson wide latitude in the escalation of U.S. troop involvement in Southeast Asia, as a metaphor and a model for the government's approach to solving systemic race-based discrimination in the War on Poverty. Calling for a "domestic Tonkin Resolution," Bookbinder urged "a declaration by the Congress and the President that we will take every step that may be necessary to ward off the enemy, to win the war against poverty and racism." Bookbinder's war metaphor, applied to a war in Vietnam already unpopular by the time of his 1968 comments, reflected the depth of Jewish organizational support for LBJ's efforts.[12]

The Culture of Poverty

As Johnson unfurled several high-profile Great Society programs, Jewish organizational leaders advanced specific group-based initiatives, backed the federal government's new approaches to social reform, and articulated arguments that would both reflect and anticipate the rise of black nationalist thinking on the national scene. They understood African American frustration over the slow pace of social change and especially of the federal government's historic foot dragging when it came to creating laws that would bring meaningful progress in the struggle for racial equality. With calls from black activists to pressure Washington into action, Jewish leaders responded with a far-reaching strategy to realize more participatory federal civil rights programs.

In April 1964, for example, the AJC offered its opinion on the concept of a "culture of poverty," first described in Oscar Lewis's 1959 ethnography *Five Families: Mexican Case Studies in the Culture of Poverty* and later embraced by President Johnson. The AJC concluded, "The persistence of poverty has created its own abortive culture so pervasive that millions of Americans feel alienated from the rest of society and denied participation in our democratic system." Poverty, the AJC explained, "perpetuated in families from one generation to the next, imprisoning the young in a web of hopelessness from which they see no escape." With that assertion, the AJC embraced what would become one of the most controversial assumptions of the Great Society; dysfunction within black families created a culture of poverty that demanded federal action to remedy.[13]

In a fascinating extension of the culture of poverty to the State of Israel, AJCongress leader Shad Polier identified weak family structure as the causal agent for social inequality among Israeli Sephardic Jews. In an August 1963 newsletter to his constituents, Polier paralleled the family experiences of African Americans in the white-dominated United States with systemic Ashkenazi discrimination against Jews of color in Israel. While African Americans struggled to improve their civic status in the United States, Polier explained, Sephardic Jews in Israel lived in homes that were "culturally deprived" with parents who "are therefore less able to aid their children in their educational efforts and less motivated to do so."[14]

The Great Society argument blaming the culture of poverty on a racist system that created absentee African American fathers, overworked African American mothers, and neglected African American children centered on research conducted by sociologist and later U.S. Senator Daniel Patrick Moynihan. In his pathbreaking and controversial "The Negro Family: The Case for National Action," Moynihan affirmed the group-based origins of American poverty and demanded a far more activist government response. Despite the legislative victories that brought the Civil Rights Act of 1964 and later the Voting Rights Act of 1965, government data showed continued downward trends for African Americans. According to Moynihan, dysfunction within the African American family, specifically the absence of fathers, prevented blacks from achieving any sort of meaningful social mobility. The rise of single-mother households, contemporaneous with increased government welfare support, implied for Moynihan that American racism, from its origins in slavery to the post-emancipation Jim Crow South and, by the 1960s, to urban America in the North, proved the causal agent for family dysfunction and its next logical consequence, systemic race-based poverty.[15]

Moynihan, as well as his colleagues in Washington and a new generation of sympathetic academic sociologists, argued that poverty tended to affect African Americans more than others because a deep and profound culture developed in poor African American households, making it very difficult for children to imagine, much less achieve, a better economic reality. In order to break the cyclical nature of this destructive culture, Moynihan pressed for legislation that he hoped would strengthen the black family by improving education for African Americans from kindergarten through to the university.

The Moynihan Report, as it was more popularly known, earned immediate rebuke across the political spectrum. Conservatives rejected its recommendations as continuing evidence of the Johnson administration's abandonment of individual rights in favor of race-based government privilege. Leftists joined many in the African American community who read the Moynihan Report as patronizing to blacks. The well-intentioned social reformer, in their view, advanced negative stereotypes in a way that ignored the impact of institutional racism. Most of all, Moynihan embraced a naive white liberal view that affirmed the virtues of an American democratic system that many of the report's critics held responsible for creating a race-divided nation in the first place.

Jewish leaders, by and large, backed Moynihan's thinking. They interpreted the report's findings as the next logical step in the struggle for racial equality, revealing fundamental shifts in the ways Jewish social justice advocates reframed their rationale for engaging in the continuing struggle for racial equality. By the era of the Great Society, Jewish leaders recognized the basic differences between Jews, who enjoyed a rapid rise in the United States, and African Americans, who still suffered from far-reaching racism. Applying that revisionist approach back through Jewish history, Rabbi Henry Cohen reminded his congregants that Jews, when offered emancipation in eighteenth-century Europe, "emerged from the ghetto with their family life intact." Jews, he explained, "were allowed to run their own community affairs and to preserve their basic institutions, and there was none more basic than the family." A typical African American, on the other hand, was "deprived of the vote, called 'boy' by men half his age, [and] educated to be a sharecropper."[16]

Challenging a conservative political critique that blamed African Americans for a mid-1960s increase in black crime, Cohen offered a text-based argument. "How should one feel about the criminal himself?" Cohen wrote in reference to a question asked by the Jewish sage Hillel. Hillel's response, that Jews should not "judge your neighbor until you have come into his place," prompted the Reform rabbi to assert, "It is ultimately impossible for a white person to put himself in the place of a Negro slum dweller." According to Cohen, American Jews did not understand nor could they comprehend the experience of blacks. For Cohen, the consensus-based ideals that brought blacks and Jews together during the 1950s and early 1960s demanded fundamental change. Only a deep and abiding respect for the differences between the two groups could move the alliance, and the struggle for justice, forward.[17]

Affirmative Action and Quotas

Perhaps the most visible group-based program of the Great Society, affirmative action, tested Jewish communal support for President Johnson's aggressive plans for racial justice just as it postured organized Jewish communal support of Black Power. While Jews once suffered under early twentieth-century antisemitic quotas that limited their social mobility, they backed affirmative action measures in the 1960s because they understood the need for a more aggressive government approach. At a time when black nationalists rejected liberal gradualism and demanded systemic changes in government, Jewish leaders understood and agreed, even at a potential cost to their own community. With their support of affirmative action, Jewish leaders once again foreshadowed support for the emerging Black Power movement. Great Society–era Jewish social justice activism demanded recognition of group status and support for government programs that gave preference to blacks.

Affirmative action, with its origins in the Kennedy administration, emerged as a response to the limitations of the rights-based civil rights strategy popularized by Dr. King in the early postwar years. The legal right to equal opportunity, Great Society policymakers noted, did not translate into real equality. African Americans remained, despite their civil rights victories, on the margins of economic, political, and social life. In order to achieve real equality, many civil rights activists argued, government must move beyond its rights-based approach and take a more aggressive stance. It must examine its civil rights failures, develop new ideas and approaches to combating racial discrimination, and take some form of affirmative action to implement its new ideas. Without these added efforts, Great Society reformers believed, the promise of racial equality would never be achieved.[18]

For African Americans, affirmative action offered the hope that generations of discrimination could be countervailed by specific, targeted, government programs meant to give deserving and worthy blacks opportunities otherwise closed to them by institutional racism. For most northern white ethnics, affirmative action only further deepened their animus for the Great Society. As Danzig recounted, the African American call for "compensatory hiring and preferential treatment" faced stiff resistance from old-time liberals because "it conflicted with the traditional liberal ideal of equal opportunity and equal treatment of people according to their individual merits." Opponents charged that hardworking whites could not gain access to Great Society programs while African Americans, solely by virtue of their skin color, enjoyed the benefits of federal largesse. As Johnson pressed for stronger affirmative action programs, working-class whites bolted, arguing that these new liberal programs amounted to nothing less than reverse racism. The color-blind society promised in the civil rights era of the 1950s, they believed, had degenerated into a color-conscious society that marginalized hardworking whites based on their racial classification.[19]

Northern Jews understood the continuing challenges facing African Americans, breaking with other northern white urban ethnics by embracing a group-centered political consciousness that demanded a more activist federal government social reform agenda. For Jews, who in the early postwar years identified more closely with African Americans and by the mid-1960s began to understand themselves as part of the white mainstream, debates over affirmative action offered a vivid, if not unique, lens into the complexities of an ever-changing approach to liberal reform. Of the major national Jewish organizations, the AJCongress took the most aggressive stance in favor of affirmative action. As early as 1963, it published "An End to Gradualism," asserting that "the most grievous error made over the years in the struggle to achieve Negro equality was the acceptance of the assumption that it could be realized through a step-by-step, evolutionary process." The left-leaning organization acknowledged that it "failed to understand historical experience which demonstrates that movements seeking justice and freedom are not appeased by limited redresses of grievances, that, indeed, such token acts only excite the desire for complete and radical change." In order to achieve success, the AJCongress concluded that it "must challenge not simply limited areas of inequality but the entire system, root, and branch, here and now."[20]

By 1968, even as much of white urban ethnic America retreated from affirmative action, Will Maslow, an attorney who started his career running field operations for President Roosevelt's Fair Employment Practices Commission during World War II before rising to the position of the AJCongress's executive director in 1960, held firm in the conviction that the federal government still needed to go "beyond civil rights" in order to remedy past injustices "that remain after the task of passing the anti-discrimination laws has been completed." As it did before, the AJCongress defended its support for activist government by linking the plight of marginalized Americans in the 1960s to the historical experience of Jews. "Just as we reject exclusion of Jews from any aspect of our society," the AJCongress affirmed in a resolution passed at its 1968 Biennial Convention, "we cannot look the other way when other minorities are in fact so excluded." Maslow called for government programs to guarantee "equality of result" rather than the more modest and generally accepted goal of equal opportunity.[21]

Religious leaders framed their support for affirmative action as a public square version of *teshuvah* or "return," the Jewish concept for repentance. In postwar America, Rabbi Henry Cohen observed, it was common practice for Jews to hire fellow Jews at the expense of better-qualified non-Jews. Extending these affinity preferences to the rest of white America, Cohen detailed the development of exclusive labor models that tended to keep whites gainfully employed and blacks on the margins of the workforce "through no fault of their own." Jewish tradition, according to Cohen, required that Jews "compensate the person sinned against for whatever harm was done him." For Cohen, that demanded support for affirmative action.[22]

In his 1967 Yom Kippur sermon, Rabbi Dov Peretz Elkins, a Conservative movement rabbi at Philadelphia's Har Zion Temple, applied the Judaic concept of *teshuvah* to American racism as well. Given the Jewish obligation "to repair the damage we have done before it can be forgiven," Elkins went so far as to demand that the U.S. government compensate African Americans victimized by centuries of racism. "In terms of the war for better education, better jobs, better homes for the black man," Elkins pleaded, "we must pay reparations." With full understanding that he was venturing onto shaky political ground in his suburban Philadelphia congregation, Elkins pressed his congregants to consider "giving the Negro more rights than the white man" in the form of "opportunities in schools and jobs and homes when he has not even on the surface earned the right to such opportunities." Only through this sort of aggressive action, Elkins concluded, can white America pay "for the damage we caused to his people."[23]

Elkins extended his defense of affirmative action by invoking Israel's social divisions. In the Jewish state, Elkins pointed out, the government already adopted its own version of affirmative action by requiring a higher grade for European Jewish children to attend high school than they did for those from North Africa. While Elkins acknowledged reverse-racism concerns, he admonished that it was "the only way that the sons of the ditch diggers will be able to gain the same opportunities that the children of the lawyers and doctors have."[24]

Jews and Whiteness

Debates over affirmative action forced Jews to reflect on their own newfound power and privilege in American society. Although Jews often explained their civil rights alliance with blacks by pointing to their common histories of oppression, federal government officials classified Jews as "white" and therefore ineligible for many Great Society programs focused on improving opportunities for communities of color. Despite widespread support for group-based Great Society programs, many Jewish leaders still took exception to the Johnson administration's decision to define American social reform strategy along racial lines. Under the Great Society's binary racial classification system, Jews became part of the white privileged class and, by extension some believed, responsible for participating in the subjugation of African Americans.

Ambivalence around whiteness complicated Jewish support for the Great Society as well as the organized Jewish community's emerging alignment with Black Power thinking. Jewish community leaders prided themselves on their own group's marginality, leveraging their outsider status as a way to demonstrate their kinship with African Americans. Postwar Jewish integration into white America undermined a key premise of the black-Jewish alliance: the two communities did not share a similar sociological reality. When black militants forced whites and Jews out of leadership positions in the civil rights organizations, they announced a basic and fundamental difference between their experience as oppressed African Americans and the privileged lives of American Jews. The more white Jews became, the more strain it placed on the idea that they shared commonalities with blacks. When blacks and Jews would later forge a new identity-politics consensus modeled after Black Power, it could only be achieved with a mutual recognition of the two group's racial difference.

While Jewish leaders appreciated the need to grant African Americans preferential treatment in the form of affirmative action, many of their coreligionists flinched when Great Society policymakers placed a racial mirror in front of Jews. As historian Seth Forman reflected, efforts to "whiten" American Jewry ended with "a series of interpretations that redefine[d] benevolent Jewish attitudes toward Blacks as primarily motivated by self-interest and, to that extent, not markedly distinct from the racist attitudes of the larger white society."[25] Jewish leaders could point to a host of polls to demonstrate their community's disproportionate commitment to liberal ideals. They prided themselves on their civil rights work and criticized the Johnson administration for understating what they perceived as the precarious position of Jews within the larger white Christian society.

The assertion that Jews had joined the white majority contradicted an American Jewish history punctuated by both activism and antisemitism. Prior to the postwar period, Jews had never enjoyed the full benefits of whiteness in American society and often had faced discrimination as members of an inferior race. Turn-of-the-century immigrants from Eastern Europe suffered from unflattering racial classifications in such popular books as William Z. Ripley's *Races of Europe* (1899) and Madison Grant's *The Passing of the Great Race* (1916). In a reference that many nativists certainly applied to first-generation American Jews, Grant warned, "These immigrants adopt the language of the native American, they wear his clothes, they steal his name, and they are beginning to take his women, but they seldom adopt his religion or understand his ideals." Kenneth Roberts, writing for the popular *Saturday Evening Post*, referred to Polish Jews as "human parasites." In the Immigration Act of 1924, Congress sanctioned a national-origins quota system that all but eliminated Jewish immigration.[26]

By the mid-1960s, though, Jews teetered on the racial divide, possessing characteristics of both an accomplished and integrated immigrant community and a marginalized religious minority all too familiar with the effects of discrimination. Restrictive quotas in education, home ownership, and hiring had all but disappeared. Jewish students matriculated at the nation's leading colleges and universities while the professional ranks boasted a disproportionate number of Jews. For the first time in modern American history, Jews appeared to resemble the white majority more than they did an ethnic minority.[27]

As anthropologist Karen Brodkin observed, "In the last hundred years, Jews in the United States have been shuttled from one side of the American racial binary to the other. Their sense of Jewishness responded to and reflected their various social places." According to Brodkin, a "whitening of Jews" occurred in postwar America. With help from a federal government that offered privilege to whites over blacks and men over women, Jews moved from an era of antisemitic discrimination to "racial middleness," a condition Brodkin described as "marginality vis-à-vis whiteness and an experience of whiteness and belonging vis-à-vis blackness." Historian David Biale put it more directly: "Whether they liked it or not (and usually they did), the Jews in postwar America had become white." With access to professional jobs, suburban homes, and the nation's top colleges and universities, Jews, according to this interpretation, became "white" and formed political opinions based more on what George Lipsitz described as their "possessive investment in whiteness" than on their history as an oppressed minority group.[28]

The whitening of Jewish America clashed with Johnson's social reform measures when the president excluded the Jewish poor from some of his Great Society programs. By pouring government resources into African American neighborhoods, Johnson hoped to minimize the effects of institutional racism and open new doors of opportunity in education, local political control, and job placement. Nonetheless, 15 percent of American Jewish families struggled to survive on annual incomes less than $3,000, the amount Johnson defined as the nation's poverty level. Most did not live in one of the president's designated poverty zones, isolating them from many benefits of the War on Poverty while people over age sixty-five constituted a majority of the Jewish poor.[29]

For example, AJCongress officials Naomi Levine and Martin Hochbaum reported that in New York City, "for a number of reasons—some internal to the Jewish community and others due to the manner in which the poverty program was created and administered—Jews have, by and large, participated only minimally in this city's poverty program." Levine and Hochbaum wanted poverty "defined by need, not geography" and criticized Johnson for excluding "the Jewish poor from participating in the anti-poverty program." Their concern was "with the Jewish poor . . . in this regard, we can say unequivocally that, in spite of the billions of dollars spent in fighting poverty . . . little of this money has gone to alleviate the plight of the Jewish poor. Indeed, the war against Jewish poverty has not yet begun."[30]

Levine and Hochbaum pointed to an August 13, 1971, report from the Economic Opportunity Office affirming that the "allegation that Jews are systematically excluded from New York's poverty program participation, while imprecise, is not totally devoid of validity." Jews faced exclusion from the Job Corps because statutes limited benefits to those "currently living in an environment so characterized by cultural deprivation, a disruptive home life or other disorienting condition as to impair his participation in other education and training programs." Similar situations existed for Head Start, small business programs, and agencies geared for maximum feasible participation. "For the Jewish poor who often live outside the prescribed poverty areas," Levine and Hochbaum decried, "this approach is unfair, unjust, and inequitable." Since Jews were not a targeted minority they did not receive their share of relief despite the fact that many lived within targeted areas of the city.[31]

The AJC's New York City office fielded complaints from constituents in Williamsburg. At an executive board meeting on March 7, 1968, AJC leader Edward D. Moldover reported that most of the antipoverty boards ignored Jews and he criticized federal government guidelines that "created injustices." At a news conference called by the AJC, Rabbi Bernard Weinberger, president of the Orthodox Rabbinical Alliance of America and a member of New York's Council Against Poverty, held firm in his support for "maximum feasible participation" but cautioned that "power must be accompanied by responsibility and accountability." Weinberger noted, "The rights and needs of every individual and every group, no matter how small, must not be ignored or lost in the shuffle." Press coverage following the news conference led to a series of meetings with local and national political leaders who promised to change their "representation formula and procedures" for greater inclusion of the Jewish poor.[32]

As Jewish leaders engaged questions of affirmative action and quotas, none offered comment on the gendered nature of the entire political debate. While contemporary journalistic accounts, as well as public and private Jewish communal sources, framed the debate in racial terms, several scholars subsequently have researched, or at least opined, on the positive impact of preferential treatment on Jewish women. Although the category "Jewish" did not qualify for Great Society programs, the classification of "woman" did. Because Jewish women tended to be better educated and in the professional workforce more than African American women (or other women of color), they benefited from group-based Great Society programs.

By the late 1960s, historian Gerald Sorin reported, nearly one-quarter of American Jewish women headed to white-collar office jobs each morning. In a 1974 article published in *Dissent*, Bernard Rosenberg and Irving Howe, author of the well-known *World of Our Fathers*, reflected on the number of Jewish women in higher education. "Paradoxically enough," they concluded, "it seems likely that Jewish women have profited from 'affirmative action' since they comprise a rather large proportion of those academic women who have suffered discrimination." A generation later, historian Leonard Dinnerstein noted that affirmative action "greatly benefited Jewish women, easing their way into law and medical schools, and ultimately into professions virtually closed to them."[33]

Other than an article in the leftist magazine, *Tikkun*, no other scholarly or even journalistic study has focused on Jewish women and affirmative action. This near-total absence of a gendered analysis points to even larger questions in Great Society–era Jewish liberalism as well as the American Jewish historiography of the 1960s. How can scholars understand the impact of group-based liberal programs on Jews if they acted on women and men in such different ways? What does it say about the construction of historical memory around the Great Society and the 1960s if little public discussion took place on the status of women as a designated minority group? To what extent did Jewish support for the group-based approach of Black Power enjoy support from American Jewish women, who better understood the structural limits of a sexist and racist nation?[34]

The absence of a gendered analysis also undermines the very rhetorical foundation undergirding the Jewish debate over affirmative action, regardless of support or opposition to group-based liberalism. Meritocracy, the idea that one's own talents, rather than one's group status, should determine social mobility, emerged as the central defining feature of affirmative action debates. Jewish opponents of affirmative action claimed falsely that these Great Society programs were "bad for the Jews." Had they considered Jewish women, then they would have had to recast their opinion, or their rationale for opposing the measures.

Similarly, proponents of affirmative action invoked the meritocracy question, concluding that marginalized groups needed the extra government support. Even though they offered support, their argument against meritocracy still assumed a male-centered "bad for the Jews" premise. The debate over Jews and affirmative action was not one of meritocracy versus reverse racism. It was about the complex internal dynamics of a Jewish community that witnessed the governmental enfranchisement of women. The complexity of that gendered approach to politics rarely emerged in contemporary Jewish debates.

Group-based liberal tensions between American Jewish leadership and federal policymakers peaked when the government adopted quotas as a possible remedy for past racial injustices. Quotas synthesized the complex dynamics between several, sometimes competing, social justices approaches. At the most basic level, the Great Society recognized that legal guarantees proved insufficient to advance the struggle for racial equality. Affirmative action programs followed as the logical next legislative step. Most national Jewish organizations backed affirmative action and understood that their status as "white" translated into exclusion from many Great Society programs.

Quotas, though, added a toxic element to the mid-1960s social justice mix: the legacy of antisemitic quotas in early twentieth-century American Jewish life. In the 1920s, backlash against massive immigration from Southern and Eastern Europe sparked a nativist movement that proved antisemitic. American Jews faced restriction on a variety of social, educational, and political fronts. Restrictive quotas marginalized Jews and other immigrant groups deemed nonwhite in the social hierarchy of the time. In one famous 1922 example, Harvard University president A. Lawrence Lowell proposed a 15 percent quota on the number of Jews admitted to the nation's most prestigious school. Similar quotas limited American Jews in their educational, professional, and social lives.[35]

Forty years later, the social position of American Jews reversed. Now part of the white majority, Jews confronted quota programs that, once again, acted to limit their access to privilege. Only this time, government policymakers wrote quota programs for the purpose of empowering marginalized groups, even at the expense of the established white majority. While self-interested whites may have supported quotas in the 1920s and opposed them in the 1960s, and self-interested African Americans the reverse, Jews proved unusual, if not unique, in their continued opposition to quotas that seemed to run contrary to Jewish self-interest in both periods. The introduction of race-based quotas in the Great Society forced the question of Jewish power and privilege to the center of communal debate just as it highlighted the unusual position of American Jews as a newfound white ethnic group that also suffered a long and recent history of persecution.

As early as 1963, the AJCongress offered a two-part analysis summarizing both opportunities and concerns. "It is hardly surprising," AJCongress leader Leo Pfeffer wrote, "that this generation of American Negroes, convinced that the Negro's rendezvous with destiny is not subject to further postponement, has little patience with what appears to it to be squeamish concern on the part of non-Negroes regarding such demands as minimum quotas for Negroes." Pfeffer compared African American demands for preferential treatment with the G.I. Bill that favored veterans who applied for civil service jobs in the government. "The moral right of the Negro community" to demand similar treatment, he argued, "is hardly less." Pfeffer broke from the consensus-based assumptions that drew blacks and Jews together in their civil rights alliance. "The anti-Semitism suffered by American Jewry," he explained, "was at its worst insignificant in comparison to the injustice and inequity which has been the life of the American Negro." He concluded that American Jews had "no moral right to condemn the Negro for demanding quotas" and that, if the roles were reversed, Jews would make the same demands.[36]

Every major national Jewish organization made opposition to hiring quotas a priority. The month after Pfeffer published his defense of quotas, the AJC offered a critique of government-sponsored quota programs. The AJC noted that it "continues to oppose the creation of a system of quotas for any group," while the ADL added that restrictive quotas were "undemocratic" and violated "the American tradition that the individual stands on his own merits." The National Jewish Community Relations Advisory Council (NJCRAC) went on record opposed to "such practices, foremost among which is the use of quotas and proportional representation in hiring, upgrading and admission of minority groups" and viewed quotas "as inconsistent with principles of equality" and "harmful in the long run to all." Agudath Israel, an Orthodox group, presented the most scathing critique of the quota system. "Quotas, described by whatever euphemisms and hidden by whatever legal language and structures have no place in America," argued Bernard Fryshman, a Talmud scholar as well as a physics professor at the New York Institute of Technology. Even the AJCongress, known for its progressive political views and willingness to break with the more moderate Jewish organizations, eventually urged its constituents to "unequivocally oppose all quotas, with no exceptions."[37]

Jewish Opposition to the Great Society

Even as American Jews backed President Johnson's 1964 election with an overwhelming majority of their votes and supported his plans for a Great Society, a small yet influential minority challenged the larger American Jewish embrace of group-based consciousness and never shared the larger Jewish affinity for black militancy or its tenets. Loyal to the political idealism of leaders such as Franklin D. Roosevelt, they charged Johnson with moving liberalism too far left. As New Deal and civil rights supporters, they feared that the abandonment of an individual rights–based approach threatened to undermine the American democratic system. Some would later switch party allegiances and become Republicans while others would continue to offer their critique from the confines of the Democratic Party. Or, as Ronald Reagan, a former New Deal Democrat, loved to quip: "I didn't leave the Democratic Party. The Democratic Party left me."[38]

This Jewish backlash played out on a number of fronts, with opposition to civil rights reform in the lead. Beginning with the 1966 midterm congressional elections, the Republican Party capitalized on growing white opposition to a more militant civil rights agenda by supporting police crackdowns on black activism, whether in the form of organized political actions intended to disrupt business as usual or more spontaneous urban unrest that often turned violent. Employing the code phrase "law and order," politicians communicated their desire for a strong police presence to squash civil rights protests. The strategy worked with Republicans, who, leveraging other political issues as well, earned impressive gains in the 1966 congressional midterms and the election of Richard Nixon to the White House in 1968.

As part of a larger reevaluation of Jews and liberalism, Nathan Glazer, an intellectual leader of what would become Jewish neoconservatism, condemned "the radical direction that liberalism has taken in American society" as antithetical to Jewish interests. Focused on Dr. King's ideal of creating a color-blind society, Glazer lamented the radicalization of politics. "We discovered to our surprise in the 1970s," he explained, "that we were creating an increasingly color-conscious society." That distressing change, he argued, grew from changes "in black thinking." As a young Jew from New York City's Canarsie neighborhood opined, "I used to be quite a way-out liberal, until twelve or fifteen years ago. But more and more I became aware of Jewish non-rights. I came to the full realization that the problems of the Jewish people were the results of Jewish liberalism."[39]

Despite American Jews' continued support for Democratic Party candidates, public opinion surveys revealed that, by and large, they shared some of the critics' concerns. When asked if they felt "more worried," "less worried," or "the same" about "violence and safety on the streets" in the previous year, 41 percent of the Jewish respondents to an August 1964 Harris poll answered in the affirmative. By 1968, though, that number rose to 52 percent. The 6 percent of American Jews who answered "less worried" about violence and safety in the streets in 1964 dropped to zero percent in the 1968 tally. With those changes between 1964 and 1968, Jews, who trailed the national average by 9 percentage points, began to reflect the rest of the nation. In New York City, Jews proved "more worried" than any other ethnic group, with 79 percent of the respondents expressing concern and just 2 percent answering "less concerned." Compared to the sample of all New Yorkers, Jews scored 12 percentage points higher, as well.[40]

Similarly, Jews in the Big Apple outpaced non-Jewish white New Yorkers when asked whether the pressures and tensions of living in New York City worsened between mid-1968 and mid-1969. Reflecting on their fears of racial violence in March 1968, 63 percent of American Jews responded that they "[felt] uneasy" compared to a national average of just 48 percent. Numbers skewed even higher for Jews as they aged, with more than 80 percent of American Jews over age thirty-five "uneasy" about racial violence. By the 1972 election, even Leonard Fein, an architect of many Great Society programs, observed that "today, the central perceived threat to Jewish interests is not intolerance, but a breakdown in law and order." The civil rights agenda, he feared, faced a law and order challenge from the right. "As McGovern is the candidate of equity," he concluded, "so Nixon is the candidate of order."[41]

On one level, Jewish opponents of the Great Society simply advanced larger political concerns over the group-status approach popularized by Black Power and embraced by the Great Society. In a March 1964 roundtable discussion on "Liberalism and the Negro" published by *Commentary* magazine, Norman Podhoretz, the magazine's editor and an early leader of this anti-Johnsonian group, observed an American Jewish polity splitting into two groups: those who favored a continuation of an individualist approach to liberalism and those who believe that government should recognize the systemic inequalities in American society and respond with public policy that recognizes race-based distinctions. Reviewing the prevailing Great Society thinking on the topic, Podhoretz recalled "the traditional liberal mentality" that rejected the notion of "competing economic classes and ethnic groups" in favor of a social concept that favored "*individuals* who confront a neutral body of law and a neutral institutional complex."[42]

Even so, Podhoretz and his allies still understood what he described as "the newer school of liberal thought on race relations" that viewed racism in systemic terms. The African American community, Podhoretz explained, "*as a whole* has been crippled by three hundred years of slavery and persecution." The earlier strategy calling for the "simple removal of legal and other barriers to the advancement of individual" blacks "can therefore only result in what is derisively called 'tokenism.'" Taken a step further, several different right-leaning Jewish groups translated Black Power thinking for their own political ends, even though their approach stood in sharp contrast to black militancy. An intellectual movement to recognize the existence and value of white ethnicity, "The New Pluralism," emerged under Jewish leadership in the late 1960s and will be explored in chapter 4. On the more populist side of right-wing politics, the JDL began as a vigilante private police force to protect working-class Jews in American cities and developed into one of the leading voices of the Soviet Jewry movement. It will be discussed in chapter 6.[43]

Church-State Separation

While seemingly unrelated to the ever-changing black-Jewish relationship, Great Society debate over federal government aid for private religious-based schools revealed a complex Jewish communal relationship to education, the proper role of government, and ultimately the positioning of the organized Jewish community on questions of Black Power. Long hallowed as a driving principle for non-Orthodox American Jews, the constitutional guarantee of a separated church and state demanded, for most American Jews, full government support of public education and absolutely no financial backing for private religious-based schools. For them, the ability to live as a Jew in the United States depended on a federal government that refused to take religious sides.

Great Society support for parochial education recalled historic Jewish fears of religious discrimination. How could a federal government in a Christian-dominated country be trusted to protect the rights of its Jewish minority if the floodgates of education funding were opened to private religious schools? Since the time of massive Jewish immigration to the United States in the nineteenth century, most Jewish leaders viewed a strong public education system as critical to continued Jewish mobility. Violating the organized Jewish community's historic commitment to a narrow interpretation of church-state doctrine introduced fears rooted in long-held assumptions about how Jews could best integrate themselves into American society.

Thoughts of a widespread Jewish move to state-sponsored Jewish day schools also threatened to weaken the public school system itself. Historically, Jews credited the public school system with their integration, acculturation, and social mobility on American shores. A free public education for all served as a great social leveler as well as the best opportunity for every child, and any child, to improve their lot. A weakening of the public schools, a necessary by-product of increased funding to private schools, violated this core priority in organized Jewish life. Given postwar Jewish social mobility, government sponsorship of private schools would also lead to a Jewish abandonment of their neighborhood public schools in favor of Jewish days or elite prep schools once off limits to Jews. LBJ's plans for federal education aid seem a violation of the most basic American Jewish communal priorities.

Within the larger Great Society frame of group-based social programs and the Black Power–inspired emphasis on strengthening one's ethnic awareness, the question of church-state separation developed into a complicated question. As Jews developed more interest in strengthening Jewish education, the thought of securing government dollars proved appealing. Although government sponsorship of Jewish schools seemed, in the old way of thinking, a threat to the continued acculturation of Jews to American life, federal dollars morphed in the Black Power era into an opportunity for unprecedented Jewish educational opportunities. A Jewish communal reversal on its interpretation of church-state separation, guided by Black Power thinking, could prove quite good for the Jews.

Ironically, Jewish communal debates over the Great Society's aid to education programs highlighted the profound differences between the nation's small Orthodox Jewish community, which tended to back John-son's proposals as a way to strengthen a fledging religious day school movement, and the larger organized community that perceived the efforts as a threat to their continued Jewish acculturation. In this case, American Orthodoxy embraced a Black Power–inspired position from the start, de-manding that the secular government harness its resources for the benefit of an activist minority group. For this community of Jews, the constitu-tional interpretations of their less-traditional coreligionists did not re-flect the tenets of Judaism. A strong separation between church and state proved antagonistic to their religious objectives because it weakened gov-ernment's ability to support Orthodox Jewish day schools, the center of learning for many observant Jews. The very group of American Jews that retreated from early postwar civic engagement on the grounds that the civil rights movement did not meet the standard as a Jewish cause took the public-square lead on federal aid to education, urging Jewish leader-ship to leverage federal dollars for strengthened Jewish identity.

When President Johnson included parochial schools in a massive fed-eral government aid program for elementary and secondary schools, al-most every Jewish group condemned the measure as a risky violation of church-state separation. With the articulation of a broader constitutional interpretation of church-state separation, these leaders believed, govern-ment policymakers threatened to undermine one of the Jewish commu-nity's most prized civil rights: the ability to express religious difference without fear of government persecution. While the group-based liberal programs of the Great Society promised special protections for perse-cuted Americans, attacks on church-state separation challenged what the AJCongress called "the basis of all freedom and the great source of secu-rity of U.S. Jewry."[44]

In a joint statement, the AJCongress, the Jewish Labor Committee (JLC), Jewish War Veterans, the National Council of Jewish Women, and the Union of American Hebrew Congregations (UAHC) objected to federal aid to support private and parochial schools. The national umbrella orga-nization for Jewish Federations agreed as well, asserting that a separate church and state "has guaranteed religious freedom for all; has served as a boon to religion; and has spared the American people destructive reli-gious conflicts." It held that "governmental aid to religiously controlled schools" would amount to "a grave disservice to both religious and public education." Officials from the SCA, comprising representatives from American Judaism's major non-Orthodox religious denominations, went so far as to meet with a government official "to establish ground rules for the evaluation and granting of funds, pointing out the need to [ensure] that the major portion of the funds were not given to churches or church institutions which were not suited for the specific community projects in mind." While the SCA supported "the humanitarian objectives of the anti-poverty program," it opposed "any channeling of Federal funds directly, or indirectly, into educational programs under the auspices of religiously controlled schools or other religious institutions."[45]

Jewish leaders labored to keep the wall separating church and state high and impregnable by engaging the American legal system. The AJ-Congress believed that "Jewish security depends not on good will but on good laws, nor on toleration of the majority but on the same Bill of Rights which protects the liberties of every American." AJCongress leader Howard M. Squadron expressed "grave concern" over sections of Johnson's bill "that required church-schooled kids to be in shared time programs to get support from public schools" and permitted federal grants "for use in 'non public elementary and secondary schools, including parochial or other sectarian schools.'" At its 1964 convention, the AJCongress "reiterated its position that any form of governmental aid to religious schools is a patent violation of the constitutional principle of separation of church and state."[46]

In 1965, the women's division of the AJCongress selected "Meeting the Challenge of the Great Society" as the theme for its biennial conference. When the president of the women's division heard that the government intended to fund religious schools in its Head Start program, she warned Sargent Shriver of the Office of Economic Opportunity that despite their eagerness "to do all we can to equalize opportunities for all children," they had to oppose "any programs which infringe on the constitutional principle of religious liberty and separation of church and state." Articulating an expansive vision of American public education, she appealed to the senior Johnson policymaker to adopt her organization's conclusion "that Federal funds to help our nation's disadvantaged children should go only to those public facilities and public institutions open to all children."[47]

In testimony to the Congressional Subcommittee on General Education, AJC president Morris B. Abram offered support for the proposed

Elementary and Secondary Education Act of 1965 on condition that "the state or federal government does not aid religion or religious education or church-related institutions." Abram suggested that Congress amend the bill to include provisions "that funds should not be used for religious purposes, that funds should be allocated under the supervision of a public agency, that citizens have the right to test the constitutionality of the bill's provisions, and that watchdog commissions supervise the administration of the bill if enacted." Similarly, the ADL recognized "the urgent need for the passage of an extensive federal aid to education act" but reaffirmed "its opposition to the use of public funds in aid to sectarian schools at the primary and secondary level."[48]

Yet organized Jewry faced opposition from both sides of the religious spectrum: Orthodox Jews committed to strong Jewish day schools and secular Jews interested in building their new more socially integrated lives in the Christian-majority suburbs. Orthodox groups applauded the federal government's reform program as a powerful tool to strengthen American Jewish life. The Religious Zionists of America, the Union of Orthodox Rabbis of the United States and Canada, the (Orthodox) Rabbinical Alliance of America, the Union of Orthodox Jewish Congregations, the Lubavitch sect, and the National Society of Hebrew Day Schools all supported LBJ's proposal without any church-state reservations.[49]

For Rabbi Israel Klavan, the executive vice president of the Orthodox movement's largest professional organization, the Rabbinical Council of America, the constitutional provision requiring separation between church and state did not preclude federal support for private religious schools. For Klavan, the principle of church-state separation limited government's ability only to support a single religious group at the expense of all others. It did not, per se, prevent government funding of many different religious groups. As long as government funding offered Americans a choice in their religious practices, then the sanctity of a separated church and state would be preserved. Klavan pressed for strengthening the many different religious groups in the United States, and considered doing so as advancing "a desirable principle which has proved most effective in the development of the American system of government and life." He demanded a pluralistic interpretation of religious freedom that encouraged a wide variety of religious groups to express themselves instead of the widespread Jewish liberal approach that sought to prevent any church or synagogue from engaging in the public square. "The beauty of the principle of religious freedom," Klavan explained, "lies in the fact that we can be different from one another and that we have every right to retain that difference."[50]

Brandeis University professor Ben Halpern backed Klavan's position at a 1971 Synagogue Council of America symposium on public aid to non-public education. "The question whether a strict ban on public aid to ethno-religious private schools is good for Jews, or essential for Jews, thus remains," Halpern argued, "prima facie, an open question." He surveyed the Jewish experience over both time and place, concluding, "Modern, emancipated, liberal Jews everywhere have universally favored our American position." Although he acknowledged that creating "cracks in the wall between public secular and religious private schools" might prove harmful, Halpern feared, even more, the possibility of a "crippling loss to our capacity to build healthy Jewish identities in America." In his estimation, the cost-benefit analysis pointed to a change in communal policy.[51]

In a *Congress Bi-Weekly* article published the following year, Seymour Siegel launched a broadside from his perspective as a political conservative. "The liberal's fascination with the public school and his dogmatic opposition to aid to religiously oriented schools," he argued, "is another example where Jewish interests and liberal ideology collide." Siegel believed that Jewish day schools held out the best hope for strengthening American Jewish identity and called out organization leaders for spending money in a fight against the federal government rather than bolstering Jewish education. He pointed to the hypocrisy of rabbis accepting tax-advantaged status when it came to their salaries or their synagogue's dues requirements while, at the same time, lobbying against similar benefits for Jewish educational centers. "Somehow," he concluded, "aiding yeshivot and day schools is impossible."[52]

On the opposite side of the religious continuum, secular Jews also urged a reinterpretation of the church-state doctrine. In New Hamden, Connecticut, for example, the local JCRC sought to end both Christmas and Hanukkah observances in the town's public schools. While it intended to protect the interests of Jewish students, the JCRC soon learned that it had inserted itself into a community of Jews that sought opportunities to learn about Christianity, even if that meant celebrations in public school. As South Orange, New Jersey, Rabbi Herbert Weiner offered, "The pressure to heighten a 'wall of separation' between church and state not only failed to accomplish its ends, but measurably heightened the wall of separation between the various elements of the community."[53]

Weiner inverted the classic argument seeking church-state separation. "There are times," he explained, "when the effort to achieve a rigid separation of church and state in a community can exacerbate religious tensions and other times when a compromise of 'principle' can bring about not only more understanding between religious groups, but even a diminution of those religious activities which make the minority uncomfortable." While Weiner understood the position of Jewish leaders who pressed for a strict interpretation of church-state doctrine, he cautioned that they "are not free to demand in the name of Judaism that every Jew must rejoice when a nonoffensive prayer is eliminated from the public schools, and they need not be excommunicated if they do not wish to join a battle for the elimination of a Christmas stamp from the Post Office."[54]

As LBJ would learn during his tumultuous years in office, hopes for a Great Society, a nation committed to social justice, devoid of poverty, and sensitive to the needs of the most marginalized Americans, proved naive. Millions of Democratic voters registered their disapproval of LBJ by abandoning their longtime political home and bolting to the Republican Party. In the 1966 midterm election, forty-seven Democrats lost their seats in the House of Representatives, and several high-profile liberal senators suffered electoral defeats. By the time candidates began to campaign for the 1968 presidential election, the War on Poverty had been defeated by both its overambitious goals and the diversion of much-needed assets to fight the war in Vietnam. When Johnson departed Washington for his Texas ranch in 1969, he left a nation divided on issues of race and a Democratic Party in disarray. Protests against Johnson's unpopular war in Vietnam added to public distrust and assured LBJ's legacy as the twentieth-century's least popular president.

For American Jews, the Great Society offered an important glimpse into the creative and dynamic tensions that defined Jewish life in the 1960s. At once marginalized and in the mainstream, Jews explored a new relationship to the state, helped define a successor philosophy to FDR's New Deal liberalism, and negotiated competing political beliefs within the large and varied world of organized American Jewry. In the final analysis, the Great Society distinguished Jews once again as white America's most liberal and progressive ethnic group just as it defined, in the clearest possible terms, their newfound appreciation for viewing American social life through a group-based lens. And when Black Power activists pressed their militant and separatist ideology onto the civil rights scene, Jewish leaders responded with overwhelming support.

American Jews and the Rise of Black Power

our months after Dr. Martin Luther King Jr. delivered his famed "I Have a Dream" speech at the August 1963 March on Washington for Jobs and Freedom, Nation of Islam leader Malcolm X offered a biting rebuke to a group of supporters in Detroit, Michigan. Lamenting the influence of white liberals in the civil rights struggle, Malcolm X took aim at King for compromising with the Kennedy administration ahead of the rally. What began as an African American–led grassroots action intended to shut down the U.S. Congress became an interracial nonconfrontational day of speeches by old-guard African American civil rights leaders and their white allies. For Malcolm X, the March on Washington typified the failure of King's consensus-driven approach to civil rights reform. Only a black-led movement, he argued, could succeed in realizing racial equality.

Employing a metaphor to dramatize his point, the Nation of Islam leader told the crowd: "It's just like when you've got some coffee that's too black, which means it's too strong, what do you do? You integrate it with cream. You make it weak." In a blistering rejection of King's embrace of white allies, the Nation of Islam leader extended his metaphor: "If you pour too much cream in, you won't even know you ever had coffee. It used to be hot, it becomes cool. It used to be strong, it becomes weak. It used to wake you up, now it'll put you to sleep." Malcolm X believed that white support for the March on Washington ruined its chances for success. "They didn't integrate it," he argued, "they infiltrated it." Once white allies joined the March, African Americans compromised themselves and their cause. As Malcolm X concluded, "It ceased to be a march. It became a picnic, a circus. Nothing but a circus, with clowns and all . . . white clowns and black clowns."[1]

The "Coffee and Cream Speech" articulated a black separatist ideology gaining traction among young African American activists increasingly frustrated with King's approach to civil rights. Black Power counted a number of different organizations among its ranks, each with its own particular understanding and approach to the struggle for racial equality. Three leading groups, the Nation of Islam, the Black Panther Party (BPP), and SNCC collectively represented a fundamental strategic break from Dr. King and his allied organizations and leaders. King's approach to civil rights activism affirmed a pluralistic vision of American democracy that valued Jewish contributions. Black Power advocates rejected it. The interracial protest marches and legal challenges that typified the movement in the 1950s and early 1960s had all but ended by the middle of the 1960s.

For American Jews, the rise of the Black Power movement marked a sea change in their approach to postwar liberal reform. Once committed to the interfaith and interracial work of early postwar civil rights leaders such as Dr. Martin Luther King Jr., American Jews developed a deeper and more honest understanding of institutional racism in the United States. As the leadership of the African American civil rights community, including Dr. King himself, pressed its agenda to the urban North, to extralegal systemic expressions of racism, and to a broader internationalist frame that included opposition to U.S. involvement in Vietnam, Jewish leaders responded with empathy and support, even as much of the emerging black militancy placed Jews in its crosshairs. As Rabbi Arthur Hertzberg said, "Perhaps the saddest element in this whole frightening picture is in the fact that Jews are the people who are best able to understand the rhetoric of Black Power, even though they are most directly on the firing line of its attack."[2]

Jewish affinity for Black Power crafted a new interracial consensus built on the rise of ethnic nationalism, identity politics, and particularist communal ambitions. Reflecting back on the civil rights movement of the 1950s and early 1960s, organized Jewry claimed common historical experiences, similar sociological marginalization, and a religious prophetic impulse as the bedrock of the black-Jewish alliance. The rise of Black Power shattered

those assumptions. Instead, Jews came to understand the basic differences between the American Jewish and the African American historical
experiences. By the mid-1960s, American Jews acknowledged their privilege as white middle-class Americans as they appreciated, even more, the
continued outsider status of their black fellow citizens. Judaism's mandate
to engage in acts of social justice required a far more sober, self-critical,
and challenging response to black inequality. Black Power animated new
Jewish views of democratic pluralism, of race and racism in America, and
the limits of Jewish liberal gradualism.

Across the Jewish communal spectrum, Jewish leaders backed Black
Power. They resonated with its themes, often drawing parallels between
the rise of black nationalist thought and the advent of modern political
Zionism, even as most black militants embraced an anti-Zionist perspective. When Black Power leaders espoused antisemitic views, Jewish
leaders urged patience and even understanding, aware that prejudicial
attitudes by marginalized blacks would not translate into actual discrimination against Jews. Most of all, Jewish leaders saw the Black Power's potential to reinvent American Jewish life. With its unapologetic advocacy
for black identity, Black Power expanded the limits of acceptable ethnic
group expression in the United States. A nation that champions the ability of African Americans to assert themselves also offers its Jewish citizens the platform to strengthen their own ethnic identities. Judaism's
prophetic mandate, in Black Power terms, meant advocacy for Jews in the
Soviet Union and Israel rather than African Americans in Mississippi and
Alabama. In the mid-1960s, blacks and Jews joined in a new consensus approach to political activism, though one very different from the one they
had known just a decade earlier.

The History of Black Power

With origins reaching back to such black nationalists as Marcus Garvey,
African American author and eventual French citizen Richard Wright first
invoked the phrase "Black Power" in a 1954 book of the same name. The
volume recounted a journey from his home in Paris to Africa's Gold Coast,
where he studied an independence movement that, in 1957, realized national status for Ghana, the first sub-Sahara African nation to break from
European colonial rule. In 1962, C. Eric Lincoln, author of *The Black Mus-*

lims in America, anticipated the rise of Black Power in an address to the Society for the Psychological Study of Social Issues. He noted the existence of no fewer than twenty black-nationalist groups in New York City alone, describing the surge as "mushrooming cults" that "keep springing up in the Black Ghettos of our great industrial cities." Predicting the rhetoric of Malcolm X and others, Lincoln noted that in the new approach to African American liberation, "blackness becomes a virtue" while "whiteness becomes a symbol of weakness and depravity, political and social decadence."[3]

The Black Power movement gained strength and focus with the election of Stokely Carmichael as chair of SNCC in 1966. Representing a new cadre of young African American civil rights activists frustrated with the slow pace of change under Dr. Martin Luther King Jr., Carmichael and his allies pressed King for stronger and more direct civil rights strategies. For Carmichael, the negative impact of white liberal gradualism doomed the consensus-centered approach of Dr. King. Unless and until white liberals stepped back from decision making, this new cohort of young African American activists believed, institutional racism would continue while power and privilege would remain entrenched within white America. As SNCC leaders argued in a 1966 position paper, African Americans were "being used as a tool of the white liberal establishment" and white liberals "have not begun to address themselves to the real problem of black people in this country."[4]

Only when African Americans led civil rights organizations, dictated strategy, and organized protests would white America truly engage with the depth and seriousness of racism. These young activists demanded black control of their own organizations and embrace of racial separatism. They demonstrated a deep cynicism with the desire and ability of white, and Jewish, liberals to advance the cause. "The role of integration is irrelevant," Carmichael blasted in May 1966, "that's not our goal." SNCC abandoned the word "nonviolent" in its acronym, renaming itself the Student National Coordinating Committee and sending the message that it had jettisoned King's uncompromising commitment to nonviolent protest. As King reflected when Black Power advocates challenged him during James Meredith's 1966 March Against Fear, "It is becoming increasingly more difficult to sell the nonviolence concept to a tired and abused people."[5]

Other African American separatist organizations grew in this era as well. In a rejection of white America and its religious heritage, the Nation of Islam linked Christianity with American slavery and the perpetuation of a racist society. Even as the Nation failed to attract a large following, the popularity of its chief spokesman, Malcolm X, offered a powerful challenge to Dr. King's accommodationist approach. In Oakland, California, the BPP, under the leadership of Huey P. Newton and Bobby Seale, armed its members for battle against white America. In one of its most high-profile actions, forty members of the BPP entered California's state capitol in Sacramento with shotguns, rifles, and pistols in plain view. Although it counted only 2,000 to 3,000 members by 1969, a Harris poll conducted by *Time* magazine the following year determined that 25 percent of African Americans agreed with the statement "the Black Panthers represent my own personal views." For respondents under age twenty-one, the positive response rate jumped to 43 percent, while nearly two-thirds of all those questioned affirmed that the "Panthers give me a sense of pride."[6]

To be sure, the growing popularity of black nationalism did not translate into full-fledged calls for creation of an African American nation-state nor to a "Back to Africa" movement reminiscent of Marcus Garvey's early twentieth-century attempt to settle African Americans in Liberia. A 1963 Harris poll revealed that just 4 percent of the African American respondents backed the creation of a separate state for blacks while 87 percent expressed disapproval. Among leaders of the organized African American community, the rejection of racial separatism proved even more pronounced: 99 percent of those surveyed registered their opposition to independent statehood.[7]

Broader African American support for even the more modest separatist goals of Black Power proved mixed at best. In 1966, A. Philip Randolph, organizer of the 1941 March on Washington effort, called Black Power "an unhappy term" with "overtones of force" that "create a sense of antagonism." Randolph's view held for the larger African American community. When asked whether they supported the end of the interracial civil rights alliance, 81 percent of the African American respondents polled in 1966 wanted continued cooperation with whites while an even higher percentage, 84 percent, of young African Americans offered similar sentiment. Bayard Rustin, the executive director of the A. Philip Randolph Institute as well as one of the organizers of the 1963 March on Washington, wrote in a 1966 *Commentary* article that "'black power' not only lacks any real value for the civil-rights movement, but . . . its propagation is positively harmful. It diverts the movement from a meaningful debate over strategy and tactics, it isolates the Negro community and it encourages the growth of anti-Negro forces."[8]

Despite African American opposition to elements of the move toward black nationalism, Jewish communal hopes for a return to black-Jewish cooperation suffered a setback when moderate black leaders who themselves worried about Black Power's rise advanced their own critique of Jewish commitment to racial equality. Negative appraisals from old-guard black leaders dramatized a critical moment in the development of the black-Jewish political alliance. While Black Power presented a separatist challenge to Jewish communal leaders, the prospect of continued interracial work surfaced deep systemic tensions between the two communities. Pressed on one side by black nationalist rejection of white allies and on the other by black moderates frustrated by Jewish compromise in the struggle for racial equality, Jewish leaders struggled to find new approaches to their social justice work.

In 1966, Bayard Rustin leveraged an invitation to speak before the AJCongress to offer pointed feedback. "Dear people," he called out, "when Jewish people run about boasting about how we Jews made it because we were intellectual, and lifted ourselves by our bootstraps, and we have such extraordinarily beautiful family life that obviously we just went up to the top like cream in coffee—well, this is hot air."[9]

Taking aim at a self-serving and paternalistic strain in the Jewish communal discourse about civil rights, Rustin chided Jews for demanding strategic and operational control of the movement's agenda. While he acknowledged the prominent Jewish role in social justice causes, he also understood the strength and necessity of keeping African Americans at the center of the fight. "If you are going to remain Jews only so long as Negroes remain nice," he blasted, "give it up." Four months later, in the pages of *Commentary*, he pressed the argument further, identifying "Black Power" as a "slogan directed primarily against liberals by those who once counted liberals among their closest friends." Rather than blaming black activists for their rejection of white allies, Rustin believed it "up to the liberal movement to prove that coalition and integration are better alternatives."[10]

Roy Wilkins, head of the NAACP, affirmed Rustin's analysis. "Boston, Massachusetts," he wrote in 1966, "has been the Mississippi of the North." Two years later, Dr. Martin Luther King Jr. argued that liberalism had failed in its bid to move beyond the impressive legislative victories of 1964 and 1965. "Today," King implored, "we are finding, too often, a quasi-liberalism which is committed to the principle of looking sympathetically at all sides. It is a liberalism so objectively analytical that it fails to become subjectively committed." Diagnosing the ills of Jewish liberalism, King criticized his onetime political allies for developing "a high blood pressure of words and an anemia of deeds."[11]

These African American critiques pointed to an uncomfortable new understanding of Jewish political activism. Viewed through this more critical lens, postwar African Americans signed on to a movement for racial equality, committed to advancing their political agenda as far as needed to achieve African American equality. Jews, on the other hand, hopped on a civil rights bandwagon dedicated only to the more limited goal of legal equality as expressed in the Civil Rights Act of 1964 and the Voting Rights Act of 1965. With the end of Jim Crow, African American critics held, American Jews declared victory and returned to their privileged lives in the northern suburbs, unwilling to address racism in their backyards or the institutional racism within society at large. As David Danzig acknowledged, the slow pace of civil rights reform inspired black frustration with white liberals, who reacted negatively to the critique. "'Black Power' with its separationist connotations," he argued, "gives shape to these fears."[12]

Jewish Opposition to Black Power

Jewish leaders shared many of the concerns expressed by African American leaders such as Randolph and Rustin. They, too, saw in Black Power the rejection of white America's most liberal ethnic group and the disintegration of King's approach to civil rights reform. For Jews who celebrated their collective support of the civil rights movement, offered a disproportionate amount of its funding, rallied in opposition to Jim Crow, and for a few risked themselves in direct-action protests, the rise of black militancy stung. It threatened to end the postwar political alliance between blacks and Jews. It purged hardworking Jewish allies from leadership in civil rights groups. Most of all, it undermined a consensus-driven image of an

American democracy that could deliver social equality for all. The rise of Black Power seemed to end a hopeful moment in American social life. For these Jewish leaders and many others who shared their concerns, Black Power wrought fears of backward movement in civil rights. By particularizing the struggle, Black Power advocates undermined the good work of white liberals in search of a color-blind society.

As early as 1964, Jewish leaders sounded the alarm over the rise of black militancy. In a memo labeled "confidential—not for publication in any form," ADL general consul Arnold Forster asked each of his regional offices to offer a candid assessment of the size, growth, and impact of radical African American groups in their cities. In the responses, local ADL officials communicated their concerns over how the black move to separatism threatened to undo a generation of interracial advocacy. They worried that, left unaddressed, blacks and Jews would suffer an inevitable political collision caused by fundamentally different understandings and approaches to questions of civil equality, freedom, and justice. ADL officials, early in the development of the Black Power movement, understood the dangers it posed and the organized Jewish community's role in the alliance's breakup.

Atlanta's ADL head Monroe Schlactus, who described himself as "extremely conservative" in his approach to identity politics, acknowledged that his office found it increasingly difficult to work with "groups of this nature." Schlactus placed his professional faith in the interracial approach to civil rights activism and lamented that Atlanta's African American civil rights vanguard wanted, in his words, "to lead and direct the entire fight." In his estimation, the ADL reached an impasse on civil rights strategy. While Schlactus understood and communicated the new trend toward separatism, he let his boss know that he remained "satisfied with things the way they are."[13]

Schlactus's analysis extended throughout the South. Charles F. Wittenstein, who served as the ADL's southeastern director, affirmed Schlactus's analysis and projected a dire warning: "If these next four years are to be anything better than an unmitigated disaster, it will require the combined and coordinated efforts of a unified Negro community with its white liberal allies." To drive home his point, Wittenstein drew connections between the emerging strategy of African American militants and the founding ideals of the American republic: "In the immortal words of

Benjamin Franklin," he explained, "we must all hang together or we shall all hang separately."[14]

Baltimore's Jason R. Silverman offered Forster a three-year perspective on black-Jewish relations in his city. In 1961, he explained, "Negro organizations sought us out to participate in joint meetings, called upon us for educational materials, etc." By 1964, he lamented, those requests proved "very seldom," leading him to conclude that "cooperation between us and Negro action organizations is not as good today as it has been in the past." In this black militant climate, Silverman needed to take the lead with his African American colleagues. "The only time I find myself relating to the Negro leadership," he wrote, "is when action is initiated from my end." When Silverman tried to work with the SCLC, the NAACP, and the Urban League to coordinate positions on a Congress of Racial Equality (CORE) boycott of Washington, D.C., schools, he revealed, "I was politely received but politely told off: that while they appreciated our cooperation they would prefer to have the Negro organizations working together as Negroes."[15]

Concern over Black Power extended to the liberal enclaves of the Northeast as well. In Boston, a bastion of white ethnic working-class Democratic voters, ADL office head Sol Kolack reported the growing marginalization of the ADL in the city's civil rights struggle. "The new militant leaders do not look to the ADL or any part of the American Jewish community for help," he explained, "because in their view our help is based on the maintenance of democratic institutions and this to them means the maintenance of the status quo." Kolack understood that, at least among a new generation of young black activists critical of his organization's moderate approach, concerns over liberal gradualism extended to his city, or perhaps proved even more severe in a city well known for its progressive past.[16]

Racial isolation moved to the west coast where Oakland ADL leader Stanley Jacobs reported that African American leaders considered Jewish leaders part of the white community and "therefore not to be trusted." Writing from the home of the BPP, Jacobs described "disengagement" between a number of local Jewish organizations and centrist groups such as the NAACP and Urban League, long-standing partner groups in the African American community. "The entire attitude of Negro leadership," Jacobs concluded, "is one of distinct coolness and even indifference toward the Jewish agencies." Reports from agencies in Buffalo, New York, Detroit, Michigan, and Missouri confirmed these experiences and findings.[17]

On the pages of various Jewish community periodicals, organizational leaders pushed back against racial separatism as part of a larger effort to return to an earlier era of cooperation. In a 1964 *Commentary* article, AJC associate director David Danzig focused his ire on what he described as the "more militant than thou" approach of the new black activists. In his estimation, racial separation as a political tool amounted to nothing more than "a reckless stance posing as a strategy, one that converts the civil rights struggle from a movement to unite Americans in support of the principle of equal rights into an open conflict between the races." Danzig's analysis spoke to the high-minded ideals of an older black-Jewish alliance that promised to bridge the racial divide rather than focus the spotlight on it. The move from coalition building to separatism threatened to divide the nation by racial status rather than promote a color-blind vision of equality.[18]

Bezalel Sherman, a member of the labor Zionist *Jewish Frontier*'s editorial board, offered a pointed affirmation of Danzig's assessment: "The Negro revolution will not succeed without the cooperation of the white man; and presenting him as an unregenerated enemy will not further the cause of equality." The editorial board of the *Jewish Frontier* went a step further, postulating that the rise of Black Power would only strengthen white racial separatists who would forge an unconventional political alliance with the objects of their racist scorn. "The Wallaces and Faubuses," it explained in reference to two well-known recalcitrant white southern politicians, "are the spiritual accomplices of the Malcolm X, Y, or Z's." Employing a wordplay linking Nation of Islam leader Malcolm X with the country's most virulent white-supremacist organization, the *Jewish Frontier* editorialists proclaimed, "The black demagogues will not be rejected unless the white bigots are. X follows from K.K.K."[19]

Jewish Support for Black Power

By all outward appearances, the rise of Black Power and its associated organizations signaled the end of a black-Jewish alliance that, at first glance, joined two American constituent groups sharing common experience, history, and purpose. The iconic image of Rabbi Abraham Joshua Heschel marching alongside Dr. Martin Luther King Jr. in Selma symbolized the highest ideals of an interracial, interfaith movement that testified to the essential similarities between blacks and Jews. This filiopietistic read on Jewish liberal activism encouraged the construction of a false narrative that congratulated Jews for their social justice passion and criticized Black Power for undoing the good work of early civil rights workers.

A closer examination of American Jewish reactions to the Black Power movement reveals a powerful, if subtle, new consensus emerging between the two seemingly antagonistic ethnic communities. As noted in chapter 1, Jewish leaders heard critique from African American civil rights leaders as early as the 1950s. Even as the public face of the movement projected an image of intergroup harmony, both blacks and Jews understood the internal challenges of waging a common fight against racism. As tensions between the two communities rose in the early 1960s, Jewish leaders maintained a keen awareness of African American concerns, leveraging both their personal relationships with black leaders as well as the public pages of their newsletters to demonstrate their willingness to respond.

In a sharp break from the early postwar public narrative of black-Jewish unity, Jewish thinkers, rabbis, and organizational leaders acknowledged that African Americans and Jewish Americans lived very different lives. American Jews enjoyed broad-based social mobility in the United States while African Americans, for the most part, did not. When Black Power activists offered loud, public, and high-profile repudiations of white allies in the mid-1960s, Jewish leaders understood the limits of their own liberalism and empathized. They stood up for Black Power thinking, offering rationales for its precepts and confidence that greater African American autonomy would advance the cause of racial justice. Not even a spike in black antisemitism fazed Jewish leaders, who offered analyses that minimized its threat to Jews. In an ironic twist, consensus still defined the coalition between blacks and Jews in the Black Power era, though the terms reflected a more honest appraisal of their strained relationship.

As early as the summer of 1963, Shad Polier supported militant blacks in opposition to the limited goals of President John F. Kennedy's proposed civil rights law. At a time when Martin Luther King Jr. and his associates completed the last details of the August 1963 March on Washington, the public persona of the civil rights movement still focused on the centrality of interracial cooperation, the import of a federal civil rights law, and the optimistic belief that conventional approaches to social change would bring civil rights victories. Black nationalists had not yet challenged the existing leadership of SCLC or even SNCC, though Malcolm X certainly viewed the status quo with contempt. At this particular historical moment, it would seem that Polier and his colleagues in Jewish communal leadership would toe the interracial consensus line, touting efforts such as the March on Washington and marginalizing separatist blacks critical of their efforts. However, this would not be the case.

In a July 1963 article published in the AJCongress newsletter, Polier refused to condemn what he described as the "revolutionary character" of African American activists upset that the nation's chief executive refused to support more aggressive priorities. Instead, Polier located the blame on whites themselves, whose support for meaningful reform he characterized as "resistant, grudging, and inadequate." Just a month later, Polier's colleague Leo Pfeffer agreed, alerting his constituents in a public report that the earlier emphasis on "color blindness" as a civil rights goal "was for yesterday." Nothing short of immediate action, to the point of revolution he explained, could achieve the new African American civil rights agenda: "His fair share of jobs, housing and education."[20]

In a 1964 exchange on the pages of *Jewish Frontier*, Leon Jick, then the rabbi of the Free Synagogue of Westchester, New York, and later a professor of American Jewish history at Brandeis University, broke with the prevailing consensus when he stressed the essential differences between the historical experiences of blacks and Jews in the United States. Jick pointed out that Jews came "eagerly" to the United States, which welcomed them as "a land of freedom and opportunity," while blacks arrived on American shores in slavery. He recalled the continued impact of racism in America, noting that the abolition of slavery during Reconstruction "meant only a new form of exploitation." While Jews enjoyed a relatively fast journey up the social mobility ladder, blacks stalled. As a consequence, American Jews tended to behave more as newly assimilated members of the white middle class than they did as a marginalized people seeking civil justice.[21]

While the regional ADL officers queried in the confidential 1964 Arnold Forster memo expressed concerns over a rise in black militancy, they also framed their assessments, in city after city, with a clear awareness of Jewish culpability in damaging relations with African American civil rights leaders. Each local leader pointed to a different Jewish communal failure complicating goodwill between blacks and Jews. Assembled together, the frank assessments offered to the national ADL office wove a complex fabric of Jewish indifference, complicity, and even occasional support of the racial status quo. With these missives, the very organization dedicated to the fight against group-based discrimination self-reflected on its own sober challenges ahead.

In St. Louis, Melvin I. Cooperman reported his own leadership was "often on the wrong side of issues." The ADL leader petitioned the national office for support, proclaiming a "crying need for Jewish community education here as elsewhere." Cooperman's request hinged on the supposition that his constituents lacked basic knowledge of racism's impact and they would benefit from the ADL's intervention. In fact, Cooperman pressed his case even further, asking that his office receive the support it needed to measure "the dimensions of Jewish community bigotry" at the same level and "in the same way in which we measure aspects of anti-Semitism." In a parting shot to his boss, Cooperman noted that even an unnamed former president of B'nai B'rith's national women's group took official positions on what he considered the wrong side of several important civil rights measures.[22]

In Detroit, Sol Littman reflected on his community's retreat from active engagement in civil rights activism, a common complaint of African American leaders toward white allies. "I, personally, regret," he wrote, "the many situations in which ADL did not vigorously and forcefully represent itself as amongst the *avant-garde* in the civil rights field." At a time when direct-action African American protests forced Jewish organizations to calibrate a response, Littman faulted his group for remaining on the sidelines. "It sure wouldn't do any harm," he urged, "if B'nai B'rith people were willing to picket jointly with CORE and NAACP in a number of key situations in which such picketing were merited and dignified." Littman's observation referenced a larger Jewish retreat from protests that centered on issues of economic injustice, often involving the business practices of Jewish businesspeople and landowners. While Detroit's black leadership had not yet expressed its upset with the ADL, Littman expected critique "in the near future."[23]

Evidence of a continuing Jewish retreat from civil rights activism extended across the country. ADL leader Mortimer Kass reported a consensus among regional directors that "Negro leadership is generally disappointed with the Jewish community." He described "disenchantment" toward "Jews, Jewish leadership and Jewish civil rights groups." Wisconsin ADL head Saul Sorrin offered his stark assessment of Milwaukee's Jewish community: "It is essentially a disappointment in terms of the profession of any Jewish liberals that they are supporters of any social changes which will bring about Negro equality." African American civil rights leaders, he concluded, shared a sense that their "friends let us down." Buffalo's Jewish community, according to its ADL leader, thought African Americans were "stirring things up too much." In Arkansas, Louisiana, and Mississippi, "the Jewish community is not fully living up to its own power, nor commitment in terms of the fact that Jewish individuals and Jewish community leaders by and large do not get involved in the area of race relations."[24]

The private arguments advanced in confidential memos by the ADL leadership in 1964 reached the American Jewish public sphere in the years that followed. During a 1969 speech to the Synagogue Council of America, Leonard Fein called out his coreligionists for embracing the racial status quo as they assimilated into the white suburban middle class. "There is the tragic fact that we are still, in many of our parts," he slammed, "a good deal lower than the angels." Jews took to bigotry, he charged, as an opportunistic way to express their newfound Americanness. "Must we not, in candor," he pressed, "ask ourselves whether some Jews have not reacted with a similar sense of liberation, happy to be American by being bigots? . . . The dirty little secret of our community, after all," he concluded, "is that its leaders have always spoken more forcefully and more radically than its followers have felt."[25]

With these analyses, the ADL leaders coalesced around a deep understanding and appreciation for the rise of black militancy. "The only trend I can discern," Littman concluded, "is one in which more and more Negroes, although not joining Malcolm X or the Muslims, are nevertheless finding themselves in separatist movements." Jerry Bakst from the New York City office concurred. "The tendency for extremists to break away in the direction of further extremism," he wrote to Forster, "is taking place all along the line in the Negro leadership—among the extremists themselves, as well as in the more responsible major civil rights groups." As a consequence, Monroe Schlactus, head of the ADL's southeastern regional office, suggested that his organization "develop greater cooperation between the more militant Negro organizations and the ADL."[26]

The same year the ADL leaders offered their Black Power premonition, Jewish leaders, organizations, and media outlets all reaffirmed the inevitability of increased black militancy. The editorial board of *Jewish Frontier* proclaimed, "There is nothing surprising in the emergence of such extremists as Malcolm X on the civil rights front." In the September 1964 *Congress Bi-Weekly*, Shad Polier wrote that "a degree of bitterness" defined the evolving civil rights movement and that "one of its natural by-products is the Black Nationalist movement." He thought it "almost inconceivable" to imagine that "extremism should not develop under the terrible pressures of a people seeking freedom and equality." The AJCongress leader described the growing black militancy as an African American fight "for entry into a promised land" as they sought "to escape the degradation and deprivations of second-class citizenship."[27]

When the black militant critique of Jews turned to antisemitism, Jewish leaders responded with relative calm, downplaying the risks it posed to American Jews. Embracing the era's emerging analysis of power relations, they differentiated between antisemitism, which posed relatively little risk to the continued social mobility of American Jews, and racism, which continued to limit African American advance. In 1964, for example, Polier acknowledged that American Jews were "in for a period of increasing anti-Semitism among Negroes," but then went on to soften his stance. While he told his followers that anti-Jewish hostility "was almost inevitable," he claimed that black antisemitism was "neither pervasive nor likely to be enduring" and argued that it touched "only a tiny fraction of Negroes." For Polier, black antisemitism was nothing more than a "passing phase" and he understood "the resentment and hostility by Negroes against white persons in these dominant positions should come as no surprise to anyone." Polier worried more about "the response of the Jew" than he did to black antisemitism, fearing that a negative Jewish reaction would cause alienation "from the struggle for racial justice."[28]

In a 1968 report to the executive director of the AJCongress, Will Maslow differentiated between prejudicial comments and actual discrimination against Jews, reporting, "discrimination against Jews and overt manifestations of anti-Semitism are at an extremely low level." When the SCA decided to focus its 1969 annual meeting on the theme "The Negro Revolution and the Jewish Question," it invited Leonard Fein to reflect on the state of black-Jewish relations. In his remarks, he warned Jewish religious leaders against making "a most serious error" by confusing "the ideological implications of the new Negro cohesiveness from its occasional anti-Semitic manifestations." Fein saw "no necessary linkage between the two" and admonished his listeners not to "throw out the baby with the bath."[29]

At a 1969 meeting of Jewish communal leaders in New York City to discuss the status of black-Jewish relations, Dr. Seymour Lachman, a dean at Kingsborough Community College who would later take a seat on the New York City board of education, defended the purge of whites from SNCC by citing the Jewish community's own need for separatism. "Because I feel a need for a certain amount of Jewish separatism," he argued, "I can therefore understand the need for a certain degree of black separatism." He explained that he would not want a marginal Jew, not to mention a non-Jew, in charge of a Jewish organization. "I can understand," he concluded, "the current Negro belief that there is a need for black men to control the black community and to evolve a black philosophy."[30]

The ADL missives affirmed the larger Jewish communal downplay of black antisemitism. Mortimer Kass reported that only a minority of his constituents wanted to "sound the alarm about the rise in anti-Jewish bigotry on the part of Negroes," while Sorrin affirmed that the "loss of confidence on the part of Negro leaders involved in direct action cannot be characterized as anti-Semitism." In Chicago, ADL leader A. Abbot Rosen acknowledged, "In the course of a more militant opposition to discrimination, Negro groups are highlighting the names of oppressors, particularly landlords." Rosen acknowledged that the lists included Jewish names, inspiring hostility from African Americans. Yet, as the Chicago leader explained, "the intent is not anti-Semitic and there is no discernible increase of anti-Semitism as a consequence of such activities."[31]

American rabbis also cautioned against Jewish overreaction to black antisemitism. In 1965, Cecil Moore, a leader in the Philadelphia office of the NAACP, made antisemitic statements in an address criticizing urban Jews for their anti-black behavior. Even as other Jews labeled Moore an antisemite and dismissed his critique as a consequence, Rabbi Judea B. Miller, a civil rights activist best known for helping to integrate the first lunch counter in Mississippi, pushed back. "I don't think we have the right to label glibly Cecil Moore an anti-Semite when he reminds us that we are phoneys," Miller blasted. "The Emperor's new clothes are not as fancy as he believes—he is naked!" While Miller labeled Moore "a fanatic," he warned his coreligionists that "dismiss[ing] him as a mere anti-Semite does not invalidate his criticism."[32]

Rabbi Henry Cohen minimized the threat of black antisemitism by moving it to the periphery of Judaic thinking on questions of social justice. In a 1966 sermon, he argued that black antisemitism proved "irrelevant to a consideration of Jewish responsibility because, in the most fundamental sense, that responsibility stems from us and not from Negroes." For Reform Jews especially, the prophetic mandate within Judaism served as a popular rationale for encouraging and explaining that movement's strong support for civil rights. Cohen, then, pressed his congregants to fulfill their "prophetic injunction to do justice" regardless of whatever antisemitism may arise. Even in the face of unappreciative blacks, Cohen pressed, Jews still needed to push forward. "We must become involved in the fight for racial justice . . . not because Negroes are deserving objects of our benevolence, but simply because it is the right thing to do."[33]

When African American college students demanded their own organization on campus, Rabbi Israel Dresner called them "black Hillel foundations," in reference to the national Jewish college student organization. Dresner considered it "a very healthy thing" for African Americans to build their own school system, comparing it to the extensive system of Catholic schools in the United States. Dresner considered "nonsense" the claim that "black anti-Semites are going to take power in America," pointing instead to the popularity of racist politician George Wallace as the real threat to the nation. For Dresner, the real danger lurked with racist white America that would, in opposition to black power, throw even more political power behind segregationist candidates such as Wallace. In that sort of America, Dresner concluded, "the Jew isn't going to be safe either."[34]

Scholarly studies repudiated the import of antisemitism as well. In a 1965 article published in *Jewish Social Studies*, sociology professor David Caplovitz discounted African American antisemitism as the probable cause of rioting that broke out in cities throughout the North. "The ghetto riots of 1965," Caplovitz believed, "did not reflect Negro anti-Semitism so much as the normal conflict between landlord and tenant, seller and buyer, creditor and borrower." AJC executive vice president Bertram H. Gold summarized a 1964 ADL study as well as a 1967 AJC report that rated anti-white sentiment as a more accurate understanding of Black Power rhetoric than antisemitism.[35]

When Stokely Carmichael declared "Black Power" on June 19, 1966, Jewish communal leaders rallied with understanding at least, and, in many cases, outright support for its strategies and tactics. Given the organized Jewish community's strong empathy for the Nation of Islam in the early postwar years, the keen awareness of the systemic differences between African American history and American Jewish history expressed even as blacks and Jews marched together in the 1950s, and the many predictions of a black militant response to the slow pace of civil rights reform in the 1960s, the strong public Jewish support offered to black militants followed as the logical consequence of longstanding communal understandings.

AJCongress officials saw in the rise of Black Power a reflection of the movement's earlier weaknesses and an opportunity to correct them. In a November 1966 article, AJCongress president Rabbi Arthur J. Lelyveld described Black Power as "an understandable and commendable surge of self-affirmation." In the wake of the Moynihan Report that criticized absentee African American fathers, Lelyveld took care to laud black men, whom he believed "must stand proudly to shape their own destiny." And when they rose to challenge established African American leadership of the civil rights movement, Black Power activists communicated, in ways the AJCongress leader understood and approved, "that the Negro masses must no longer be content to rely on the beneficence of friendly whites or on the mediation of those few Negroes who had 'made it' into the middle class." For Lelyveld, the new emphasis on African American political autonomy affirmed "that 'black' was 'good.'"[36]

In 1967, *Congress Bi-Weekly* featured an article by Leonard Fein affirming the limits of white liberalism and the need for stronger African American control of the civil rights movement. "Black power itself is, if anything," he wrote, "a reasonable response to the predictable failure of integrationism." White America refused to accept desegregation at the same time that African Americans stood firm in their desire for equality. In that environment, Fein argued, Black Power offered a path for the African American community to "gain its due." Only a Jewish retreat from it earlier hands-on approach to civil rights activism would work. "Tomorrow, or the day after, or the day after that," he implored, "we shall have to come to terms with the fact that it is for the Negro to decide, and not for us, how much his Negroness shall matter." Fein believed that the Black Power movement offered African Americans an opportunity for self-respect as it forced Jews to confront what he described as "the massive task of learning how to see the Negro as a man."[37]

As an organization, the AJCongress took up the question of Black Power at its 1968 biennial convention. In a resolution its membership approved, the organization linked African American calls for heightened ethnic awareness to the Jews' own need for strong communal bonds. "As a people that has always stressed its own identity," the resolution declared, "Jews understand this process and know that it can only be resolved by those who are directly involved." The AJCongress defended the purge of Jews from civil rights organizations, arguing that the time had come for American Jews to take responsibility for their own religious community. In terms of African American political autonomy, the Jewish advocacy group understood that "the black community will and must, in large measure, direct its own future within the framework of a democratic society." Ultimately, the AJCongress pledged to work with black groups in support of their separatist goal.[38]

Even the more centrist AJC defended Black Power when its associate director David Danzig defined the Black Power movement in a September 1966 article in *Commentary*. He framed this new form of African American advocacy as consistent with American democratic principles. "This effort to encourage Negroes to see themselves as a power bloc, and to act as one," he wrote, "is entirely in keeping with American minority politics, and yet an attempt is apparently being made by both the advocates and the opponents of 'black power' to present it as something of a departure." He pushed back against Jewish critics of Black Power, arguing that its detractors failed to look deeply enough at the issues facing African Americans. "Rarely, in the course of all the excitement over 'black power,'" he argued, "did anyone seek to deal with the realities underlying the current thrust of Negro social action."[39]

Two years later, AJC executive vice president Bertram H. Gold added his support during a presentation to the 1968 National Conference of Jewish Communal Service. The slow pace of legal change, he understood, demanded a more activist African American agenda. Playing to those critical of the new movement, Gold acknowledged, "the separatist aspirations on the part of blacks today have bothered us white Jewish liberals," noting that "they seem so contrary to our cherished notions about integration." Still, he pressed, "Many of these aspirations, particularly those related to group growth goals, are a necessary and inevitable stage which we must be ready to accept, given the circumstances of American life today." Gold lauded Black Power for its emphasis on "black initiative, black self-worth, black identity, black pride." He looked to its interest in developing a strong African American economy and political base as well as its focus on cultivating a new generation of black leaders. Ultimately, he believed, Black Power's separatist orientation would serve as nothing more than a needed pause so that African Americans would be able to recreate their interfaith alliances "as psychological, social, and political equals."[40]

In a December 1966 symposium on the fast-changing relations between blacks and Jews, Brandeis University professor Ben Halpern defined a new consensus, affirming the necessity of black militancy while he paralleled the African American effort to the Jewish people's own history of discrimination. He argued that he was "unable to sympathize with Jewish liberals shut out by the slogan of Black Power and characterized Jewish protests against white civil rights purges as 'puerile' and 'self-indulgent.'" Halpern "fully under[stood]" the African American impulse to embrace Black Power, arguing that "it would be foolish and self-destructive of the Negroes to take any other course . . . The Negroes want to run their own show."[41]

Others at the symposium defended their support of Black Power by invoking the Great Society–embraced sociological theory that located an ethnic group's access to power as the most important determinant in assessing a minority group's opportunities for social mobility. Because African Americans still lingered on society's margins, they could not enter into coalition with Jews, who had already achieved status in mainstream America. As Rabbi Arthur Hertzberg urged, "The issues between Jews and Negroes are not misunderstandings between the two groups, but hard questions about power and position." Because Jews enjoyed privilege, Hertzberg's line of thinking went, they could not really empathize with the racial oppression of their African American colleagues nor could they immerse themselves in the civil rights struggle as deeply as they believed. When Stokely Carmichael purged whites from civil rights leadership, Hertzberg understood. "Not even one's best friends can be the leaders," he sympathized, "in a struggle in which their personal futures, and those of their children, are not involved." The rise of black nationalism, the purge of whites from civil rights organizations, and even the rise of black antisemitism all grew from the basic power differential between the two groups.[42]

Jewish leadership's understanding and empathy for the growing Black Power thinking extended as well to the religious sphere, where rabbis embraced the growing militancy in black America. In a March 1968 sermon at Philadelphia's Conservative-movement synagogue Har Zion, Rabbi Dov Peretz Elkins celebrated Black Power and placed blame for African American frustration squarely on white America. "If indeed there is a way for the black to pull himself up," he implored, "then it is by the bootstraps of Black Power." In a play on the popular African American slogan, "Black is beautiful," Elkins reminded his congregants, "We have always felt that being Jewish is 'beautiful.'" For Elkins, the notion that God created all people in God's image extended to that popular slogan. "Why not then foster slogans such as 'Black is beautiful,'" he asked his congregants, "because it's the color God gave them." Elkins considered the rise of Black Power a logical consequence of American racism and he understood its genesis and purpose. "The black must feel that it's beautiful to be black," he concluded, "before he can achieve the self-respect that we have taken away from him through slavery, repression, and racist discrimination."[43]

For Rabbi Arnold J. Wolf, an outspoken leftist rabbi from Chicago who served as well as a visiting faculty member at the Reform movement's seminary, the Hebrew Union College-Jewish Institute of Religion, the African American community, and not American Jews, faced the greatest threat in the United States. In a 1969 address to the Synagogue Council of America, Wolf critiqued Jewish leaders who still held on to the view that blacks and Jews shared a common American experience. "I think we suspect that somehow the Negro community, the black community, has inherited in America our covenant fate." Calling out the rapid economic mobility of American Jews, Wolf charged, "If anyone is in danger of Auschwitz in America, it seems clear to me that it is not the upper-middle-class Jewish community with all of its appropriate defenses. It is the black community which is threatened with genocide, not we."[44]

Although American Jews did face threats from time to time, Wolf acknowledged, African Americans faced a more sinister threat from liberalism itself. "The enemy of the black is the very system which the Jew thinks is his defense," he argued. "The system which has admitted us, coddled us, approved of us, promoted us, protected us is the very system which the black sees as the enemy. . . . For the black," Wolf urged, "the enemy is no person, not even any group, but the liberal establishment itself, which for them is American racism incarnate." With these assertions, Wolf challenged his coreligionists to consider the irony of their own support for racial equality. "So we defend, quite against our own real interests," the rabbi concluded, "a system in which we have a place and they have none."[45]

When Jewish religious leaders sat with their Christian colleagues to decide on a theme for their 1968 New York regional conference, they chose "Black Power—A Positive Force," inviting Roosevelt University's Charles V. Hamilton, coauthor with Stokely Carmichael of *Black Power: The Politics of Liberation in America*, to deliver the keynote. Reform Rabbi Roland B. Gittelsohn of Boston's Temple Israel, himself a member of President Truman's 1948 Committee on Civil Rights and an activist from the 1950s who supported congregants jailed during Freedom Summer in Mississippi, entered the new era of black-Jewish relations with strong support for black nationalism. "The positive aspect of black power," he argued, "is its search for ethnic identity. This, we Jews of all peoples should be able to understand and approve. The American Negro today is in this respect retracing precisely the experience of American Jews a generation or two ago."[46]

Gittelsohn rejected criticisms of Black Power as destructive, framing it instead as an empowering movement that encouraged African Americans "to throw off the shackles of intramural colonialism, to reject selection of his values and goals by the white community, to assert a large measure of control over his own life." He drew parallels between the experiences of middle-class suburban Jews and working-class African Americans in the nation's urban centers. "The citizens of Brookline and Newton and Scarsdale and every other suburban community control the policies of their children's schools," he reminded his brethren. "Black Power means that Negro parents want no less authority and privilege for themselves."[47]

In a 1969 CCAR brochure published in observance of Race Relations Shabbat, Reform movement clergy urged their congregants to be "especially understanding of this painful withdrawal into separatism and nationalism." They recalled the failure of the European Enlightenment to properly integrate Jews into the larger Christian society, the experience of Theodor Herzl, founder of modern political Zionism, at the Dreyfus Trial as he realized that Jews could never live as equal citizens in a non-Jewish nation, as well as early Zionist leader Leon Pinsker's realization that liberal integration could never succeed in nineteenth-century Eastern Europe. African Americans, the CCAR understood, were following the same path as Jews centuries earlier. American Jews, therefore, should "understand the overriding need of a powerless people, sick with self-hatred, to gain dignity and pride along with a fair share of economic and political power." As a community that itself faced marginalization, "who for so long were the 'Jewish problem' and were considered unworthy of being granted full civil rights, should better understand the black man and the 'negro problem.'"[48]

Conservative movement rabbi Jacob Chinitz called for his coreligionists to emulate Black Power. In a ten-point program he called "Jewish Power," Chinitz sought to leverage black consciousness to help build stronger Jewish identity. In a move that would help build a new identity politics–based consensus between black militants and Jewish ethnic revivalists, Chinitz pressed for the introduction of Jewish studies courses in both high schools and colleges as well as the creation of what he called "distinctive Jewish dress." In this Conservative rabbi's thinking, American Jews in the Black Power era could retrieve the ancient Jewish customs of their tradition-bound ancestors by wearing a *tallit katan* (prayer shawl under one's clothing), a *kippah* (head covering), and grooming one's hair short. In a larger critique of organized Jewish life, Chinitz pressed his congregants to rally against their secular-based communal leaders, especially Jewish Community Federations that he considered too divorced from Jewish ritual and practice.[49]

In a rare statement from the Orthodox community, Yeshiva University professor Rabbi Jerry Hochbaum, who served as well as a consultant to the National JCRAC, told the 1969 meeting of the Rabbinical Council of America that "the Jews should be sympathetic to the development of a more positive Negro self-image." As he explained, "No group can appreciate so deeply as the Jews the growing interest among Negroes in black identity." In this case, the desire among African Americans to maintain a particularist sense of identity aligned with Orthodoxy, which struggled against the same assimilationist forces in American society. Even as the public expressions of identity proved quite different, Hochbaum understood that movements for black pride and Jewish pride shared important similarities in a postwar political culture that sought and then celebrated interfaith engagement in its earlier years.[50]

American Jewish support for the emerging Black Power movement challenges a widely held yet mythical understanding of the black-Jewish alliance. Far from the Cold War anti-Communist narrative demanding a benevolent political coalition across religious and racial lines, Jewish leaders struggled in relationship to their own social mobility, their deep awareness of racism's impact on African Americans, and the strategy and tactics necessary to move their progressive agenda forward. Through this lens, the apparent splintering of the movement in the late 1960s can be seen instead as the beginnings of a new identity politics–centered approach to social reform. Even as Jews faced marginalization from their historic civil rights allies, they saw in the Black Power approach tremendous new potential for their own ethnic identities. Soon after African American nationalists pressed their black-centered political agenda, American Jews would turn inward as well, emulating Black Power tactics in a new campaign for heightened Jewish identity.

Turning Inward: Black Power and Jewish Youth Movements

Criticizing the historic, if not heroic, Jewish commitment to African American racial equality during the civil rights movement of the 1950s and early 1960s, Myron Fenster, a Conservative movement rabbi from Shelter Rock Jewish Center in Roslyn, New York, wondered why American Jews took such a great interest in the well-being of non-Jews at the apparent expense of their own coreligionists. "Let me admit to feeling sad and cheated," he lamented at a 1966 symposium on black-Jewish relations, "when some marvelously idealistic college kid is ready to lay down his young life to inch along the Negro struggle but would not lift a pinky to save the whole Jewish enterprise from oblivion." Fenster's observation surfaced a deeper political and religious dynamic at play among Jewish civil rights workers. Even as Jews represented a disproportionately large number of white activists, few connected their social justice work to organized Jewish life. While a case can be made locating their progressive politics in Jewish tradition, young Jewish liberal activists in the 1950s and early 1960s most often applied a more secular rationale for their civil rights commitments, aligning with SNCC and CORE instead of the organized religious world of Fenster.[1]

While Fenster's lament accurately described a small subset of American Jews who still clung to some sort of interracial alliance, he missed a larger and far more important strategic shift underway among American Jewish social justice advocates. Faced with the rise of black nationalism and its particularist orientation, American Jews stood at an inflection point in their own political and ethnic consciousness. As Rabbi Balfour Brickner, the associate director of the Reform movement's commission on social action, observed in a 1972 address, American Jews faced "the most vexing dilemma" in their entire American Jewish experience. Should American Jews focus on "particularistic, exclusively Jewish, matters" or remain committed to "the more universal" approach that "has nourished the American Jew and given us succor?" For Brickner and the larger American Jewish community, the answer proved clear: "We are turned inward."[2]

Jewish leaders saw in Black Power an opportunistic moment for their own communal priorities. During a 1969 gathering on black-Jewish relations, for example, Reform rabbi Israel Dresner suggested that Jews could "benefit from the sudden thrust of the black people" and asked, "Why do we condemn black kids who suddenly wear their hairdo African or wear African clothing?" In the rise of black ethnic and racial awareness, Dresner saw the possibility of "suddenly tomorrow, a million American Jews" walking "into their white-collar jobs wearing a kaputah, a beard, and a shtreimel [referencing traditional Jewish dress and appearance]."[3]

Dresner's support for a stronger and more public Jewish profile conflicted with a Reform movement once ideologically committed to assimilation as the strategy of choice for American Jewry. From its origins in the late nineteenth century, American Reform Judaism rejected Zionism, minimized the use of Hebrew in religious services, and considered the laws of kashruth, keeping kosher, outdated and irrelevant to modern life. Only in the identity-politics culture of the 1960s could a Reform religious leader call for stronger Jewish identification with tradition while linking that move to the examples set by African American activists. Dresner played seemingly competing social trends simultaneously: a turn toward a deeper level of Jewish ritual observance while embracing the latest trends in the larger culture. The new identity-politics consensus developing among blacks and Jews blurred the boundaries between the religious and the secular.

Leonard Fein agreed. At the 1969 meeting of the Synagogue Council of America, the associate director of the Harvard-MIT Joint Center for Urban Studies argued that Jews would be the "unintended beneficiaries" of a black nationalist movement that would give "more elbow room for Jewish assertiveness." From his background helping develop Great Society programs alongside Daniel Patrick Moynihan, Fein understood firsthand the development of black militancy in the mid-1960s. As a Jewish observer, he appreciated the ways in which these larger social developments could play out in his own ethnic community. While he understood that the new developing consensus lacked the sort of intentionality of the earlier black-Jewish alliance, Fein still pressed for Jews to leverage the changing racial dynamics for their own benefit. In his own subsequent career, Fein did just that as he founded the independent Jewish periodical *Moment* magazine, created Mazon: A Jewish Response to Hunger, and helped form Americans for Peace Now, a progressive Zionist group.[4]

Purged from leadership positions in civil rights organizations, inspired by the unapologetic approach of Black Power, and modeling tactics employed in several of the larger protest movements of the era, Jewish activists pressed a multifaceted agenda to revitalize American Jewish life. In what Brandeis University professor Jonathan Sarna called a "great American Jewish awakening," American Jews took aim at Jewish organizations for their lack of commitment to serious Jewish education, pressing for the creation of community-based Jewish day schools. This new generation of more traditional Jews increased their level of Jewish ritual observance, challenging their parents' more assimilationist postures. They rejected the synagogue as the sole center for Jewish religious expression, while women, marginalized from more traditional religious life, demanded equality in worship, lay leadership, and ultimately, the rabbinate. As Harold R. Isaacs argued in a 1972 *Commentary* article, the Black Power–inspired "great shaking up and shaking out" of the black-Jewish alliance gifted Jews the opportunity "to rediscover what there might be for them in their Jewishness."[5]

In one sense, the turn inward signaled an impressive revitalization of American Jewish life. Jews pushed out of civil rights organizations by a more militant African American community critical of white liberal gradualism and by a New Left movement taking aim at Zionism rejected their historic consensus-based civic role in favor of a return to Jewish tradition. The grandchildren of Eastern European Jewish immigrants, in an approach originally described by University of Chicago sociologist Marcus Lee Hansen, rejected the assimilationist posture of their parents' generation in order to reclaim the tradition of their grandparents. According to Hansen, immigrants wanted nothing more than to rid themselves of their Old World past, raising their children as assimilated Americans. The grandchildren, critical of their parents' abandonment of heritage and culture, waxed nostalgic for what they considered the authentic ethnic knowledge of their grandparents. With the religious and ethnic revival of young Jews in the mid-1960s, the three-generation cycle from tradition to integration and back to tradition appeared complete.

But the Hansen model did not describe the mid-1960s American Jewish turn inward. Although many participants and observers lauded the return to tradition as a sign of revitalized Jewish life, in fact the American Jewish religious revival borrowed more from Black Power than it did from any imagined Jewish past. At a time when American Jews ascribed their new-found Jewishness to their own tradition, they actually were reflecting a larger Americanist trend. Black Power expanded the limits of acceptable ethnic group expression in 1960s America. The social protest movements of the day offered the strategies and tactics needed to bring institutional change. By leveraging the two, Jewish activists became more American even as they pressed for heightened Jewish expression. In essence, the more Jewish these efforts seemed, the more secular they became.

The generation of Jews that turned inward during the mid-1960s grew up in a postwar religious world typified by interfaith outreach and religious accommodation. Fueled by an expanding American economy, the opening of affordable suburban communities, and a desire to take their place in the middle class, Jews fled their historic homes in city centers for the expansive space, greener surroundings, and quieter neighborhoods of the American periphery. Living side by side with Christian neighbors, Jews engaged a host of questions unknown to them in their urban environs. How can Jews maintain their religious identity in a community where they are a numerical minority? How will they respond to the normalization of Christian holidays, both in the civic sphere and in the public schools? What does it mean to be different, especially at a time when the Cold War trumpeted the virtues of a consensus-based democracy?

In most cases, postwar Jews embraced a more universalist approach to religious life, celebrating what famed sociologist Will Herberg would later call the Protestant, Catholic, Jewish triad in American life. Clergy formed and expanded interfaith dialogue organizations, developed a

National Brotherhood Week, and touted the Judeo-Christian values that bound religious America into a single cohesive whole. The Conservative movement's rabbinical arm offered permission for suburban Jews to drive their cars to synagogue on Shabbat, a practice otherwise forbidden by Jewish law. When government policymakers in 1957 wondered whether they should add a question to the 1960 census on religious affiliation, the AJCongress spoke for a broad consensus when it issued a statement "unequivocally opposed" to the idea. In similar fashion, and as articulated in chapter 2, Jewish organizations favored strong public schools and a strict separation of church and state, recoiling when parochial school advocates pressed for government support.[6]

Framed in terms of American Jewish accommodation to an era's larger social and political culture, the consensus-based interfaith approach of postwar Jews followed the same path as their more identity-based children in the 1960s and early 1970s. Both groups emulated the religious and ethnic expression of the non-Jews around them. In the 1950s, the American dream of middle-class status, home ownership, and social acceptance from their neighbors encouraged Jews to leverage Christian religious expressions as tools to advance their own integration into their emerging communities. In the spirit of interfaith and intercultural understanding, Christmas observance, if matched by opportunities for their children to teach the Hanukkah story or show their classmates how to play the dreidel game, strengthened the case for a pluralist democracy embracing the religious differences of its citizenry.

The Black Power–initiated splintering of the Jewish and African American communities masked a deeper, more important, and powerful symmetry that aligned their activism for a new age. When Jews began a religious revival in the mid- and late 1960s, they often employed language that celebrated a return to tradition and boasted of strengthened American Jewish life. Yet, their turn inward proved less a move toward Jewish tradition than it did a reflection of a new era's political status quo: identity politics. Even as American Jews called out their impressive efforts revitalizing Jewish life, that sort of ethnic activism could occur only within the larger political context of 1960s America. And because the nation's larger move to heightened ethnic awareness began in the African American community, the turn inward proved more black than Jewish. In their personal lives and in the political work that grew from it, young Jews borrowed from black nationalism to strengthen their Jewish knowledge, observance, and consciousness. Within a decade, they launched a series of identity-building efforts that brought Judaism more into the public square, pressed back against the assimilationist-based consensus ideals of the 1950s, and created conflict with organized Jewish leaders accused of selling Jewish life short.

Black Power's rejection of interracial coalitions placed identity politics at the heart of the public square. It affirmed a pluralistic approach to American democracy, encouraging distinctive ethnic, religious, and, later, gender groups to lobby for their particular needs as part of what cultural theorist Horace Kallen once described as an American "symphony of sounds." What early cultural pluralist thinkers such as Kallen envisioned as complementary instruments blended together in harmony, Black Power advocates framed in more separatist and power-centered terms. Institutional racism, they understood, translated into an orchestra with some instruments that enjoyed musical dominance as well as others that did not. For cultural pluralism to work in 1960s America, all ethnic sub-groups demanded the right to be heard. The symphony, then, must feature all its instruments with equal strength.[7]

The New Pluralism

Jewish leaders responded by articulating a new approach to American ethnic life, "The New Pluralism," which sought ways of integrating Jewish, African American, and white ethnic groups into the Black Power–inspired understanding of cultural pluralism. With the separatism of Black Power and the Great Society's emphasis on communities of color, Jews faced an ethnic America divided by racial status and a social identity increasingly understood more as privileged and white than as marginalized and persecuted. The purge of white liberals from civil rights organizations led to a larger fear of polarization among onetime allies. American Jews especially understood that their ascension into the middle class complicated their relationship with African Americans, as well as with other communities of color. How would blacks, whites, Jews, and other ethno-religious minorities coexist in an identity politics–rooted democracy? How could the politics of Black Power, translated across the national landscape, evolve a new vision of cultural pluralism inclusive of all?[8]

The New Pluralism negotiated a path between the racial separatism typical of Black Power and the desire, especially among white urban northern ethnics, for inclusion in the identity-based politics of the day. At a 1969 gathering to discuss the tense relations between blacks and Jews, City University of New York history and political science professor Seymour Lachman, who later that year joined the New York City Board of Education, pressed for creation of a new theory of cultural pluralism that could, in his mind, "help enhance Judaism in America and lead to continuation of our survival." Playing on the seemingly competing themes of early postwar accommodation and 1960s ethnic expression, Lachman wanted Jews to enjoy the freedom to integrate into the larger society, or, if they chose, to live "amongst our own people."[9]

For Lachman and other innovators of the New Pluralism, the rise of black-identity politics anchored their work. Lachman understood that forging new understandings of pluralist democracy "is what I believe the masses of blacks are trying to do with black power." San Francisco–based JCRC leader Earl Raab recognized that "the black Revolution is spurring the Jewish community—and America—into a renewed understanding of pluralistic politics." By pressing for what historian Arthur Goren called an "awakening of ethnic and racial identity," New Pluralism advocates sought a vision of American democracy that recognized the needs and interests of all ethnic Americans, regardless of racial status. As Goren explained, the New Pluralism offered hope for a new consensus between otherwise disparate groups. "Only if public policy responded to the legitimate grievances and needs of the ethnic group hitherto ignored if not scorned," he urged, "would it be possible to stop the 'polarization' of American society into black and white, haves and have-nots."[10]

Among Jewish communal leaders, Irving Levine, the AJC's director of education and urban planning, took the lead in the organized Jewish community's efforts toward imagining a new approach to cultural difference in the United States. "Pluralism," Levine affirmed, "is as American as cherry pie." He sought a *via media*, a middle ground, between the consensus-based models of the early postwar years and the Black Power separatism of the mid-1960s. The AJC leader focused first on the needs of working-class white ethnics whose inclusion in a new model of cultural pluralism addressed contemporary fears of a polarizing ethnic America. At a time when more and more white ethnic Americans abandoned the civil rights cause, Levine sought ways to enlarge the identity-politics tent. In the midst of a growing focus on African American–based ethnic activism in the mid-1960s, Levine held, "whites, too, have the right to assert a strategy." An approach to pluralist democracy that cut across racial lines, he hoped, would lay the groundwork for "bridge building" and eventually to "coalition building" between groups that splintered with the separatist ideology of Black Power.[11]

Levine launched his efforts in the fall of 1967 with a call to action on twenty-one different social issues that plagued the nation and alienated white ethnics. In anticipation of a national conference to explore how American Jews might benefit from a new approach to cultural pluralism, the AJC leader asked for guidance on how white ethnics might engage government policymakers about rising crime, high taxes, health insurance, urban planning in their neighborhoods, support for parochial schools, childcare, and the plight of unskilled workers. Levine counted almost 150 attendees at the first National Consultation on Ethnic America held at Fordham University in 1968.[12]

After the conference, the AJC created the National Project on Ethnic America, which, in 1974, became the Institute on Pluralism and Group Identity. During its life span, the AJC efforts sponsored ethnicity-based workshops to assist community organizations address topics such as "The Media and Ethnicity" and "Establishing a Human Relations Program on Your College Campus." The Jewish organization examined the relationship between one's ethnic identity and mental health issues as well as the role of women in a pluralist nation. As Arthur Goren concluded, the AJC's efforts proved a navigation "between the new pluralism and soft pluralism, between sanctioning group privileges and a laissez-faire approach to ethnic group life."[13]

The New Pluralism, in its mediation of race-based and ethnic-based categories, positioned American Jews as an ideal, if not unique, group to lead the effort toward a new interracial political consensus. Stung by the dissolution of FDR's New Deal Coalition after the race-based political agenda of LBJ's Great Society, white urban northern ethnics tended to bolt from their onetime progressive ideas in favor of a backlash meant to point out the particular challenges that working-class whites face in their day-to-day lives. Jews, who have moved back and forth across the racial divide, enjoyed the unusual opportunity of empathizing with each side of the racial continuum, even as groups both black and white sometimes doubted whether Jews fit comfortably on their side of the racial continuum. With the New Pluralism, American Jewish leaders struggled, mostly without success, to find common political ground between white and black Americans.

The Campus Environment

The Black Power–inspired Jewish ethnic revival played out first on the college campus, where young Jews, who once answered their need for political activism by joining free speech or civil rights groups, turned inward, discovering a host of Jewish-centered issues worthy of their attention. As Donald Feldstein, an education consultant hired by the National Jewish Welfare Board to study college-age Jews, reported in 1970, "It is no longer embarrassing or 'out' to belong to a group on the college campus with the word 'Jew' in the title." He noted "literally scores" of Jewish groups forming on college campuses across the country with "aggressively Jewish" missions that imitated "the spirit, the style, and the tactics of the New Left and black militants." The same year, the AJCongress announced, "On college campuses (and off them), young Jewish men and women are creating a kind of 'new Judaism' that has been described as activist-oriented and communal rather than middle-class and congregational."[14]

In the classroom, Jewish students sought a strengthening of university-level Jewish studies. As political science professor Daniel Elazar reported in a 1971 *Midstream* article, when "blacks began to demand 'black studies' programs in the universities, young Jews countered by demanding more extensive Jewish studies programs under the explicit label, with no masks." Jewish students internalized the era's Black Power–inspired identity politics to gain what their parents' generation did not: a sense of themselves as unapologetic and deeply informed Jews. As Leonard Fein observed, "Jewish students are learning to respect themselves as Jews by listening with care to what their black peers are saying." They took lessons from Black Power that, as Fein explained, "they did not, and, in fact, could not have learned from their own fathers, who have been so wrapped up in making Judaism easy that they have, on the whole, made it trivial as well." Even Yeshiva University, the flagship school for Orthodox Jews, reported that a program designed to bolster Jewish knowledge for less identified students grew from 43 enrollees in 1956 to 264 participants in 1964.[15]

Heightened Jewish student awareness extended as well to the faculty ranks where the growing interest in black studies offered Jewish academics a path for strengthening course offerings in Jewish studies. Beginning in the late 1950s and especially through the 1960s, scholars across disciplines refocused their scholarship and teaching to include the study of people and topics historically ignored by the academy. Immigration and labor historians wrote books on ordinary, working-class people, rejecting existing approaches that focused narrowly on white male elites. In the wake of the civil rights movement, black intellectuals criticized what cynics called "dead white man's history" in favor of a social history frame that explored, for example, the lived experiences of African Americans during slavery. Other scholars joined the mix with new fields developed in Chicano studies, American Indian studies, Asian American studies, and women's studies.[16]

The rise of ethnic studies politicized the university, as its proponents sought to bring the larger social challenges of the nation into their research and their classrooms. Just as civil rights workers focused their passion for change in grassroots activism, a new generation of scholars leveraged the university as a training ground for the next generation of change agents. The university itself, they understood, reflected the inequities of the larger culture just as it offered the educational frame necessary to inspire its graduates to hop on the social justice bandwagon.

In a theoretical approach known as "the identity project," the university's mission focused on the goal of strengthening the ethnic identities of its graduates. A course on the sociology of race, for example, demanded that its students engage their own racial status as part of the course curriculum. Rather than following the traditional university model of detached, third-person critical inquiry and analysis, ethnic studies professors taught, researched, and wrote in real time, integrating identity politics into their day-to-day profession. Student and faculty passion for this wholesale change in the university's purpose led to a five-month student and faculty strike at San Francisco State University during the 1968–1969 school year. It ended only when administrators created the nation's first, and still only, College of Ethnic Studies, offering students a number of new majors and guaranteeing faculty the ability to design their curriculum as they wished.

Jewish faculty efforts coalesced in the fall of 1969 when interest in the field of Jewish studies inspired a group of younger scholars to break from the old-line professional associations in religion and create their own group, the Association for Jewish Studies (AJS). As AJS historian Kristin Loveland explained, the development of the new Jewish academic group "was a result of the postwar expansion in university course offerings and the 1960s proliferation of area studies, which also included African American, Latin American, and Asian American studies." Jewish professors, she explained, leveraged the newfound emphasis on ethnic studies to "resituate Jewish studies" in the larger academy. As intellectuals, Jewish studies professors strove to refine, develop, and strengthen their discipline while, in a bid to the era's appreciation for particularist advocacy, "realiz[ing] the uniqueness of the Jewish experience as a field worthy of study from its own perspective."[17]

The AJS embraced the identity project approach innovated by black studies. As Columbia University sociology graduate student David Glanz wrote in *Congress Bi-Weekly*, "Regular programs in Judaica were demanded and legitimized as parallels to black studies courses." In its earliest iteration, the AJS required that all its members identify as Jews, leading one of the organization's founders, Rabbi Irving "Yitz" Greenberg to acknowledge that "more is at stake in Jewish studies than increasing research and teaching efforts in the field." At a time when American Jews were "turning inward from universalism to particularism," Loveland explained, scholars faced intense pressure to link their scholarly work with issues of "communal relevance."[18]

Over time, though, the AJS retreated from its staunch identity-based position. Jewish studies scholars feared that too great an emphasis on using university-level Jewish studies courses as tools to help students become more identified as Jews would compromise the critical analytic approach central to scholarship, or at least to the traditional rules of academic inquiry. Rabbi Greenberg worried that "too close an identification with the concerns of the Jewish community and for the Jewish civilization" would undermine a scholar's credibility. A Jewish studies professor, he worried, would appear to favor one interpretation of Jewish life over others. He thought that sort of identity-centered teaching belonged to congregational rabbis, who could use their denominational status to direct their congregants' thinking. Scholars needed to remain theologically neutral. Ruth Wisse, another AJS founder who developed the field at

McGill University before her move to Harvard University, agreed, urging her colleagues to do all they could to "provide an alternative to immediate applicability."[19]

As the AJS debated it nature and purpose, scholars across North America gravitated to the new association. While its first annual conference at Brandeis University counted just forty-seven attendees in 1969, the numbers nearly doubled, to ninety, for the 1971 meeting. By its fourth year, the AJS counted 269 professors and in 1989 had grown to 443 delegates. At the 2016 meeting, more than 1,100 academics attended more than 190 different sessions. The AJS's growth mirrored increased enrollments in Jewish studies courses, as reported by Bill Novak and Robert Goldman, who, in 1971, affirmed "many students are currently engaged in some form of Jewish studies, whereas two and three years ago they were not involved in even the most elementary process of such learning."[20]

Academic interest in Jewish studies extended beyond the university classroom. UC Berkeley's Hillel chapter, for its part, offered students a variety of extracurricular learning opportunities. A review of its February 1970 calendar showed that Jewish undergraduates could join a free seminar on Hasidism, a joy-filled form of traditional Jewish expression that enjoyed a renaissance among countercultural Jews in the 1960s. A Hebrew language course promised to connect young Jews both with their tradition and with the modern State of Israel, while another course focused specifically on Jewish participation in the era's radical movements.[21]

When the Hillel leadership determined that their building needed a new veneer, it staged a "paint-in," playing on the language of the sit-in movement in order to provide "an opportunity for free expression on the walls of Hillel." A national review of college campuses determined that by 1971, a dozen universities offered students decision-making power to develop noncredit courses at each school's version of a Free Jewish University. In 1972, Berkeley Hillel expanded its ambitious education program by creating a "Free Jewish University," and offered first-semester classes on Soviet Jewry as well as Jewish mysticism. Two years later, historian Fred Rosenbaum formed Lehrhaus Judaica, recreating a Frankfurt, Germany-based school originally created in 1920 by German Jewish philosopher Franz Rosenzweig.[22]

Within the religious sphere, UC Berkeley students, disappointed with what they called the "usual boring services you find at Hillel," organized the Union of Jewish Students (UJS), a self-described radical group committed to bringing Jewish expression into the broader Jewish community. In the fall of 1967, the UJS designed its own High Holiday religious service for the second day of Rosh Hashanah, the Jewish New Year. Student organizers appealed to undergraduates across the university's religious, ethnic, and racial landscape, attracting some 200 participants. Reflecting both its physical proximity to Oakland, California, and its close ideological kinship to Black Power, the UJS decided to replace the central feature of a Jewish religious service, the reading of the Torah, with a sermon by Black Panther leader Bobby Seale.[23]

The students' articulation of Judaism as a religion rooted in the imperatives of social justice as expressed by the work of the BPP situated them at the nexus between a more tradition-bound interpretation of Jewish life and the realities of the Berkeley-based identity-politics scene of the 1960s. They conflated Black Power with Judaism in an organic expression of their lived experiences as children of the social protest era. While many of their parents' generation probably faulted them for undermining the sanctity of the High Holidays, their rejection of synagogue life as well as of their own Hillel group revealed a new brand of Jewish expression deepened by the students' serious engagement in the larger identity-politics culture surrounding them. The UJS strengthened its Jewishness by embracing the era's secular political culture.

Outside of the university, Jewish students took the knowledge they gained in Jewish studies courses, the tactics they learned from the era's social protest movements, and their inward-turning desire to focus on a strengthened Jewish life to challenge established Jewish leadership. As Professor Ronald I. Rubin explained in a 1973 *Tradition* article on the Jewish ethnic revival, "Jewish youth had not abandoned liberalism; they simply redirected it to a new target—Judaism." In the early 1960s, young Jews traveled to the South in order to participate in grassroots actions aimed at eliminating Jim Crow. By the early 1970s, Rubin observed, "they 'sat in' as they had in the past, but in new quarters, the Jewish offices." Instead of confronting white racists, Jewish social justice activists took aim at "the Jewish 'establishment.'" The "generation gap" that helped define the broader countercultural resistance of American youth toward their parents extended to Jews, who looked for ways to reinterpret Jewish expression for their own times.[24]

Students took aim at the Jewish Community Federation model. Created in the early twentieth century as a centralized fundraising and grant-giving agency, Federations grew into what Los Angeles Jewish Federation Council president Barbi Weinberg described as "secular Jewish institutions" focused mainly on "providing for the health and welfare needs of Jews." Typically, synagogues and religious schools remained on the periphery of Federation strategy, priority, and funding. In many communities, Federation lay leadership, typically representing the community's wealthiest givers, gravitated to the philanthropic organization because it offered a means of identifying as a Jew without the theological or educational demands of religious observance. In the postwar period especially, Federations played a central role in the capital construction projects necessary to build Jewish institutions in the suburbs. As Hillel Levine, then a Ph.D. candidate in sociology at Harvard, reported in his analysis of nationwide Federation grant making in 1967, only 14.1 percent of the $44 million annual giving supported Jewish education, while "low Jewish content" organizations such as Jewish community centers counted twice as many Federation dollars in their budgets. By the late 1960s, the Federation's legacy stood in sharp contrast to the emerging Jewish turn inward.[25]

In April 1971, the San Francisco Jewish Liberation Project (JLP), the Stanford Union of Jewish Students, and a host of Bay Area Jewish educators and youth leaders joined together to form the Jewish Education Coalition (JEC). The new group quickly mobilized when the San Francisco Federation threatened to close Brandeis, the city's Jewish day school. Employing language from Malcolm X, the JEC promised "to make public, by any means at our disposal, all the evidence of the Federation's refusal to adequately educate its children." Taking aim at the assimilationist approach of their parents' generation, the JEC proclaimed "a new Jewish youth—committed to Jewish life, not assimilation and showpieces." The radical political group envisioned a dynamic, transformational, and relevant Judaism for its generation. "Hidden beneath the empty edifices of synagogues and Sunday schools," the JEC proclaimed, "we have discovered an almost forgotten but vibrant tradition."[26]

Under the leadership of Sherman Rosenfeld, the group of self-professed radical students took over the San Francisco Federation building, staging what it called a "pray-in." In a May 1971 letter, Rosenfeld charged that the Federation, a nondemocratic organization, responded only to the wishes of its small group of wealthy donors. "Such individuals," he argued, "apparently define their Jewishness in terms of the checks they write, not in terms of real commitment to Jewish values." Rosenfeld's group took aim. "We are young Jews . . . concerned that the kind of Jewish education people of our generation are receiving is turning them away from Judaism," they proclaimed in a broadside titled "A Challenge to Federation Priorities." With capital letters to accentuate their message, they listed "swimming pools and high paid Jewish bureaucrats" under the heading, "WHAT WE DON'T WANT." Under the heading "WHAT WE WANT," they pressed for "new Jewish projects and Jewish actions." For the protesters, the takeover of the Federation building meant more than "a mere physical occupation," as they insisted on observing the Sabbath and engaging in formal Jewish learning during the action.[27]

In a 1969 article published in the *Jewish Liberation Journal*, Tsvi Bisk, who later immigrated to Israel and worked as a research historian for the Labor Party, offered a Jewish revivalist strategy that linked Jewish tradition to tactics borrowed from the era's larger political culture. He expanded on the essential critique offered by the UC Berkeley students, moving the debate off campus and into the heart of Jewish organizational life. Taking aim at what he described as "the disgusting ostentation of Jewish bar mitzvahs and weddings," Bisk lambasted American Jews for constructing "magnificent Frank Lloyd Wright–type synagogues to show the goyim that we can do it too" even as they proved "absolutely lacking in Jewish content."[28]

Instead, Bisk, in a move consistent with an emerging group of young Jewish leftist activists, called for a redirection of Jewish communal funds "from glory-seeking prestige projects (such as hospitals) to the more immediate needs of Jewish education." He sought inclusion of modern Hebrew as well as courses in Bible and Talmud within the curricula of synagogue-based religious schools. Leveraging the direct-action protest culture of the New Left, he sounded the call: "Confrontation tactics of an educative and influential nature within a Jewish framework should begin immediately." Playing on sit-in movement tactics, Bisk called for teach-ins "focused on Hebrew language instruction." To dramatize the protests, he pressed for these actions in public places, to be seen by many, conducted by "long-haired radicals" in order to embarrass what he called the "Jewish establishment" as well as highlight the educational apathy in organized Jewish life.[29]

As Jason Porth recounted in his aptly titled thesis on progressive Jews in the 1960s, "Left Out," Jewish activism reached back to the high school level as well. In early 1969, students in Minneapolis, Minnesota, responding to Afro-centric messaging, offered their principal a list of eleven demands that sought to communicate what a Black Power movement would look like if it were framed in Jewish terms. With a flair for the dramatic, students insisted that "all school books shall be read from right to left" in order to align with Hebrew-language binding. They asked that "all food dispensers shall issue only kosher food" and that "separate dispensers shall be provided for meat and dairy dishes." In a play on the tradition of the Jewish bride circling her groom seven times during the wedding ceremony, students threatened that, should their demands go unheeded, "the Jewish students will march seven times around the school building, sounding the shofrot [ram's horns], until the walls will cave in, as they did in Jericho." If "Black was beautiful," then, as their petition concluded, "Being Jewish is beautiful," too.[30]

Aware of the larger forces at play with Jewish youth, national Jewish organizations responded with what the AJCongress called "the intensification and broadening of its adult Jewish education programs." Leveraging the social justice mind-set of the new generation, the AJCongress pledged to create study guides detailing Jewish social justice work, support the creation of social action committees, and encourage Jewish college students to host conferences engaging the relevant social and political questions of the day. In this way, the top-down leadership structure of the organized Jewish community responded to the more populist-centered Jewish ethnic turn inward. Jewish leaders understood that they needed to listen if they wanted to remain relevant and compelling in the generation to come.[31]

Jewish Day Schools

Efforts by Jewish young people to strengthen Jewish education extended to Jewish day school education, especially among non-Orthodox Jews, for whom secular public education proved the historic standard. For a generation of Jewish students raised in the suburbs, Jewish education typically amounted to synagogue-based supplemental school, culminating in a bar or bat mitzvah experience. Infused with a larger American culture that valued one's ethnic heritage, the new generation of Jewish leaders demanded that their organized communal leaders step up in support of Jewish day schools, considered the gold standard for intensive Jewish learning and living. In a dramatic break from earlier generations of American Jews, the new efforts for day school education extended beyond the Orthodox, who maintained an effective monopoly on that approach to Jewish learning.

Prior to the 1960s, only the Orthodox backed this intensive approach to Jewish learning. Yeshiva College (later Yeshiva University), founded in 1928 as the successor institution to the Rabbi Isaac Elchanan Theological Seminary, sought to combine the mandates of traditional Jewish life with the contemporary realities of America. It created the first-ever intensive Jewish high school for girls in 1948. Six years later, Yeshiva opened Stern College for Women. And, in 1955, Yeshiva University launched its Torah Leadership Seminar with twenty-eight enrollees. It also developed programs focused on offering intensive Jewish learning to young people raised in non- or minimally observant homes. Thanks in part to the increased interest in Jewish day school education, newly observant Jews founded a number of Orthodox synagogues, including New York's Lincoln Square Synagogue. In 1954, Orthodox leaders formed the National Conference of Synagogue Youth to focus efforts on encouraging children from adolescence through their teenage years to follow Jewish law in their everyday lives. Chabad rabbis stepped up their campaign for greater ritual observance with outreach to Jewish college students filling university dorms thanks to the G.I. Bill–inspired boom in higher education. These efforts led Nathan Glazer, in a series of articles appearing in 1956, to identify an Orthodox-centered "Jewish revival in America."[32]

Early postwar Reform Jews rejected Jewish day school education, investing their future as American Jews in an approach that sent their children to public schools during the day and supplemental synagogue-based religious schools in the afternoons and weekends. A 1953 survey by the Reform movement's National Federation of Temple Brotherhoods, for example, showed that "over 90 percent wanted nothing to do with Jewish all-day schools." When Rabbi Joachim Prinz, then a candidate for the AJCongress presidency, affirmed in 1958 that if the organization were serious about the "survival of the Jewish people" then it would back Jewish day schools, Justine Wise Polier objected. "Day schools," she believed, proved "inimical to the public-school system" and led to an "undesirable Jewish self-isolation."[33]

Four years later, Wise Polier's organization went on record opposed to federal aid for parochial schools, calling it a "clear violation of the constitutional principle of church and state—a violation that would bring in its train all the evils that the constitutional provision was designed to prevent." Even as Milton Himmelfarb noted a growing anti–public school sentiment among American Jews in a 1960 *Commentary* article, he concluded that the number of students interested in Jewish day school education amounted to a tiny fraction of the population. "After all," he explained, "Jews are fewer than 3 percent of the American population, and it is unlikely that the absence from the public schools of 3 or 4 percent of that 3 percent, or even 15 percent of it, can make a difference nationally, or even much of a difference locally."[34]

Non-Orthodox Jews softened their stance toward Jewish day school education with the rise of Black Power–inspired identity politics. As Columbia journalism professor Samuel Freedman argued, the expansion of Jewish day schools followed renewed Jewish enthusiasm after the 1967 Six-Day War, the movement to save Soviet Jews, and, cast most broadly, "the replacement of the melting pot ideal by the model of an ethnic mosaic." While just 35 Jewish day schools served a total of 7,700 students in 7 communities in 1940, some 323 day schools as well as 83 Jewish high schools served 63,500 students in 117 communities in 1965. By 1975, the number of day schools had surged to 425, with 138 high schools and a total of 82,200 students enrolled.[35]

In a stunning reversal of prewar numbers, a 1967 survey revealed that the Reform and Conservative movements each accounted for about a third of the total number of Jewish day school students, while the Orthodox numbered just 21.5 percent. The remaining schools had no movement affiliation. As Conservative movement rabbi Jacob Chinitz declared, proponents of "Jewish Power" "should without shame or apology, promote the building of more private, parochial, day schools within our Orthodox, Conservative and Reform, and secular movements." For political scientist Daniel Elazar, writing in a 1971 *Midstream* article on American Jewish life, the day school movement, which he described as "substantial," marked "a sharp departure from the thrust of Jewish interests during the modern era when Jews tried desperately to break down all barriers that might keep them out of general schools and were even willing to sacrifice the Jewish education of their children on behalf of integration."[36]

The call for better Jewish education gave pause as well to the organized Jewish community's historic opposition to government funding of private religious schools. Tsvi Bisk, recognizing the ability of Jewish day schools to deliver a much higher level of learning, urged his coreligionists to take a page from the Catholic community's Great Society notebook and support federal aid to parochial schools. In this view of pluralist democracy, different religious groups would be encouraged to deepen their knowledge and practice to advance a nation that, while not preferring one group over another, encouraged every religious denomination to develop itself as best it could.[37]

Government support of religious education, then, strengthened the nation by respecting and encouraging religious difference. Bisk extended his rationale to public schools as well, asking educational officials to offer Hebrew in districts with large Jewish populations. With this request, Bisk succeeded in keeping religion out of the public school system while he found creative ways to strengthen Jewish education and identity. Because modern Hebrew grew from the development of the Zionist movement, Bisk's proposal, mirroring the contemporaneous rise of black nationalism, also strengthened American Jewish Zionism.[38]

While the African American–led embrace of identity politics encouraged Jews to strengthen their children's Jewish educations, the growth of non-Orthodox Jewish day schools also reinforced existing Jewish concerns over the quality of racially integrated public schools in northern cities. White flight, which counted large numbers of Jewish students retreating from public schools after court-ordered desegregation led to busing programs, increased demand for private schools, Jewish or not. In New York City, Jewish parents pulled their kids from the public schools, creating Brooklyn's first Reform movement Jewish day school.[39]

Cities across the country followed suit by forming community day schools. In Los Angeles, the founding board of Valley Beth Shalom's day school counted parents who sought the school because they wanted their children to receive intensive Jewish learning unavailable in the public schools, while other parent leaders, who envisioned the school primarily as an escape from the Los Angeles Unified School District, pressed for a curriculum that taught the least amount of Jewish studies necessary. As

Leo Pfeffer of the AJCongress proclaimed in spring 1967 testimony before the New Jersey Senate Committee on Education, Jews "go there [to day schools] not because they love God but because they are afraid of the Negro." Then-Temple University political scientist Daniel Elazar believed "the all-day school movement was clearly strengthened by the fact that many Jews were caught in changing neighborhoods where the public schools deteriorated before they were ready to move." As a result, Jewish parents weighed their options: remaining in the public school system, moving their children to private schools, or resolving an increased desire for Jewish education by creating or strengthening Jewish community day schools.[40]

The Jewish Left and Communal Protest

On the larger American Jewish scene, leftists redirected their political efforts from secular causes to Jewish ones. Immersed in the radical politics and counterculture of the mid-1960s, young Jews pressed for heightened Jewish identity in a far-reaching critique of organized Jewry's status quo. In 1964, a group of students under the leadership of Cornell-educated city planner David Gurin organized themselves into group called "the Zealots" in order to protest Jewish landlords who overcharged African American residents of their apartment buildings. On April 29, 1964, they delivered a letter to the New York Board of Rabbis demanding they "seek out the slum owners in their congregations and to threaten them with denunciation from the pulpit and even *herem* or excommunication if they fail to repair and maintain their properties." Calling on their religious leaders to "uphold our historic standards of social justice," protesters attached a list of some 250 Jewish landlords with the demand that "the House of Israel must be cleansed of those who exploit the poor."[41]

Two years later, Michael Tabor, who would later help organize Kibbutz Micah in Pennsylvania as a reflection of his own socialist agricultural upbringing, Arthur Waskow, founder of the Institute of Policy Studies and later a rabbinic leader in renewal Judaism, and Sharon Rose, an organizer of the Jewish Campaign for the People's Peace Treaty, created the Washington, D.C.–based Jews for Urban Justice (JUJ). "We must use our individual and collective resources to force change in the attitudes and institutions of the Jewish community and of the larger American society," the Jews for Urban Justice proclaimed. "As Jews of today, we must heed the words of the Prophets and act." In the fall of 1967, the Jews for Urban Justice did act, staging a public protest at a well-known Washington, D.C., synagogue, calling out its members for their "insensitivity" on the needs of migrant workers, open housing, and support of the nation's welfare system.[42]

"After completing our study on social action in the Jewish community," JUJ organizers explained, "we were shocked by the insensitivity of Jewish organizations to social problems." Trained in civil rights organizations such as SNCC, CORE, and Students for a Democratic Society (SDS), these young activists expanded their mandate to include a broad array of leftist causes. They organized a boycott of a Jewish-owned supermarket that continued to sell California table grapes, the object of a United Farm Workers boycott effort; conducted a "Freedom Seder" utilizing Arthur Waskow's *The Freedom Seder: A New Haggadah for Passover*; created a radical Jewish Sunday school; and sponsored a national conference of Jewish radicals.[43]

Tsvi Bisk extended his communal critique beyond organizational leaders, calling unethical Jewish landlords to task for their business practices. Immersing his protest call within Jewish tradition, Bisk demanded that Jewish slumlords face review by Jewish courts and called for the creation of a Talmudic Research Committee to find other textual guidance in support of protest. He reminded his brethren that Jewish law "allows one to challenge the congregation at a certain point in the service to demand justice, and the service cannot continue unless the complainant is heard."[44]

Jews and the Counterculture

The 1960s counterculture worried Jewish leaders, who feared that young Jews would reject Judaism in favor of Eastern religions. At a time when Jews constituted just 2.5 percent of the overall population, some 15 to 18 percent of Hare Krishna members, 6 to 8 percent of the Unification Church, and 9 percent of the Church of Scientology claimed Jewish ancestry. As actor Theodore Bikel proclaimed during a visit to UC Berkeley's Hillel, "Many young Jews turn to Buddhism or other Eastern cults to find a hook on which to hang their spiritual coat. Look first in your own attic." In response, Jewish religious leaders searched for ways to integrate traditional Judaism with elements of the larger Eastern-leaning religious precepts so popular in the late 1960s. The Black Power–inspired emphasis on particularist identity, the countercultural embrace of alternative religious forms, and an American Jewish turn inward all combined for a hippie-inspired redefinition of American Judaism.[45]

In 1967, Rabbi Shlomo Carlebach, a leader among neo-Hasidic spiritual leaders, envisioned a Jewish application of the era's ethnic activism. Young Jews, he believed, "found that the Blacks of their generation were finding their Black identity, the Chicanos were finding their Mexican identity, the Chinese, the Japanese, et cetera." Carlebach understood that all of these American youth were "reaching for their own ethnic identities," embracing pluralistic approaches to American life. "All of them dissatisfied," he understood, "with our melting pot." In his estimation, Jewish children raised in postwar America were just "nominally Jews." They became Jewish only because their parents were Jews and not because Judaism offered any transformational qualities. At a time when Jewishness meant engaging in "the boring cycle of Jewish education," a generation of young Jews sought spiritual meaning and direction from other faith traditions. Meanwhile, Rabbi Carlebach charged, their parents stood "hopelessly by on the sidelines, bemoaning the loss of our children, but doing little more than wailing and wringing our hands over the loss of this generation which has rejected our values or lack of values." By the mid-1960s, pushed out by civil rights groups and encouraged to seek their own sense of themselves, young Jews, as Carlebach explained, had "been deprived of the benefit and knowledge of the Book, the Torah."[46]

His remedy: a House of Love and Prayer (HLP) rooted in the countercultural lifestyle of San Francisco's Haight-Ashbury neighborhood. Opened in the heyday of the 1960s, the House of Love and Prayer operated on the principle that "when you walk in, someone loves you," and "when you walk out, someone misses you." Given the increasing popularity of Eastern religion, drug use to alter one's mind, and astrology as a supernatural way to gain life guidance, Carlebach reasoned, young Jews might be encouraged to return to their own religious tradition if it could be presented in terms better understood by the counterculture. As one HLP student explained, "When I met Rabbi Shlomo Carlebach, it completely changed my life. Shlomo taught me one thing: I can get high without drugs. Our great rabbis and teachers have been getting high for centuries on Torah and prayer. On Shabbos. On Love."[47]

Within the religious world of American Jews, even the once-assimila-tionist Reform movement pressed for heightened ritual observance. In a 1969 discussion of the troubled relationship between blacks and Jews, Rabbi Israel Dresner called for the creation of "Reform yeshivot." In 1975, the Reform movement introduced a new *siddur* (prayer book), the *Gates of Prayer*, to replace the *Union Prayer Book*. In order to accommodate more tradition-bound Reform Jews, the new *siddur* could be purchased as ei-ther a left- or a right-opening book. The Reform movement's residential summer camps stepped away from classic American folk songs and began teaching Hebrew and Zionist music, transforming more secular camp ac-tivities into sessions with specific Jewish themes, educational programs, and immersive Jewish life.[48]

In one of the best-known expressions of a Jewish religious revival mod-eled on the larger radical politics of the era, Arthur Waskow authored the 1969 *Freedom Seder*. Playing on the Passover theme of slavery and redemp-tion, Waskow linked the historic experience of Jews to other racial and ethnic minorities struggling for freedom. The *Freedom Seder*, he explained, "tried to develop the liturgy in ways that assert the liberation of the Jewish people *alongside* the liberation of the other peoples—not theirs as against ours, or ours as against theirs." In Waskow's *Freedom Seder* version of the Jewish festival, the Warsaw Ghetto Uprising during World War II paral-leled the Black Power protests of the 1960s. And, with a U.S.-led war raging in Southeast Asia, Waskow connected Jewish redemption from the bond-age of slavery in Egypt to the Vietnamese fight for their national freedom and autonomy. To accentuate his point, Waskow welcomed Father Dan-iel Berrigan, an anti–Vietnam War protest leader listed as one of the FBI's most wanted, to his original 1969 Columbia University Freedom Seder.[49]

Revivalists pressed against the structures of the organized Jewish com-munity as well. From a religious dissatisfaction born in suburban syna-gogues of the 1950s, a group of young Jews sought a reinvention of Jewish prayer outside its traditional geographic bounds. As Rabbi Everett Gen-dler of the JTS reflected in a 1971 article, synagogues proved "ecologically untenable, economically unjustifiable, and religiously questionable." The very business model of the synagogue, he explained, demanded that con-gregational rabbis and boards increase their membership "to a size which precludes the very intimacy and warmth which people rightly seek from religious involvement." By 1967, political scientist Daniel Elazar explained, the postwar tendency of synagogues to emulate the style and decorum of Protestant churches failed to attract a new generation. Elazar thought the early postwar allure of assimilationist Judaism proved "less attractive" to young Jews, whom he described as "'turned off' by Judaism as a 'churchly' phenomenon in a secular age."[50]

Instead, sociologist M. Herbert Danzger argued, "the ethnic turn inward of the mid-1960s" inspired young Jews to reinvent Mordechai Kaplan's Reconstructionist approach to Judaism, and especially his emphasis on the *havurah*, a less formal group of Jews who gather outside of the synagogue to celebrate their religious lives together, for their times. Impressed by the work of Father Daniel Berrigan, who created a radical underground church for his parishioners, JTS rabbinic student and later Reconstructionist Rabbinical College president Arthur Green led an effort to create a similar group for Jews. He rallied support from Columbia University student Alan Mintz, who also served as head of the Conservative movement's national youth group, and Brandeis University Hillel director Rabbi Albert Axelrad, to create Havurat Shalom in Somerville, Massachusetts. With a dozen students, a faculty that included Renewal Judaism's founder Rabbi Zalman Schachter-Shalomi, and a board that counted Brandeis University professor Nathan Glazer, Milton Himmelfarb, Hillel directors Max Ticktin and Richard Israel, as well as Conservative rabbis Jack Reimer and Hershel Matt, Havurat Shalom opened as a seminary dedicated to training future religious leaders in a countercultural form of American Jewish expression. Its curriculum demanded a four-year course of study that could lead to rabbinic ordination through an existing religious authority.[51]

On the West Coast, another group of young Jews formed the Aquarian Minyan in Berkeley, California, in 1974. Self-described as "a group of individuals in the process of becoming a native Jewish spiritual community," the Minyan welcomed individuals with "deep roots in the tradition" as well as those without strong Jewish knowledge. Emulating the countercultural spirit of nearby San Francisco, the group's founders named their group "Aquarian" because it "implied the acceptance of the unconscious, nonrational parts of our being and it also set up a distinction between those Jewish groups in which ten men constituted a 'minyan' and a group which believed every living being could be part of a minyan if the intention for 'connection' existed."[52]

Like their Boston counterpart, the Aquarian Minyan worshipped in their members' homes, following the lead of Rabbi Zalman Schachter-Shalomi, who played an important role in guiding the group. Schachter-Shalomi pressed the Minyan to focus on Jewish mysticism, which he thought offered its members a powerful and spiritual approach to Judaism. As Minyan founder Reuven Goldfarb remembered, many of the group's countercultural members had already immersed themselves in "Eastern spiritual paths, psychedelics, encounter work, and other cleansing therapies, both physical and cognitive," that made for a more natural transition to the mystical tradition. In their religious services, the Aquarian Minyan employed guided meditation along with small, intimate discussion groups meant to encourage members "to confront and befriend their inner selves." By 1976, the Minyan counted several hundred attendees at High Holiday services.[53]

Jewish residential summer camps integrated the nation's larger political currents as well, refashioning their very missions to reflect a Jewish turn inward in the late 1960s and beyond. As early as 1919, Jewish summer camps welcomed campers as a way to continue Jewish education and engagement throughout the summer months. Camps tended to follow particular theological or ideological movements, with Yiddish-speaking socialist camps, Hebrew-speaking Zionist camps, and a variety of Orthodox groups forming their own summer retreats. In 1941, Shlomo Bardin founded the Brandeis Institute in California "as a retreat at which young adults raised in nonreligious homes could experience Jewish living," while the Conservative movement's Camp Ramah system opened its first camp in northern Wisconsin in 1947 with the mission of developing "those qualities in boys and girls which will best prepare them for leadership in the American-Jewish community." Yeshiva University opened Torah Leadership Seminars in 1952.[54]

By 1970, Ramah counted nearly 3,000 campers in seven different sites throughout the country. As Marshall Sklare reflected in a 1972 *Midstream* article, Camp Ramah's Palmer, Massachusetts, location created a summer experience that sought to "integrate the Ramah program into youth culture." With that, the Jewish summer camp could "provide a Jewish alternative for campers of high school and college age who were attracted to youth culture." Apparently, the experiment proved effective beyond the camp's expectations. Camp leaders reported drug use among campers, a precipitous decline in the level of ritual observance, the introduction of nonkosher food, and a risqué camper-led presentation of the Broadway musical *Hair*. Ramah ended its program with a nationwide edict discouraging any other locales from following their lead.[55]

In the world of Jewish literature, publication of *The Jewish Catalog*, a how-to book designed to emulate the Whole Earth Catalog, reflected the intensity of the Jewish religious turn inward. Second in Jewish Publication Society sales only to the Hebrew Bible, *The Jewish Catalog* emerged, in the words of writer William Novak, as "the most vivid and concrete expression of a new religious impulse in Jewish life." For a generation of Jews raised by parents who did not offer lessons in day-to-day Judaism, *The Jewish Catalog* gifted a page-by-page remedy. In a series of chapters, readers learned how to knit their own *kippot*, bake their own challah, and create their own *talitot*. One part Jewish immersion and one part 1960s counterculture, *The Jewish Catalog*, according to Novak, combined "the hitherto mutually antagonistic modes of liberalism and traditionalism." Readers enjoyed the best of both their American worlds. It was, Novak concluded, "the largest and most successful adult education program that American Jewry has ever experienced."[56]

The rise of modern feminism in the 1970s coalesced with the American Jewish turn inward to inspire a movement for gender equality within Judaism. The emergence of Jewish feminism owed part of its genesis to the identity politics of the Black Power era. As Gloria Steinem explained in a 1969 article, "Finally, women began to 'rap' (talk, analyze, in radicalese) about their essential second-classness, forming women's caucuses inside the Movement in much the same way Black Power groups had done." In her later analysis of the era, Professor Sylvia Barack Fishman agreed, concluding, "Feminism was born in an environment that nurtured ethnic pride and assertiveness, fostered scorn for the perceived hypocrisies of a conformist consumer culture, and encouraged social activism on behalf of civil rights and other movements." At a moment when the larger political culture encouraged folks to "do your own thing," Fishman thought it "perhaps inevitable that Jewish feminists turn their attention inward."[57]

Just as Jews involved in other social justice movements in the mid-1960s experienced antisemitism and purges from their onetime progressive allies, Jewish women faced marginalization for their perceived white privilege as well as their support of Jewish nationalism and the State of Israel. At a time when many women experienced discrimination

in a male-dominated society, Jewish women reported double marginalization: as women in a man's world and as Jews in an increasingly antisemitic feminist world. Jewish feminism, Professor Ellen Umansky argued,
"emerged as a means of asserting both Jewish visibility within the feminist movement and feminist consciousness within the U.S. Jewish community." T. Drorah Setel, a student rabbi and coordinator of the Feminist
Task Force of New Jewish Agenda, lamented, "I am unseen as a feminist
among Jews and unseen as a Jew among feminists." Brandeis University
professor Joyce Antler recalled pushback she received as a Jewish woman
during a conference that featured presentations by black, Latina, and Irish
Catholic women. "Jewish women are just white middle-class women," the
conference organized told her, "there is nothing that differentiates them
from the ruling majority. There is no reason to treat them as a specialized
minority or to devote any of our time to their particular experience."[58]

The Jewish feminist movement grew in response, fashioning what
Fishman described as "a new—in many ways unique—variety of feminism." The intellectual leadership of Jewish feminism emerged in 1971
when women organized themselves into prayer groups and study groups,
applying a gendered analysis to Jewish text and exploring new possibilities for a reinterpretation of Jewish law. In New York City, one of these
groups developed into Ezrat Nashim, an activist group comprised of
women from Judaism's Conservative movement that took its name from
the double meaning of the Hebrew phrase "the strength of women" as well
as the name of the women-only section of the synagogue.[59]

In 1972, Ezrat Nashim issued a direct one-and-a half-page manifesto,
"Jewish Women Call for Change," demanding recognition as witnesses in
Jewish law, the ability to initiate divorce proceedings, admission to both
rabbinic and cantorial school, power equity in Jewish organizations, and
equal status as men in fulfilling Torah's commandments. As early Ezrat
Nashim member Susan Shevitz reflected, "We served as cantors and congregational leaders at camp and at teen services. But in the adult congregational world there was no room for the woman skilled in liturgy or
sermonizing or Jewish studies." The group presented its demands at the
1972 meeting of Conservative rabbis and it served as the guiding principles of their gender-equality activism. In 1974, activists created the Jewish
Feminist Organization, dedicated to "nothing else than the full, direct and

equal participation of women at all levels of Jewish life — communal religious, educational and political."[60]

Among Orthodox Jews, women sought a strengthening of their roles within the contours of Jewish law, even as tradition-bound rabbis debated the limits and possibilities of gender-based religious renewal. As the historian of American Orthodoxy Jeffrey Gurock explained, women began their work in arenas outside of religion, demanding the right to join synagogue boards. With governance power, women could effect positive change without engaging the limits of Jewish law. Later, a few rabbis experimented with various approaches to women's involvement in prayer. At the University of Wisconsin, Madison, for example, women gained the right to read Torah because the student-led service opted to restrict all participants in that section of the service to women. By 1972, Orthodox women formed their own prayer services and, in one case, New York City's Lincoln Square Synagogue developed a monthly women-only service to accommodate a more gender-balanced approach to prayer.[61]

Although it took more than a decade to achieve the goal of women's rabbinic ordination at JTS, Ezrat Nashim as well as other Jewish feminist voices succeeded in harnessing the social protest culture of the era for women's inequality. The Reform movement's Hebrew Union College-Jewish Institute of Religion ordained Sally Priesand, who began her rabbinic studies in 1972 without a guarantee of ordination, while the Reconstructionist Rabbinical College accepted women from its inception in 1969, graduating Sandy Eisenberg Sasso as its first woman rabbi in 1974. Amy Eilberg received ordination from JTS in 1985.[62]

The counterculture inspired a broad range of Jewish revivalist movements, each playing off the larger political currents to inspire a Jewish turn inward. These efforts on the domestic front paralleled an expansion of the American Jewish turn inward on the international scene, where the rise of Black Power thinking encouraged Jewish-centered political advocacy on a global scale. Thanks in large part to the rise of black militancy, American Jews embarked on a campaign to save Soviet Jewry and, especially in the years after 1967, strengthen the State of Israel.

Black Power,
American Jews,
and the Soviet
Jewry Movement

By all outward indications, the Soviet Jewry movement emerged a decade too late. The most opportune time to launch the Soviet Jewry movement, if leveraging the larger anti-Communist mood of the nation stood at the center of its strategy, would have been in the early postwar years. The policy of containment and the Truman Doctrine that followed obligated the federal government to resist Communist expansion. Eisenhower's embrace of NSC-68 set a policy founded upon the then-secret assertion that the Soviets' very mind-set demanded global control. The rise of Joseph McCarthy as the nation's most visible and threatening anti-Communist ideologue translated foreign policy fearmongering to the home front, where careers faced certain doom under his cloud of suspicion. A national anti-Communist consensus this strong would have paved a long and smooth political road for Soviet Jewry activists to follow.

Yet in the early postwar years, American Jews by and large resisted particularist political expression, seeking instead interfaith and interracial alliances that trumpeted Jews' status as fully integrated Americans. The anti-Communist consensus, even as it seemed to align the needs of Soviet Jews with the national security interests of the nation, inspired a political culture antagonistic to a Soviet Jewry movement. Most American Jews and the organizations representing them proved content to focus their time and money on a continued assimilation into suburban middle class and a social justice agenda focused on civil rights abuses at home. During the 1950s and early 1960s, organized Jewry focused its particularist efforts on rebuilding Jewish institutional life in the suburbs and its political work on the universalist goals of interfaith and interracial cooperation.[1]

To punctuate the relative American Jewish indifference to Soviet Jewry in the early postwar period, the State of Israel, as part of its larger mandate to ingather Jews, pressed for Soviet Jewry emigration from its very creation in 1948. Without the pressures of a continuing acculturation to American suburban life or the need to find a compelling political argument for the U.S. Congress or president, Israel's leaders integrated their own version of a Soviet Jewry movement into the Jewish state's very raison d'être, the ingathering of the exiles.

The Israeli government did not need convincing. As early as 1952, Isser Harel, chief of Mossad, Israel's intelligence agency, convened a meeting of former Soviet Jews to organize an Israeli effort to place covert teams on the ground in the Soviet Union for the purpose of documenting abuse and supporting eventual emigration to the Jewish state. They formed a Liaison Bureau that directed Israeli advocacy efforts for Soviet Jews. The difference between early postwar Soviet Jewry activism in Israel and its relative quiet in the United States focuses the question of historical causation: given their relative lack of involvement in the early postwar years, what inspired American Jews to take up the cause of their Eastern European coreligionists in the mid-1960s?[2]

Black Power and the Emergence of the Soviet Jewry Movement

Black Power activism inspired American Jews to internalize the call for identity politics. The fight for Soviet Jews emerged, then, as the next political step for Jewish liberals once dedicated to African American civil equality. If black nationalists pushed Jews out of domestic social justice causes, arguing that each ethno-racial group must take care of its own, then a movement to save Soviet Jews developed as the logical response. As historian William Orbach wrote, "Jewish youth, possibly influenced by black activism and rejecting their parent's lethargy, demanded decisive action on behalf of Soviet Jewry." While the antisemitic policies of the Soviet government could have triggered American Jewish interest a decade earlier, Orbach understood the delay. The "growing disillusionment with the civil rights struggle, in the face of increasing black militancy," he concluded, served as inspiration for Jews to ride the era's new "ethnic wave."[3]

In a fascinating twist on the American Jewish embrace of Black Power thinking, the Soviet Jewry movement burned the postwar consensus candle at both ends. While other Jewish endeavors in this period tended to eschew the anti-Communist themes of the 1950s in favor of the new identity-based political strategies, Soviet Jewry activists employed Cold War tactics as an important way to gain broader support. Rooted in the fundamental belief that the Communist superpower discriminated against its Jewish minority, the Soviet Jewry movement leveraged anti-Communism to propel its efforts for free Jewish emigration from the Eastern Bloc. Soviet Jewry activists understood that Main Street USA, and especially its representatives in Congress, never abandoned anti-Soviet thinking.

As delegates to the 1964 Conference on the Status of Soviet Jews proclaimed in their declaration of purpose, "Our purpose is not to exacerbate 'cold war' tensions. Our aim is to mobilize public opinion into a worldwide moral force which will save the Jewish community of the USSR from spiritual annihilation."[4] By linking the religious needs of Jews to the larger anti-Communist political climate, leaders of the Soviet Jewry movement gained critical support from conservatives as well as liberals, rural Americans in addition to city dwellers, and, most important, the politicians elected to represent all of them. In both houses of Congress as well as the White House, the Soviet Jewry movement enjoyed support far beyond its relatively limited number of Jewish constituents. With this approach, the leadership of the Soviet Jewry movement built a groundswell of support for its particularist cause.

On the other side of the political spectrum, Soviet Jewry activists also emulated the strategies and tactics of black militancy, pressing their particularist needs to the center of their activism, and creating, without apology, a Jewish-centered movement that placed their religious community first. They rallied in the streets, politicked on Capitol Hill, and created a far-reaching coalition of American Jews across the denominational and political spectrum. In their own version of Malcolm X's "by any means necessary," American Jews secreted religious objects to Soviet Jewish "refuseniks," risking arrest and expulsion in a larger effort to secure civil equality for their brethren. Thanks to Black Power, American Jews engaged in forms of public identity and political protest that their 1950s suburban parents never could have imagined. In one fell swoop, the Soviet Jewry movement leveraged Cold War consensus thinking with Black Power's singular focus on ethnic consciousness to strengthen Jewish life thousands of miles from the United States.[5]

The rise of the Soviet Jewry movement also owes a debt to an emerging Holocaust consciousness. Just as a generation of Black Power–inspired African American youth took issue with the more accommodationist political approaches of their parents' generation, Soviet Jewry activists, along with their brethren engaged in the other social justice causes of the time, opposed the apparent silence of American Jews during World War II. During the war years, allied victory demanded accommodation to the federal government's military stance. Jews could not challenge President Roosevelt on his response to the plight of European Jewry for fear of facing charges of disloyalty. The U.S. government's incarceration of 67,000 U.S. citizens of Japanese descent testified to the harsh injustices possible when a democracy goes to war and the near impossibility of waging opposition campaigns.[6]

By the 1960s, though, the social justice status quo flipped as the civil rights, free speech, and later anti-Vietnam War protest movements encouraged young people to bring democracy into the streets and rally for their causes in the most public and even confrontational ways. For American Jews, that meant a break from the compromising stance of the World War II generation. As Jacob Birnbaum of the Student Struggle for Soviet Jewry (SSSJ) proclaimed at the organization's founding, "We who condemn silence and inaction during the Nazi Holocaust, dare we keep silent now?" In one of the SSSJ's early handbooks, Birnbaum linked the Soviet Jewry cause to the attempted genocide of the Jews in stark terms. "Though there are no gas chambers in the Soviet Union, our people there —the surviving remnants of Hitler's massacres—are being destroyed in their innermost humanity."[7]

The JDL took out an advertisement in the March 26, 1970, *New York Times* proclaiming, "In 1942, when we learned of Auschwitz—we did nothing . . . In 1970, when we know of the national and spiritual destruction of Soviet Jewry—Where is the unceasing effort? Where are the huge crowds?

Where are the huge protests?" Thanks to the rise of identity politics, Soviet Jewry movement activists could align themselves with a new consensus that demanded particularist advocacy. The generation of young Jews coming of age in the 1960s and early 1970s would not be, as a Soviet Jewry bumper sticker of the era proclaimed, "the Jews of silence."[8]

Despite their ability to leverage Cold War anti-Communism with Black Power–inspired identity politics, Soviet Jewry activists still faced challenges from within. Jewish organizational leaders resisted the more confrontational tactics of the young Soviet Jewry activists. As they did in many Jewish communal priorities, establishment leaders considered quiet, behind-the-scenes dialogue the best strategy for winning concessions from the Soviet government. By engaging in direct-action protest, they feared a spike in Soviet antisemitism and a harsh reaction by Communist authorities against their Jewish population. The younger activists, on the other hand, cured in the social protest movements of the 1950s and 1960s, disagreed. Only direct action in the spirit of the sit-ins, boycotts, and public protests of the civil rights era would motivate Soviet leaders to soften their anti-Jewish stands. Although the organized Jewish leadership eventually joined the cause, forging a common American Jewish effort proved difficult.

In the immediate postwar years, only a few American Jewish organizations engaged the plight of Soviet Jews. The JLC extended its workers-rights mission to the Soviet Union, where it called attention to repression of Jewish cultural life but did not address the religious rights of Soviet Jews. Orthodox groups rallied for Jewish religious freedom, though their efforts could best be characterized as limited. In the 1965 edition of the *American Jewish Year Book*, Jerry Goodman, the founding executive director of the American Jewish Conference on Soviet Jewry (AJCSJ), criticized national Jewish leaders for ignoring the plight of Soviet Jews. Prior to 1963, he charged, the AJCongress, B'nai B'rith, and NCRAC "remained unconvinced of the special nature of anti-Jewish discrimination in the U.S.S.R." Goodman took issue with the "quiet diplomacy" approach of national Jewish leaders, who limited their expressions of concern to "low-echelon Soviet officials" and accepted their assurances that "there was no Jewish problem in the U.S.S.R." Early work on behalf of Soviet Jewry could be characterized more as a conglomeration of disparate Jewish organizations reaching out to their brethren than as any sort of coordinated movement.[9]

Reform rabbi Allan Levine's experience championing the Soviet Jewry cause dramatized the limited scope of early organizational efforts. A participant in the 1961 Freedom Rides who endured incarceration in Jackson, Mississippi for his civil rights activism and led a 1963 sit-in protest against police brutality in the North, Levine faced rebuke from many of his senior colleagues when he took up the cause of Soviet Jews. He pressed the CCAR to back direct-action protests. After the professional rabbinic organization refused, he urged it to "take our cue from civil rights organizations in the United States." Levine, a self-described "young Turk" in the Reform rabbinate, demanded "public demonstrations and direct nonviolent action on a nationwide basis to dramatize the plight of our people." He failed in his effort. "The older men, who are also the leaders," he explained, "felt that the best ways to approach the Russian situation were leadership conferences and talks and expressions of alarm presented by Jewish leaders to Embassy officials."[10]

Levine took his desire to emulate African American protest strategy to the founder of the State of Israel, David Ben-Gurion. Reflecting the official CCAR position, Levine wrote, "Those who disagree with us argue that such demonstrations are contrary to American foreign policy, are undignified and might generate anti-Semitism rather than motivate pro-Jewish sympathy." Hoping that the Jewish world's best-known nationalist would back a more aggressive Soviet Jewry strategy, Levine posed a direct question: "Mr. Ben-Gurion, do you think . . . that public active nonviolent demonstrations such as picketing and sit-ins would help, OR be detrimental to the welfare of Soviet Jewry?"[11] At that moment, Levine postured as an American citizen sensitive to U.S. foreign policy interests, a Jewish leader concerned about the potential for increased antisemitism in the Soviet Union, and a social justice activist intent on translating civil rights strategies into the burgeoning movement to aid Soviet Jews. He wanted to challenge his senior colleagues by connecting the Soviet Jewry movement to the African American civil rights movement.

The Early Movement to Aid Soviet Jews

The transition from sporadic and more individualized efforts to a broad-based campaign began in the fall of 1963, when three different Soviet Jewry groups emerged in a two-month period. This rapid mobilization of

Jewish activists reflected a number of important changes within American Jewish life informed both by the historic consensus-framed alliance of the early civil rights years as well as by the ethnic nationalist reframe of identity politics in the mid-1960s and beyond. In October, leftist writer and journalist Moshe Decter convened a Conference on the Status of Jews by innovating a strategy that would define the Soviet Jewry movement: leverage non-Jewish allies with appeals to the larger Cold War political climate. The high-standing luminaries Decter recruited included U.S. Supreme Court justice William O. Douglas, U.S. Senator Herbert Lehman, and famed socialist leader and many-time presidential candidate Norman Thomas. Next, Decter built alliances with African American leaders, crafting a consensus-based Soviet Jewry effort on the interracial civil rights model. Labor leader Walter Reuther signed up and, in Decter's greatest strategic victory, so too did Dr. Martin Luther King Jr.[12]

At the conference meeting, Decter sought a consensus strategy that joined the Jewish-directed goal of aiding Soviet Jews with the larger anti-Communist imperative in American politics. He characterized Soviet state-sponsored oppression as a violation of conscience. In a political climate that framed American exceptionalism as the antidote to the Communists' persecution of its minorities, Decter and his colleagues leveraged a wide-ranging group of political allies. With support from religious leaders across Christian denominations, the Conference adopted an "Appeal of Conscience for the Jews of the Soviet Union," listing seven different Soviet violations of human rights, each an offense to mainstream America. In that context, the Jewish call for religious freedom placed the particular desire of Jews to defend their coreligionists in the Eastern Bloc as an expression of American patriotism. With Decter's tactical approach, the Soviet Jewry movement rallied a base of support across religious and political backgrounds.[13]

Yet Decter also played American identity politics to his advantage. His tactical approach to the Soviet Jewry movement mimicked the larger social protest movements of the era. When he initiated a more activist and grassroots political agenda, he earned the respect and support of Justice Douglas, who turned both to Rabbi Abraham Joshua Heschel and Synagogue Council of America leader Rabbi Uri Miller for their support. Douglas pressed the two influential rabbis to engage in public protests similar to those waged in the civil rights movement. Heschel, well known for his work alongside Dr. King, backed Douglas and Decter with appeals to both the National Conference of Presidents of Major Jewish Organizations and the NJCRAC. Heschel demanded Jewish organizational leaders frame the Soviet Jewry movement through the same lens as his earlier social justice causes. "If we are ready to go to jail in order to destroy the blight of racial bigotry," Heschel pressed, "if we are ready to march on Washington in order to demonstrate our identification with those who are deprived of equal rights, should we not be ready to go to jail in order to end the martyrdom of our Russian brethren?" Failure to do so, he warned in a December 13, 1963, letter, would force him to create a national Soviet Jewry organization himself.[14]

These calls resonated with African American civil rights leaders, who drew parallels between the two movements. "The attempt to liquidate spiritually the Jewish people in Soviet Russia," Martin Luther King Jr. wrote, "is something that we must not allow." King repeated his civil rights–era claim that "injustice anywhere is a threat to justice everywhere" and "injustice to any people is a threat to justice to all people." He argued that his status as an African American and as one who lived far from the Soviet Union did not mean he could "stand idly by" while Soviet Jews, whom he referred to as his "brothers and sisters," suffered. In King's estimation, "The struggle of the Negro people for freedom is inextricably interwoven with the universal struggle of all peoples to be free from discrimination and oppression." King closed with an affirmation that he would "not remain silent in the face of injustice."[15]

Herbert S. Caron, a Harvard University Ph.D. in psychology, followed Decter's lead when he organized the Cleveland Committee on Soviet Anti-Semitism (CCSA). Skeptical of the organized Jewish community's willingness and ability to engage in the struggle for Soviet Jewry, Caron emulated strategies from the era's larger social protest movements to build the CCSA into an independent, grassroots, activist organization. Caron's formula— rejection of established Jewish organizations, an embrace of Cold War anti-Communism, and use of civil rights movement–inspired public protest to draw particular attention to the needs of Soviet Jews—guided the CCSA as it became one of the earliest and most important grassroots advocacy groups in the emerging movement.

The Student Struggle for Soviet Jewry

This activist approach enjoyed the full support of Jacob Birnbaum, a British-born observant Jew, whose organization, the SSSJ, would emerge as one of the Soviet Jewry movement's most important groups. Birnbaum also rejected quiet diplomacy and called for public protest to "show our government that we really do care deeply for our cause, that far from letting up, we shall enormously increase our efforts to mobilize a tidal wave of public opinion." He drew direct parallels between the civil rights movement and his vision for helping Soviet Jews. As Birnbaum affirmed in one of his organization's early handbooks, "Many young Jews today forget that if injustice cannot be condoned in Selma, USA, neither must it be overlooked in Kiev, USSR." In a coalition-building bid, Birnbaum and the SSSJ also strengthened their strategic approach by inviting Christians to join them in an interfaith fast that framed the Soviet Jewry movement as an effort to achieve a common goal of religious freedom.[16]

Birnbaum's interest in Soviet Jewry reflected a larger trend in the movement: the mobilization of America's Orthodox Jewish community, historically detached from any sort of grassroots activism, into identity politics. In the early postwar years, Orthodoxy resisted involvement in the civil rights movement, considered a secular protest movement of little relevance to Jews. Yet the rise of Black Power, and its renewed focus on ethnic particularity, appealed to a population of American Jews who cherished their Jewish identities and searched for ways to realize their tradition-based lifestyle in a pluralist democracy such as the United States. The Soviet Jewry movement brought both of those impulses together.

By applying otherwise-secular political strategies to help their co-religionists abroad, Orthodox Jews could fully engage the American body politic, strengthen Jewish life, and remain true to their own religious convictions. Some two-thirds of SSSJ's membership defined themselves as Orthodox, with almost all educated within the Jewish day school system. In a 1973 survey on Jewish identity, SSSJ members tallied a mean score of eight on a nine-point scale. On one march, SSSJ protesters employed Jewish ritual objects, including a Torah, a shofar, and prayer shawls, to focus a religious lens on political change. At another, activists referenced the Passover seder and the Jews' status as slaves in Egypt. Yeshiva University students organized a "Talmudic Teach-In" with Rabbi Aharon Lichtenstein, who taught Jewish textual demands for freeing the captive. As Vanderbilt University sociologist Shaul Kelner summarized, "The Soviet Jewry movement brought the seder out of the home and into the public square."[17]

Still, not all observant Jews followed along. Some leaders from the Orthodox movement worried that public activism would compromise the well-being of Soviet Jews. Chabad, for example, feared that the Soviet government would sever its lines of communication with Eastern Bloc Jews in order to punish American Jews for their activism. Agudas Israel, part of the more traditionally observant Orthodox community, rejected direct-action protest out of fear that it would only cause Soviet authorities to mete out revenge on the local Jewish communities. In November 1963, for example, Agudas Israel criticized "the highly publicized aggressive tactics that various Jewish organizations have adopted regarding the situation of the Jews in Soviet Russia."[18]

With growing support across religious denominations, the sssj went to work. At an April 27, 1964, organizing meeting held at Columbia University, Birnbaum and law student Glenn Richter called for a public demonstration just four days later. On May 1, 1,100 activists took to the streets. By August 1964, the sssj mobilized some 2,000 protesters to demonstrate in the historic center of New York Jewish immigrant life, the Lower East Side. Calling for at least one public protest each month, the sssj developed a set of organizational priorities that included a robust education program. Emulating the "Freedom Schools" within the civil rights movement, Birnbaum directed parallel efforts across the Jewish community. Children spending their summers at residential Jewish camps received informational kits that offered both background information on the plight of Soviet Jews as well as suggestions on how each camper could begin organizing in protest. As sssj historian Amaryah Orenstein explained, "Having absorbed a belief in the redemptive power of protest from their counterparts in the Civil Rights Movement, ssrj activists would seek to arouse the conscience of Americans of all faiths with dramatic but lawful direct action that spotlighted the moral and humanitarian nature of their cause."[19]

sssj leaders leveraged Dr. Martin Luther King Jr.'s use of biblical reference to strengthen their efforts. As the veritable "People of the Book," sssj leader Glenn Richter understood, Jews enjoyed strong public identification with religious-based arguments for social justice. When the SSSJ planned its next demonstration, it chose the Battle of Jericho as a theme for the effort, as Orenstein explained, "to connect the campaign for Soviet Jewry to the Black Freedom struggle." As Jericho organizers advertised in a flyer meant to recruit new Soviet Jewry protesters, "Jewish students are all aflame—and creditably so—about Selma. But injustice in the Ukraine must also be fought. Though it is distant [it is surely] not more distant than Vietnam."[20]

Jacob Birnbaum, referencing the powerful impact of African American spirituals in civil rights work, hired a lyricist to write protest songs with specific instruction to employ one of two themes, "Let Them Live (as Jews) or Let Them Leave" and *"Am Yisrael Chai"* ("The People of Israel Lives"). As Orenstein understood, "The stirring image of nonviolent Civil Rights protesters singing about freedom in the face of police brutality certainly reinforced for Student Struggle for Soviet Jewry founder and National Director Jacob Birnbaum the potential to mobilize the masses through the emotional power of song." Their collective efforts worked, as 3,000 activists participated in the April 1965 Jericho event and grew to 15,000 by a 1966 march focused on the theme of *geulah* (redemption).[21]

Expanding the Soviet Jewry Movement

Even as these grassroots efforts gained strength, the organized Jewish community clung to its less confrontational approach. Soviet Jewry activists complained about generational differences that stymied their ability to organize within established Jewish groups. The first national organization dedicated to fighting for Soviet Jewry, the American Jewish Conference on Soviet Jewry, which counted twenty-four different groups on its membership list, resisted calls for direct-action protests. Soviet Jewry activists responded by applying similar direct-action tactics employed against Soviet authorities to force their own communal leaders to act. As Orenstein explained, "Just as militant African Americans answered Stokely Carmichael's clarion call for Black Power, members of Student Struggle for Soviet Jewry became more outspoken in their demand for a radical solution to the Soviet Jewish problem—mass emigration."[22]

After a trip to the Soviet Union, Columbia University student Hillel Levine formed the Emergency Committee for Soviet Jewry and took immediate aim at the slow-moving strategies of the Jewish community's organized leadership. Joined by six of his classmates, Levine presented a list of demands at an April 1968 planning meeting for the AJCSJ. Levine and his crew made their position clear: "If there is no positive evidence that the necessary funds will be allocated for the creation of effective machinery, we feel it our obligation as concerned Jews to picket this Conference publicly protesting abdication of responsibility and this insult to the Jews of the Soviet Union."[23]

They faced a recalcitrant group. "We were, of course, asked to leave," Levine remembered, "but we made it clear that we were going to stay and be heard." A standoff followed with the students speaking, the committee leadership ruling them out of order with a reprimand, only to be ignored by the activists, who continued to make their case. From the perspective of the established Jewish leaders, the exchange amounted to nothing more than "youthful rebellion." Levine, for his part, thought it "amazing how people can devise catchphrases to shield themselves from truth." Three Philadelphia rabbis suffered the same fate when they formulated a plan to picket the Soviet Embassy in Washington, D.C. While the AJCSJ leadership rebuffed the effort, the rabbis succeeded in their goal only because the Israeli embassy backed them.[24]

The following year, hundreds of students went to the Jewish Community Federation's General Assembly in Boston demanding money for Jewish education and an "independent Soviet Jewry budget." To punctuate their commitment to their goal, the protesters staged a sit-in. In October 1971, Soviet Jewry activists went so far as to borrow the very language of the early civil rights movement when they planned a cross-country "Freedom Bus" carrying Soviet Jewish refuseniks as well as American Jewish activists to raise awareness for the plight of Soviet Jews.[25] On a journey featuring speeches and rallies in communities between Washington, D.C., and Seattle, organizers distributed educational information and invited people to view an ADL-created Soviet Jewry exhibit intended to bolster young Jews' "relationship to Judaism, Soviet Jewry and Israel." In each city, activists scheduled rallies that included the local mayors, who proclaimed "Soviet Jewry Day" in their communities. They hosted public rallies, ran workshops on both the high school and university levels, spoke at churches, and sought coverage from local media.[26]

Soviet Jewry activists from a variety of organizations gained political strength for their particularist movement by emulating the public relations and communications strategies of the secular social reform efforts around them. In order to draw attention to the plight of American prisoners of war in Vietnam and Southeast Asia, anti-war activists designed and sold bracelets, each adorned with the name and rank of a missing U.S. soldier. In similar fashion, the Orthodox movement's youth division, the National Council of Synagogue Youth (NCSY), designed a "Prisoner of Conscience" bracelet. On a 1971 flyer that included an order form for the bracelets, as well as Soviet Jewry buttons, bumper stickers, and posters, Soviet Jewry workers proclaimed in a large headline banner: "The POWs are coming home. The POCs are still in chains!" The NCSY described its product as a "simple nickel-plated bracelet" that "shows the name of a prisoner, the words 'prisoner of conscience,' the slogan 'Let My People Go,' and a bent Jewish star in chains, a symbol of the oppression of Soviet Jews."[27]

In similar fashion, the SSSJ produced buttons with the slogan "Russia is not healthy for Jews and other living things," a Soviet Jewry movement version of the popular anti–Vietnam War slogan, "War is not healthy for children and other living things." On another button, the activist group leveraged the racial binary of the civil rights movement to create an image of a black hand holding a white hand over a black-and-white Soviet Jewry image. Another button invoked Holocaust consciousness when it asked, "Are We the Jews of Silence?" When Moscow hosted the 1980 Olympic Games, the SSSJ issued two commemorative buttons. The first, "Berlin 1936. Moscow 1980. Olympics of Oppression," drew historic parallels between Nazi Germany and Communist U.S.S.R. Another framed a swastika with the words "Six Million Dead" next to a Soviet symbol questioning "Three Million More?" Finally, the Jewish Organizing Project, as part of the Freedom Seder, designed a button with a clinched fist in the spirit of the famed Tommie Smith and John Carlos Black Power protest at the 1968 Mexico City Olympics.[28]

The Jewish Defense League and Soviet Jewry

If politics makes strange bedfellows, then the Soviet Jewry movement brought an unusual alliance between the African American left and the American Jewish right. In the African American community, Black Power defined the leftist vanguard. Among American Jews, the JDL claimed the mantle for the activist right. Both sought the primacy of ethnic differentiation and advocated a populist response often at odds with each community's more established leadership. More than any other Soviet Jewry group, the JDL translated the prevailing Black Power–inspired nationalist sentiment into advocacy for Jews.

As part of an emerging neoconservative critique that rejected the group-based liberal thinking dominant in Jewish America, Rabbi Meir Kahane formed the Jewish Defense Corps, later renamed the Jewish Defense League, in 1968. With a charismatic personality, grassroots approach, and focus on Jews ignored or marginalized by the Jewish community's formal leadership, Kahane built an organization dedicated to working-class and elderly Jews left behind in urban America. A staunch Jewish nationalist, Kahane injected a no-apology mind-set into his defense of Jewish interests on the local, national, and international levels.[29]

The JDL embraced vigilante tactics to provide private security to Jewish city dwellers in neighborhoods that transitioned to majority African American residents. In New York, the JDL created a summer camp that combined Hebrew lessons with self-defense classes and rifle shooting. The JDL's membership counted a disproportionate number of Orthodox Jews, young Jews, and Jews from working-class backgrounds and neighborhoods. By the end of 1971, it counted chapters in most of the nation's major cities. Ultimately, the JDL claimed a membership of some 8,000 people located in seventeen cities and twenty-four college campuses.[30]

Kahane took particular issue with American Jews who focused their political activism on universalist social movements such as civil rights and free speech. He objected to mainstream Jewish organization leaders who embraced gradualist approaches to social change. "I was very upset," he explained, "that young Jews didn't give a damn about being Jewish anymore." Recalling the disproportionate Jewish presence in the civil rights, anti–Vietnam War, anti–Cold War, and United Farm Workers boycott movements, Kahane blasted that young Jews "were fighting for blacks, for the Vietcong, for Cubans, for lettuce, but not for themselves." Only with a militant Jewish approach, he believed, could the JDL succeed in "protecting Jewish socioeconomic interests and promoting Jewish ethnic pride, particularly among Jewish youth."[31]

Even as it harbored deep-seated racial animus against African Americans, the JDL embraced Black Power ideology, finding ways to redefine it for their right-wing Jewish activism. As Amaryah Orenstein recounted, Kahane believed that the Black Power movement "constituted both a cause and a model for Jewish Power." In the JDL leader's estimation, Black Power activists "did more with their sit-ins and street demonstrations than all the respectable Negro organizations combined." By employing black nationalist approaches to social change, Kahane worked to develop a new, more activist image of Jews, whom he believed suffered for their apparent aversion to militancy. "It is the Jewish problem," he explained, "which must come first for the Jew just as, rightfully, the Black problem must come first for the Black, or the Irish problem for the Irishman." Even as Kahane understood the risks associated with employing violence as a tool for social change, he also made sure to acknowledge that it "sometimes worked." The JDL's motto "Never Again" resonated with Malcolm X's "By Any Means Necessary" and Stokely Carmichael's impulse to abandon the expressed nonviolence of SNCC. Kahane thought the time had come for Jews to learn about "the kind of pride preached by [Black Power leader Eldridge] Cleaver."[32]

Kahane understood the symmetry between his organization and black militancy, holding particular affection for the BPP, organized in Oakland, California, as a high-profile response to police violence against African Americans. By leveraging its legal right to arm itself in public, the BPP organized groups of rifle-toting blacks to observe police actions. Eventually, BPP chapters opened in cities across the country. The BPP advanced an impressive new image for African Americans as well. Rather than remaining silent in the face of American racism, or embracing the unconditional nonviolent approach of Dr. King and other mainstream African American civil rights leaders, the BPP sought high-profile actions that would communicate a sense of power, self-respect, and agency among African Americans. In one of its boldest moves, members of the BPP entered California's state capitol building in Sacramento fully armed.

These images impressed Kahane, who saw in black militancy an answer to Jewish powerlessness, especially in the post-Shoah world. Kahane aligned himself with the Black Panther's racial separatism, even as his Jewish exclusivity earned him rebuke from the Jewish mainstream. "There is no question," Kahane explained in his defense, "that despite the effort to paint us as racists—which is incredible nothingness—we certainly do feel and understand a great many of the things that, for example, the Panthers say." A 1971 editorial in *Jewish Frontier* described the JDL as "a breed of 'Jewish Panthers'" whose bold activism proved "unlike the sniveling Uncle Jakes of the Jewish community." In an article on campus life published by *Jewish Frontier* later that year, Philip Horn compared the JDL to the Black Panthers, acknowledging that while "each attempts to give its constituents the impression that the other represents the dominant thinking within its ethnic group . . . the role that each group plays within its own community is similar." Even repudiations of the JDL affirmed its links to black militancy. As New York AJC head Haskell L. Lazere proclaimed in a 1970 article, the JDL proved "an aberration of American and Jewish life" because its vigilante approach drew it to the "Black Panthers, Minutemen, [and] White Citizens Council."[33]

Blacks and Jews could understand one another in an era of identity politics and, from the rightist perspective of the JDL, Black Power and Jewish militancy shared a common tactical approach. In the JDL founder's estimation, Jews living in the diaspora, like African Americans, struggled with government's marginalization of their religious group. Even as the Great Society appeared to separate African Americans from Jews in its designation of minority racial status, Kahane and the JDL understood an underlying consensus: recognition of group status mattered. Individual rights–based liberalism gave way to a new public appreciation of difference. Both groups, Kahane affirmed, needed "to use unorthodox or outrageous ways" to achieve their goals. "On this," he proclaimed, "we don't differ. We don't differ on their wanting to instill in their young people ethnic pride. Not at all."[34]

Those ways included an abandonment of nonviolent Jewish protest. Although Kahane affirmed that he did "not preach violence for its own sake or unless absolutely necessary," he still pushed back against those "who would tie our hands and limit us to respectability." Just as Oakland's BPP leveraged Second Amendment rights to gun ownership to protect African Americans from police violence, the JDL created neighborhood patrols to protect Jews from perceived African American threats. While BPP members carried weapons, JDL activists donned distinctive berets, wore their own uniforms, and armed themselves with chains and baseball bats.[35]

The BPP and the larger Black Power movement reminded JDL leaders of the modern Zionist movement. With specific focus on the right-wing Revisionist branch of Zionism, the JDL paralleled the plight of blacks in the

United States with the need for Jewish nationalism in what was British-Mandate Palestine. The JDL saw in black militancy the same sort of ideology and tactics Revisionist Zionist leader Ze'ev Jabotinsky and his allies advanced for Jews. During the 1968 High Holy Days, Kahane proclaimed "Operation Haganah," employing the name of the underground pre-State Jewish army to launch an effort by JDL members to protect inner-city Jews as they walked to their local synagogues for prayer.[36]

The JDL, arguably more than any other American Jewish group, stoked the Soviet Jewry fire by taking aim at the more diplomatic strategies of the established national Jewish organizations. At a 2,000-strong Soviet Jewry rally at Hunter College on December 27, 1970, protestors wore pins that said "Up Against the Wall, Mother Russia," offering a Jewish take on the popular rally cry, "Up Against the Wall, Motherfucker." Kahane often employed that slogan to communicate his level of passion. At that very rally, Kahane, referencing two refuseniks given the death penalty in the Soviet Union, threatened the Soviet leader with violence: "Listen, Brezhnev, and listen well: if Dymshits and Kuznetsov die, Russian diplomats will die in New York. Two Russians for every Jew!" Later, Kahane ordered his followers "to break any and every law" if it meant aiding Soviet Jews and demanded that rabbis in New York City endure arrest on behalf of their coreligionists as they did for African Americans.[37]

The Anti-Defamation League rejected JDL tactics, especially its slogan "Never Again," a reference to the need for post-Holocaust Jews to fight against the possibility of another attempted genocide. It pushed back against the JDL-inspired notion that "seems to see American Jews as living in a fiercely hostile society, living, as it were, in Nazi Germany or in Israel surrounded by forty million enemies." That supposition, the ADL proffered, proved "a presumptuous insult to those who died in the Holocaust and to those who live in real peril in the Middle East today." The NJCRAC rejected the JDL as "destructive of public order and contributory to divisiveness and terror." While it acknowledged that "Jews must not tolerate anti-Semitism, as black citizens must not tolerate racism," the NJCRAC understood that "the answer to such provocations cannot be found in clubs or physical battles."[38]

Instead, the NJCRAC preferred a more moderate approach. "The evils of our society and the extremists in our midst," it concluded, "must be countered through peaceful processes consistent with democratic goals."

The left-leaning AJCongress, in a 1971 private memo to its division and chapter presidents, reported that the JDL "ideology was undemocratic, its functioning harmful and its influence deleterious to the best interests of American and world Jewry and particularly Soviet Jewry." The organization forbade its professionals from inviting JDL members to speak at its meetings. In 1970, the AJCSJ, with twenty-six national Jewish organizations and community councils, called the JDL "misguided zealots."[39]

Tensions between the mainstream Jewish community and the JDL came to a head in May 1969 when *Black Manifesto* author James Forman launched a high-profile campaign against white churches demanding $500 million in reparation for African American slavery. When he threatened to take his appeal to New York City's Temple Emanu-el, the congregation's rabbi, seeking a way to navigate a difficult and complex situation, offered Forman the opportunity to speak. Kahane bolted, discounting Forman's claims as well as any responsibility for American Jews. "Most Jews came here in galleys long after the Blacks were freed," he proclaimed. With a promise to prevent Forman from ever entering the synagogue, Kahane blasted, "Blacks deserve nothing from us and that is what they will get." Members of the JDL showed up with weapons that included baseball bats, chains, and pipes, ready to ensure that the Shabbat service continued without interruption. As Kahane explained to a reporter for the *Jerusalem Post*, the JDL "would be only too glad to welcome him to the Temple, but that he should come prepared to end up in the hospital." While Forman never showed up, Kahane leveraged the standoff's publicity to advance his new branding image of Jews as strong and powerful.[40]

The Soviet Jewry movement animated the different ways American Jews harnessed the ideology and tactics of the Black Power movement to strengthen their own religious community. Young Jews pushed out of Mississippi turned instead to the Soviet Union. Orthodox Jews typically uninvolved with public life sprang into action. Leftist Jews modeled their struggle for the Eastern Bloc brethren with strategies that borrowed from the larger secular social protest movements of the time. And right-wing Jews saw in Black Power an opportunity to advance their own nationalist agenda. The Cold War, long the target of leftists, reemerged as the most powerful political strategy to mobilize broad-based support for massive Jewish emigration even as the Soviet Jewry movement remained the largest and most particularist of the many Jewish turns inward.

Black Power and American Zionism

n a 1966 *Midstream* article, Rabbi Arthur Hertzberg, author of the canonic *The Zionist Idea* and instructor at Columbia University, took aim at American rabbis for their apparent indifference to the Zionist cause. In the pre-state era, he argued, American rabbis formed the nucleus of a small but important American Zionist movement, urging congregants to back the call for a Jewish state, lobbying government leaders for friendly policies, and pressing ambivalent Jewish organizations to offer public support for the Zionist movement. In the years since Israel's creation, Hertzberg blasted, rabbis retreated. Fears of dual loyalty, the emergence of Jerusalem rather than New York as the new "center stage" of Zionism, and the strength of a consensus-based approach to American politics meant that "no one can today make a major career within American Jewry through Zionist political activity." The postwar rabbi, Hertzberg understood, "is expected to symbolize the new Jewish role as part of a new American "we." Although Hertzberg focused on rabbis, his analysis pointed out the broader consensus-based political culture that discouraged a public embrace of Jewish nationalism among American Jews.[1]

Eighteen months after Hertzberg published his diatribe, American Jews across the nation rallied after Israel's victory in the 1967 Six-Day War. Young American Jews added a junior year in Israel to their college programs while their parents poured money into various Israel emergency appeals. The Left, so ingrained with an anti-Israel and anti-Zionist flavor, faced resistance from Jewish activists unwilling to compromise their nationalist aspirations amid charges of Israeli colonialism and imperialism. Compared with earlier Israeli military victories and even the Jewish nation's very founding in 1948, the American Jewish reaction in June of 1967 confounded organizational leaders. What inspired such a rapid about-face for American Jews on the question of Zionism? Why did American Jews jump to Israel's defense, even when it meant a break from many of their historic left-leaning allies? How did an American Jewish community reluctant to engage identity politics in the 1950s emerge by the late 1960s as a strong, vocal defender of its nationalist aspirations?

Black Power gifted American Jews a new appreciation and enthusiasm for Jewish nationalism, redefining the very meaning of what it meant to be an ethnic American and helping inspire an unprecedented growth in American Zionism. If African Americans could advocate for black nationalism, so too could Jews press for their version of national sovereignty. And they did. Thanks to the expansion of identity politics inspired by Black Power advocates, Jews discovered a new Americanist pathway to the modern Zionist movement. Dual loyalty concerns eased as American Jews, from the halls of organizational leadership to rallies on college campuses across the country, articulated an unapologetic defense of their people's right to national self-determination. In the 1950s and early 1960s, support for the Zionist cause as anything more than a humanitarian movement for the world's oppressed Jews complicated domestic civic status. Thanks in part to Black Power, advancing a Zionist agenda in the American public square proved good for the Jews.

The nationalist aspirations binding Black Power advocates with American Zionists seemed ironic at first. In the larger historiographic understanding of black-Jewish relations, it would appear that the political dynamics surrounding American Jewish support for the State of Israel offered yet another example of a fundamental political split between the two onetime civil rights allies. As African American civil rights activists purged whites and Jews from leadership positions in their organizations, they also aligned themselves with the Palestinian cause, calling out Israel's post-1967 territorial expansion as evidence of the Jewish state's failed policy of imperialism and colonialism. Progressive Zionists, to be sure, rejected that critique and split from both the New Left and the radical African American community. Still, the Left's larger rejection of Cold War political assumptions brought strong condemnation of Israel's governmental policies and of Zionism as a political ideology. As Hebrew University political science professor Shlomo Avineri explained, "The fact that

Israel is supported by America and that part of this support derives from circles that regard Israel as a 'bastion against the spread of communism,' causes the Israel-Arab conflict to be viewed as one aspect of the Cold War, with Israel as the protagonist of American interests."[2]

Despite these outward differences, the rise of black and Jewish nationalism in the late 1960s evidenced yet another facet of the new identity-politics consensus emerging between blacks and Jews. Black nationalists and Jewish Zionists saw eye-to-eye even as they engaged in high-profile disputes over one another's positions, strategies, and tactics. Jewish leaders, and American rabbis especially, saw in African American calls for Black Power a repetition of Jewish history. They linked the political ideologies and tactics of modern Zionist leaders in the late nineteenth and early twentieth centuries to African American calls for greater autonomy in the 1960s. As historian Seth Forman explained, "Jewish leaders were conspicuous for the frequency with which they compared Black Power with Zionism, often without the slightest sensitivity to the differences between the two nationalist impulses in both theory and practice, or to their vastly different implications for Jewish life in the United States." In a few instances, American Jews and some Israelis themselves sought to import a Black Power mind-set to social reform efforts in the Jewish state itself. By the same token, African American activists, even as they criticized Jewish nationalism in their public pronouncements, made no effort to hide their ideological kinship with Zionist thinkers, whom they quoted in their own advocacy work. For blacks and Jews, the rise of Black Power recreated the interracial civil rights alliance of an earlier era, though in a very different form.[3]

Early American Zionism

When the modern Zionist movement emerged in late nineteenth-century Eastern Europe, few American Jews embraced the cause. Central European American Jews who arrived in the United States some fifty years before Herzl's famous 1897 First Zionist Congress in Basel, Switzerland, rarely thought of leaving a nation that offered so much to its Jewish citizens. Two generations of acculturation to American life situated this group of Jews in the middle class, with religious freedom and little anti-semitism. The notion that Jews needed their own national homeland failed to gain traction; as one of the nation's best-known rabbis, Isaac Mayer Wise, famously declared in 1897, "The new messianic movement over the ocean does not concern us at all." A year later, the Reform movement's synagogue arm, the UAHC, announced it was "unalterably opposed to political Zionism" because "the Jews are not a nation but a religious community." For them, indeed, "America is our Zion."[4]

When nearly two million Eastern European Jews opted to leave their homes for new surroundings in the late nineteenth and early twentieth centuries, almost all picked the United States as their destination. Ottoman-controlled Palestine welcomed roughly 100,000 Jewish immigrants before the British took control of the area after the Great War (World War I). The opportunities afforded by a rapidly expanding industrial economy in America inspired more Jewish migration than the socialist or even religious allure of rebuilding the Jews' ancient homeland. In just a few years, New York City grew to international prominence as a new center of world Jewish life. While Eastern European Jews and their U.S.-born children held Zionism closer than their Central European-descended coreligionists, almost all opted to express their support of a Jewish homeland from their homes in the United States.

The rise of Louis Brandeis and his famous 1915 defense of American Zionism swelled the Jewish nationalist ranks to unprecedented levels. "Loyalty to America," he wrote, "demands rather that each American Jew become a Zionist." Brandeis, who would become the nation's first Jewish member of the U.S. Supreme Court, equated Zionism with Americanism, integrating Jewish nationalism into the pluralistic fabric of the nation. If Irish Americans claimed a connection to their Irish national heritage, he argued, Jewish Americans should be able to reclaim their national homeland as well. Yet, in a stipulation that would set American Zionism on an ideological collision course with its European counterpart, Brandeis rejected aliyah, immigration to Palestine, as a requirement for American Jews.[5]

With Hitler's ascension to power in Germany, American Jews stepped up their support for the Zionist cause as a humanitarian necessity for European Jews. The CCAR softened its earlier anti-Zionist stance and most national Jewish organizations embraced the creation of a Jewish state, though often with stipulations to address their dual loyalty concerns. Even so, when David Ben-Gurion pronounced Israel's independence in

May of 1948, American Jews limited their support of the new nationalist project to domestic political advocacy, pilgrimage tours, and charitable donations. For the most part, American Zionists held true to the Brandeisian stipulation: no immigration.

In the years between the establishment of the State of Israel in 1948 and the rise of Black Power in the mid-1960s, few American Jews embraced the Zionist movement with enough conviction to unsettle their lives in the United States and move to the Jewish state. The Cold War anti-Communist consensus celebrated American democracy and its ability to assimilate a diverse population. Throughout the 1950s, average annual immigration from the United States to Israel topped out at just 361. Even as that number nearly doubled, to 699, between 1960 and 1966, it still represented a minute fraction of an American Jewish population estimated at 5.3 million people. The postwar era in the United States celebrated the primacy of interfaith ecumenicism, interracial political alliances, and the ability of Americans to solve the social and political issues that divided them. Few offered meaningful critique of the prevailing consensus and almost no one considered American life so terrible that they would need to leave.[6]

American Jewish interest in the Zionist movement of the 1950s focused almost exclusively on the humanitarian needs of Holocaust refugees. Across the Jewish organizational spectrum, American Jews offered political and philanthropic support for Israel as a necessary response to the Nazi's attempted genocide. In the years after World War II, onetime non-Zionist American Jewish groups eased their dual loyalty concerns and proclaimed themselves Zionist, though with the stipulation that their support for Israel did not imply a rejection of Jewish life in the diaspora. In a famous 1950 Jerusalem exchange, AJC head Jacob Blaustein and Israeli prime minister David Ben-Gurion struck a public compromise: American Jews would back the Jewish state while Israel's leadership would respect the primacy of their coreligionists' American citizenship. As late as 1955, the AJC warned, "The intensive public efforts of American Zionists to influence our government on behalf of a pro-Israel policy may create a situation of conflict between American Jews and the Government." The AJC worried that mobilizing Jews in defense of the Jewish state "may tend to give rise to the charge of dual loyalty."[7]

This approach to American Zionism, labeled "checkbook Zionism" by its detractors, informed postwar Jewish America. At its 1960 annual meeting, for example, Alan Stroock, chair of the AJC's Committee on Israel, proclaimed, "Israel speaks only for its citizens and in no way speaks for the Jews of other lands." And, as he imagined the decade ahead, he announced, "We will be operating more as the American Jewish Committee, rather than the American *Jewish* Committee." Among American Jews, the rise of early 1960s social protest movements did not translate into support for the Zionist movement. Young Jewish activists tended to follow the same political path as described by Stroock, joining secular organizations in political struggles that did not engage overt Jewish issues. Although activism in the civil rights, free speech, and anti-war protest movements could be linked to Jewish imperatives, the growth of leftist causes in the early 1960s did not include many calls for Jewish nationalist expression.[8]

Black Power and American Zionism

As early as 1964, American Jewish leaders paralleled the growing African American call for Black Power with the modern Zionist movement's own tactical struggle between the centrist Jewish army and more militant Revisionist groups. For Rabbi Allan Levine, the question went to the very core of his own social justice work. Born and raised in Montreal, Canada, Levine immigrated to Israel in 1955 before moving to the United States and earning rabbinic ordination at the Reform movement's Hebrew Union College-Jewish Institute of Religion. In 1961, he began a four-year stint as a Freedom Rider before joining Dr. King on the Edmund Pettus Bridge during the famed 1965 Selma march.[9]

In the midst of his civil rights work, Levine wondered whether the nonviolent approach to social change proved most effective. Given the violence he witnessed, shouldn't he and his African American colleagues take up arms against their oppressors? Didn't Zionist leaders confront a similar question when faced with both Arab and British violence? Seeking guidance, Levine included questions on Zionism in his January 1964 Soviet Jewry letter to Israeli prime minister David Ben-Gurion. The American civil rights rabbi asked the founding father of the Jewish state whether he thought "the terror and violence of the Sternists and Irgun were catalytic agents in the attainment of Israeli independence."[10]

Even though Ben-Gurion rejected the violent tactics of the right-wing Jewish militias, perhaps, Levine wondered, Israel's prime minister had grown more respectful of his adversaries' tactics over time. Drawing a direct parallel between Zionist activism in British-Mandate Palestine and American Jewish involvement in the civil rights movement, Levine wondered whether "in retrospect . . . the independence of Israel could have been achieved without terror and violence or by the same direct nonviolent method used by those of us involved in the struggle for freedom and civil rights in the United States." Although Ben-Gurion's response, if any, is unknown, Levine's query reveals a fundamental similarity between the movement for African American equality in the United States and the Jewish people's struggle determining the nature and limits of their own call for national independence. In essence, Levine wanted to know whether Black Power's eventual abandonment of nonviolence enjoyed Jewish nationalist precedent.[11]

Just four months later, Shad Polier offered similar thoughts at the AJCongress's 1964 Biennial Conference. Watching the rise of black militancy on the American scene, Polier drew a direct parallel to Ben-Gurion's struggle to unite the various Jewish military factions at the time of Israel's independence. While Rabbi Levine wondered whether African American civil rights workers might need to emulate Revisionist Zionist groups in their militancy, Polier concluded that black activists certainly would. He empathized with African American frustration over centrist political strategies that demanded nonviolence. Instead, he saw in Zionist history a model for contemporary black militancy. Referencing the Revisionist militant group Lechi (Freedom Fighters for Israel), known by the British as the Stern Gang, Polier claimed: "To the British people, the Stern Gang in what was then Palestine was no less extremist than the Black Muslims are in the eyes of the American people."[12]

In the estimation of this left-leaning Jewish communal leader, the "Stern Gang was fighting for political freedom" and "fighting to open the doors so that Jews who had survived the hell of Nazism could enter into the promised land." In similar fashion, Polier concluded, "The Negroes are also fighting for entry into a promised land and to escape the degradation and deprivations of second-class citizenship." Polier, who certainly rejected the tactics of both Revisionist Zionists and anti-Zionist black nationalists, still believed the civil rights movement would follow a similar course among African Americans as Lechi did among Zionists. "The Jews of Israel overwhelmingly repudiated the Stern Gang and placed their trust in the Haganah," Polier concluded, "so, too, the overwhelming majority of the Negroes of America repudiate Elijah Muhammad and Malcolm X, his former disciple and now the would-be new prophet of Negro nationalism."[13]

Across the Jewish communal spectrum, Jewish leaders and intellectuals understood and articulated a clear connection between the growing militancy of African American civil rights activists and the Jews' own fight for national power after an attempted genocide against their people. For Hertzberg, SNCC leader Stokely Carmichael amounted to nothing less than "the most radical kind of Negro Zionist." While Carmichael endured harsh critique from many in the organized Jewish community for his abandonment of uncompromised nonviolence in civil rights strategy, Hertzberg understood his predicament. In the rabbi's mind-set, Carmichael faced a question well known to Jews: at what point do the abuses of a government demand a violent response?[14]

Hertzberg framed Carmichael's dilemma through the lens of Jews suffering under Nazism in World War II. He supported Carmichael's position because he remembered the plight of German Jews, "who felt most violently angry at the sight of Hitler and most hurt by the good people who stood aside." Hertzberg looked beyond the harsh rhetoric of Black Power, drawing attention to the core issues it sought to redress. "What Mr. Carmichael is asserting is Zionist in more fundamental respects than the anger that it is expressing," Hertzberg explained. As postwar Jews knew too well, "no community has any real position in this nasty world unless it translates its appeals to conscience into the beginnings of a power base, both economic and political, of its own." Hertzberg concluded, "This was precisely what all the Zionist theorists, from Herzl through Borochov, were talking about."[15]

The 1967 Six-Day War

With strong American Jewish affinity for black nationalism established, the 1967 Six-Day War between Israel and her Arab neighbors tested the onetime political allies. While the old-line African American leadership of the civil rights era backed the Jewish state after its military victory, Black Power activists along with most in the larger New Left political bloc renounced the post-1967 Israeli occupation of majority-Arab lands in East

Jerusalem, the West Bank, Gaza, and the Golan Heights. At a time when many Jewish leaders understood the rise of black militancy, equating it to pivotal moments in Jewish history, they also faced increasing anti-Israel, anti-Zionist, and at times antisemitic tension from many of those same African American activists. Although nationalist Jews and Black Power–inspired African Americans did reach a new identity politics–based consensus in the late 1960s, that consensus would include continued disagreements over Israeli government action and the right of Palestinians to enjoy their own national self-determination.

American Jews across the organizational spectrum emerged in the post-1967 period with unprecedented support for the Zionist cause. For them, the rise of Black Power opened the gates to free and open nationalist expression on American shores. Translated inward, Jewish leaders leveraged black nationalism to legitimate their own Zionist activism, even when their support of the Jewish homeland conflicted with the anti-Israelism of very black militants who paved their activist road. For American Jews, Black Power–inspired identity politics combined with an impressive Israeli victory to motivate unprecedented philanthropic giving, pilgrimage tours, long-term study opportunities, and, in some cases, immigration to the Jewish state. In what seems a moment dripping with political irony, American Jews placed Black Power thinking at the center of their Zionist campaign to delegitimize Black Power anti-Zionists.

When Egyptian leader Gamal Abdel Nasser mobilized his army on May 15, 1967, and soon thereafter ordered United Nations peacekeepers out of the Sinai desert, closed the vital shipping lanes at the Straits of Tiran, and called on his Arab neighbors to join him in a "holy war" against Israel, he triggered a profound realignment in both American Jewish political activism and the relationship between blacks and Jews in an era of Black Power. As historian Clayborne Carson wrote, the 1967 Six-Day War "signaled a shift from the universalistic values that had once prevailed in the civil rights movement toward an emphasis on political action based on more narrowly conceived group identities and interests." For Jews, as Murray Friedman observed in a 1969 *Commentary* article, the combination of Black Power and Israel's victory in the 1967 Six-Day War offered "alienated Jews" a platform to discover their Jewishness.[16]

The timing of the 1967 Six-Day War could not have been better for

American Jews. Some three years after the rise of Black Power, the purges of Jews from civil rights leadership, and emphasis on each ethnic group "taking care of its own," Jewish activists stood primed for mobilization. Israel's dramatic victory revealed deep fractures in the relationship between anti-Zionist African American activists and Jewish leftists committed to the Jewish state. At the same moment that almost all American Jews expressed strong support for the State of Israel, celebrating an image of Zionists as strong, powerful defenders of Jews in a post-Holocaust era, militant blacks doubled down on their opposition to a regime that now occupied Arab lands and declared East Jerusalem part of its sovereign capital. This inflection point in black-Jewish relations set the two communities on opposite Zionist courses. Black Power supporters rejected Jewish nationalism out of hand, while American Jews leveraged ethnic America's new appreciation for particularist enterprises by rallying to Israel's defense.[17]

Especially in the years after 1967, black nationalists articulated a narrative of Zionism founded upon the belief that Jewish Israelis, in a colonial exercise, created the State of Israel by dispossessing the indigenous Arab population of its land. Zionism, far from its historic definition as a utopian vision combining socialist principles with nationalist aspirations, became an expression of imperialism and one of an ever-expanding list of progressive concerns. As Nathan Glazer observed, "The Arabs are seen as a people in rebellion against Western imperialism, a force with which Jews as a people are seen to be allied." Because the United States, in this estimation, advanced an imperialistic foreign policy and supported the State of Israel, the Jewish state promoted imperialism itself. American Jews, once understood as allies of African America because they understood what it meant to face persecution, emerged in the post-1967 era as partners of a white Israeli government responsible for subjugating its people of color, the Palestinian Arabs. The black-Jewish alliance of the 1950s became the black-Arab alliance of the 1960s.[18]

Soon after the war ended, Black Power activists published a series of vitriolic articles criticizing the Jewish state. In its newsletter, SNCC offered thirty-two "documented facts" dating back to the founding of modern political Zionism in 1897, blaming the Zionist movement for the Mideast conflict. In its June 1967 issue, the editors of *Black Power* published a poem calling for the mass murder of Israeli Jews:

We're gonna burn their towns and that ain't all,
We're gonna piss upon the Wailing Wall,
And then we'll get Kosygin and DeGaulle,
That will be ecstasy, killing every Jew we see in Jewland.

In other instances, editors wrote that Zionists created the State of Israel through "terror, force, and massacre," published an antisemitic image of Israeli defense minister Moshe Dayan with dollar signs replacing his military uniform's stars, and printed a blurred photo purported to capture a 1956 Jewish massacre of Arabs in the Gaza Strip.[19]

The black nationalist critique of Zionism extended to the United States as well. SNCC program director Ralph Featherstone, after identifying Israelis as Jewish oppressors, argued that the term applied as well to American Jews. Referencing the continued presence of Jewish merchants and landlords in urban America, Featherstone labeled as "Jewish oppressor" any of "those Jews in the little Jew shops in the ghettos." SNCC leader Stokely Carmichael concurred. At the 1968 national meeting of the Organization of Arab Students, Carmichael remarked, "We have begun to see the evil of Zionism and we will fight to wipe it out wherever it exists, be it in the Ghetto of the United States or in the Middle East." In a New Year's Eve 1970 edition of the *New Year Times*, BPP leader Eldridge Cleaver declared that his group "fully supports Arab guerillas in the Middle East." Later, he expanded his critique to affirm, "Zionists, wherever they may be, are our enemies." These binational proclamations gained currency when CBS News commentator Richard C. Hottelet reported that Al Fatah, a branch of the Palestine Liberation Organization, considered training Black Panthers for combat in Israel in order to "prepare them for a sabotage and assassination campaign in the United States."[20]

In Chicago, the 1967 National Conference for New Politics passed a resolution, created by the black caucus, denouncing Israel for engaging in an "imperialist Zionist war." When black activists pressed Jewish delegates to accept the anti-Zionist statement, a group elected to vote with their feet and exited the conference. AJCongress leader Rabbi Joachim Prinz, who preceded Dr. Martin Luther King Jr. on the dais at the famed 1963 March on Washington, appealed to the famed civil rights leader for support after the resolution's passage. King, though, hedged his response, denouncing the black caucus but also letting Prinz know that "I must confess that I, too, was greatly disappointed because we always expect our Jewish brothers to be our strongest allies if for no other reason than the fact that they had a common oppression."[21]

Jewish leaders pushed back against black anti-Zionism. AJCongress president Rabbi Arthur J. Lelyveld resented Black Panther support of Al Fatah and rejected their "unacceptable vituperation against all supporters of the State of Israel," while AJCongress executive director Will Maslow penned a report, "Israel, Africa, Colonialism and Racism: A Reply to Certain Slanders," refuting black nationalist charges that Israel acted as "a creature of colonialism, a stranger to Africa and a racist society in the Middle East." In May and June 1967, Lelyveld as well as the famed actor and political activist Theodore Bikel resigned from SNCC in protest. Heightened Jewish nationalism in an era that valued identity politics placed Zionist Jews and anti-Zionist blacks on a collision course. Yet, their interracial clash reflected two political opponents playing the same identity-politics game. Blacks and Jews internalized ethnic nationalism in conflicting ways, though they joined one another as unapologetic advocates of their own group's self-interest.[22]

Black Power anti-Zionism hit hardest among leftist Jews who felt the strongest kinship with African American militants in the years before the Six-Day War. If one could make a list of all the New Left's political imperatives, radical Jews would share near-perfect alignment, with Zionism as the singular exception. Although some Jewish leftists rejected Zionism and maintained their unconflicted place in the Left, most struggled to reconcile their progressive understanding of Zionism with the rejectionist rhetoric emanating from Black Power supporters after 1967. The Six-Day War forced a decision point for Jewish radicals: continue their alliance with black militants and renounce the State of Israel or break with the Left and defend Zionism on their own.

After Eldridge Cleaver journeyed to Algiers in defense of Al Fatah, the radical Jewish Liberation Movement (a leftist group that initially backed the BPP) flinched. "Let it suffice to say," Itzhak Epstein, an organizer for the Students for a Democratic Society and secretary-general of the North American Jewish Student Network, bristled, "The Panthers have declared themselves to be the enemies of my people's national aspirations, and supporters of those who want to commit genocide against us. Whatever justice there is in the Panthers' own struggle, I must view them from now on as my enemies." As Epstein reflected, the split between leftist Jews and Black Power advocates upset a political alliance that otherwise joined radical blacks and Jews in a common purpose. "Even if I were a superaltruistic liberal and campaigned among the Jews to support the Panthers' program," he concluded, "I would justifiably be tarred and feathered for giving aid and comfort to enemies of the Jews. I would rather it were not this way, but it was you who disowned us, not we who betrayed you."[23]

M. J. Rosenberg, then the Hillel director at Temple University and later a political activist on Capitol Hill, took aim as well. Targeting the New Left's Students for a Democratic Society (SDS), Rosenberg rejected the black nationalist depiction of Jews as "racist Zionists." In a 1969 article published in New York City's well-known alternative newspaper, *Village Voice*, Rosenberg lined up contemporary black antisemitism with a Jewish history steeped in anti-Jewish animus. "We must see him for what he is," Rosenberg charged, "just another *goy* using the Jew as the available and acceptable scapegoat. We must then fight him with all we have." Faced with untangling the Gordian knot between his leftism and his Zionism, Rosenberg asked: "Did I have to choose between the Fatah-supporting SDS and the ultra-middle-class lox-and-bagel breakfast club Hillel society?" His answer proved clear: "If I must choose between the Jewish cause and a 'progressive' anti-Israel SDS, I shall always choose the Jewish cause." In the post-Holocaust world, Rosenberg concluded, "we retain but one supreme value—to exist. Masada will not fall again." With that, Rosenberg leveraged Black Power's most familiar slogan in opposition to black militancy itself: "When the issue is survival, we must prevail 'by any means necessary.'"[24]

The Six-Day War could not have been better timed. With three years of rising black nationalism, calls for whites to leave the interracial alliance and focus on the needs of their own communities, and a simultaneous Jewish ethnic revival in the religious, cultural, and educational spheres, American Jews responded to Israel's 1967 victory with uncompromising support and enthusiasm. Israel's fast and stunning victory infused a sense of Jewish pride unseen in the history of American Zionism. Eased (by the rise of Black Power) from dual loyalty concerns, American Jews voted for their Jewish homeland with their wallets, their voices, and even their feet. As Professor Steven M. Cohen reported, "An autonomous Jewish student movement arose on American campuses" committed to supporting, among other Jewish-centered issues, the State of Israel.[25]

A special emergency campaign brought over $100 million between the closing of the Gulf of Aqaba on May 23, 1967, and the end of the war on June 10. The UJA campaign, which recorded $64 million during its 1966 effort, burst at the seams with a $241 million total in 1967. United Jewish Appeal official Abraham Harman suffered from the best possible fundraiser challenge: "We had an administrative problem how to handle the flow of money." Despite a U.S. government ban on travel to Israel, 10,000 American Jews registered their interest in taking civilian jobs in Israel with either the Israeli consulates or with Hillel, the nationwide campus Jewish organization. Ultimately, 1,000 American Jews gathered their passports, traveled to Israel, and volunteered in nonmilitary roles so that Israelis would be free to protect the Jewish state. In New York City, 150,000 Jews rallied for Israel. According to estimates by Arthur Hertzberg, a third of the Jews rallying to Israel's defense "lacked any organizational Jewish ties" and came to their newfound Zionism from the civil rights and anti-war movements.[26]

For young American Jews already enrolled in Hebrew University's study abroad program in May, 1967, the impending war presented a more immediate question: should they honor their parents' cables urging them to return home as well as the U.S. embassy's call for all U.S. citizens to leave the country, or should they remain in Jerusalem for the duration? After a student meeting to discuss the situation, every single American Jew opted to stay in the Jewish state. "My existence as a Jew," one explained, "was being threatened simultaneously with the threat against Israel." Others followed their lead. The number of American Jews planning travel or study trips to Israel increased by 400 percent after the war. During the 1967–68 academic year, 177 students matriculated at Hebrew University's junior-year study abroad program. The next year, that number jumped to 478. By 1969, it reached 529 and continued to grow to 612 in the 1970–71 academic year. The rate of aliyah for American Jews increased almost 50 percent in the year after the war. While about 7,500 American Jews immigrated to Israel between 1948 and 1967, that number swelled to 30,000 in the years between 1967 and 1973.[27]

In the broader community, national groups upped their commitments to the Jewish state as well. The AJCongress reversed its long-standing opposition to aliyah when, at its May 1968 Biennial Convention, delegates passed a resolution affirming "the responsibility of American Jewry to help foster and promote the principle of aliyah to Israel." Crafting an argument linking the American and Israeli Jewish communities, the AJC pressed for creation of more work-study programs in Israel for American students as well as opportunities for American Jewish professionals to share their skills for the "upbuilding of Israel." In the fall of 1968, the AJC launched an intensive Hebrew language program, sold "A Taste of Hebrew" textbooks, and started "Hebrew through Conversation" weekend retreats for adults interested in strengthening their connections to Israel. The AJC imagined a new partnership with the Jewish state that would promote American Jewish immigration for those who wished to create new lives in Israel and strengthen Jewish leadership in the United States for those who chose to return. The AJC Commission on Jewish Affairs also wrote discussion guides on Zionism.[28]

In large measure, America's Orthodox Jewish community tended to stay on the margins of social activism. It considered engagement in the secular world a diversion from Jewish life, rejecting the Reform movement's emphasis on prophetic Judaism as a mandate for political involvement in secular America. With Israel's victory in 1967, though, Orthodoxy faced its own identity-politics question: did the military threat to the Jewish homeland and its eventual liberation of East Jerusalem and other holy sites in Judea and Samaria encourage a political about-face? Should Orthodox Jews join others in the American Jewish community as they rallied for Israel in the public square? By and large, they answered in the affirmative. As a journalist reported in 1967, Orthodox Jews "evolved into an ethnic pressure group, much the same in character as other ethnic groups."[29]

While this study tracks changes in Jewish identity politics throughout the postwar period, it typically examines a changing cohort of Jewish leaders over time. Those active in the early postwar years, holding true to King's consensus approach to social justice work, tended to retire from activism before Black Power advocates pressed an identity-politics agenda seemingly at odds with the 1950s approach. Simply put, Jewish organizations may have demonstrated some internal political consistency in their support for African American strategies and tactics over time, but the individuals who led those groups and formulated those opinions tended to change. Rabbi Roland Gittelsohn of Boston's Temple Israel offers an unusual historical perspective as his career spanned the entirety of postwar civil rights work. Through his example, we can glean from at least one source how the changing political nature of black-Jewish relations was interpreted over an expansive thirty-year span.

In 1947, Gittelsohn emerged as a national figure with his appointment to President Harry S. Truman's civil rights commission. When direct-action protests began in the South in the 1950s, Gittelsohn backed the efforts, encouraging his congregants to engage in grassroots civil rights work and reaching out to his colleagues in Mississippi to assist when they were jailed for their opposition to Jim Crow. The Boston rabbi personified the middle-class northern Jewish liberal passionate about civil rights and willing to join King's interracial alliance to advance racial equality. After black militants pressed back against white allies and Gittelsohn's own record of achievement as a civil rights advocate, it would seem the rabbi would take pause. Instead, Black Power proved opportunistic for the Boston rabbi, who leveraged identity politics to strengthen the Zionist cause after 1967.[30]

Frustrated with American Jews and the rabbinate in particular for emphasizing the religious aspects of Judaism at the expense of Jewish peoplehood, Gittelsohn pressed for stronger American Jewish ties to Zionism. When he took over leadership of the CCAR, the Reform movement's professional rabbinic association, he moved its annual meeting for the first time to Israel. "In authentic Judaism, religion and nationalism have always been inextricably intertwined," he urged in a 1972 *Midstream* magazine article following that visit. "Anyone who distorts that tradition to make it appear as only religion or only nationalism will have concocted an aberrant monstrosity which will not be authentic Judaism." Two years later, Gittelsohn expanded his critique to a broader audience. "We American Jews have too often acted as if Judaism were only a religion," he lamented. Accusing his brethren of ignoring "the reality that much in Judaism goes beyond what the world normally calls religion," Gittelsohn pressed American Jews to expand their Jewish expression to "every corner of life."[31]

The Black Power movement, in Gittelsohn's estimation, achieved in the African American community precisely what he longed to do among his own coreligionists. "The Black Power advocate is the Negro's Zionist," he implored. "Africa is his Israel." Rather than focus attention on the animus between blacks and Jews, Gittelsohn urged his coreligionists to empathize with black nationalism, which, in his analysis, "should not be at all difficult for us to accept and approve." Gittelsohn, like Allen Levine and Shad Polier, linked the left-leaning black nationalist cause with right-wing Revisionist Zionists. He paralleled the historic experiences and frustrations of early Zionists seeking an end to British rule in Mandate Palestine with the unrest that occurred for blacks in urban America. Referencing the decision by members of the Jewish militia Irgun to detonate a bomb inside the British military headquarters at Jerusalem's King David Hotel, Gittelsohn expressed understanding for the mind-set of African Americans who grew similarly frustrated with their loss of autonomy in a racist United States. Responsibility for "ghetto violence must be shared by white America," he urged, "which has been much too insensitive for a century to Negro anguish and need."[32]

Other American rabbis shared Gittelsohn's view. Reform rabbi Israel Dresner, recalling his civil rights work with Stokely Carmichael, described the SNCC leader as brave. "We, as Jews, knowing what happened in Europe, knowing that the Zionist analysis of Europe . . . unfortunately proved accurate," Dresner explained, "sympathize with and understand some of these black extremists who see America as being for the black man what Europe was for the Jew." Rabbi Dov Peretz Elkins simply affirmed, "Black Power is nothing more and nothing less than Negro Zionism."[33]

Even M. J. Rosenberg in his larger critique of black anti-Zionism understood the new emerging consensus. "It is as a Jew," he wrote, "that I must accept black nationalism." Reflecting on others who drew parallels between Zionism and the rise of Black Power, Rosenberg affirmed that even though "the black nationalists may or may not be the equivalents of militants of the early Zionist organizations, and Malcolm X may or may not be a black Vladimir (Zev) Jabotinsky, . . . surely the parallel is there." Rosenberg linked the Zionist movement with both African American nationalist calls and the North Vietnamese struggle for independence from U.S. military forces. The only difference between the three, he believed, was that "the Jewish struggle has seen its greatest aim realized, however tenuously." Paralleling the civil rights struggle in the United States with the emergence of a renewed interest in ethnic nationalism, Rosenberg concluded, "Black nationalism and Jewish nationalism will exist concurrently. To accept one, you must accept the other." Rosenberg understood, in language that demonstrated the emergence of a new consensus approach to the black-Jewish alliance, that "the black is America's Jew and a common fight can be waged."[34]

The rise of identity politics and American Zionism coincided with the rise of a Jewish counterculture discussed in chapter 4. The larger threads of each of these revivalist movements intertwined in the wake of Israel's 1967 military victory. In August 1977, Rabbi Hanan Sills, a founder of the Jewish Renewal movement, created a one-week kibbutz experience in rural Mendocino, California, with the theme "Joys of Jewishing and connecting with our Jewish roots." As Sills explained, the California kibbutz immersion provided "a place to have a Jewish experience on the land for those of us who don't want to go to Israel to get that connection." Participants enjoyed the typical camp experiences of evening campfires, silk-screen art classes, hiking, and swimming but added the more countercultural activities of organic gardening and yoga. Jewish rituals included a *mikvah* (ritual bath), immersion in kabbalah, Hasidic dancing, and Yiddish music. In the Santa Cruz mountains several hours' drive south of Mendocino, campers at the Reform movement's UAHC Camp Swig could elect to live in tents on the grounds of their own Kibbutz B'nei R'im, created by Israeli staff answering the American Jewish call for greater immersion in Jewish nationalist culture.[35]

American Zionism Aids Black Power

The influence of Black Power worked in reverse as well when African American leaders coopted Jewish historical narratives to advance their own political goals. While not the focus of this book, the development of black-Jewish relations in the period of identity politics played in both directions. Black leaders leveraged Jewish examples to improve their own group status. They admired American Jews for their ability to organize collectively, support a communal infrastructure, and, most important, maintain a sense of autonomous identity in the diaspora. While Black Power leaders offered specific praise for Jewish legacies in the 1960s and beyond, the cooperative relationship between black and Jewish nationalism predates the limits of this study.

As early as 1919, African American intellectual W. E. B. Du Bois wrote, "The African Movement means to us what the Zionist Movement must mean to the Jews, the centralization of race effort and the recognition of the racial fount." In the postwar years, Du Bois later argued, Zionism developed into a practical necessity, given the refusal of most nations to settle Jewish refugees from the Holocaust. In 1920, Back-to-Africa leader Marcus Garvey echoed Du Bois's thinking when, at a meeting of his United Negro Improvement Association (UNIA), he commented on "a new spirit, a new courage" among black nationalists that "has come to us simultaneously as it has come to other peoples of the world." Focusing specifically on the rise of modern political Zionism in the 1920s, Garvey punctuated: "When the Jew said, 'We shall have Palestine!,' the same sentiment came to us when we said, 'We shall have Africa.'" At the same meeting, Reverend J. W. H. Eason proclaimed, "Old Glory, when you come back, won't you cry aloud and recognize Palestine for the Jews officially, Ireland for the Irish officially, and Africa for the African officially?" The American Jewish Yiddish press called Garvey's black nationalist anthem, "Ethiopia, Thou Land of Our Fathers" "The Negro Hatikvah." A. Philip Randolph noted important parallels between African American aspirations and Zionism as well.[36]

In the postwar period, several of the most important African American civil rights leaders acknowledged the contribution of Jewish nationalism to the black cause. Roy Innis, the national director of CORE, reminded his constituents that "Jews caught in Egypt in the time of the Pharaoh did not talk about revolution against what was the most powerful and formidable military machine of the time. They talked about liberation—separating themselves from Egyptians." Innis proclaimed, "We black nationalists, too, must speak of separating ourselves." Bayard Rustin acknowledged the parallels between Jewish and black nationalism, even as he pointed out their inherent differences. According to Rustin, the particular history of African America, of forced immigration and slavery, differed in the most fundamental ways from the Jewish call for a return to Zion. "When Jews talk about Israel," he explained in a *Midstream* article, "they are talking about a place where they have sons and daughters, and cousins and friends; where people speak the language which has been theirs for centuries." African Americans, on the other hand, lack a direct connection to their ancestral homelands. Few can even identify their family's country of origin, while centuries of slavery and racism stripped blacks of many of the most important cultural, linguistic, and economic elements necessary for state building. Ultimately, Rustin believed it "counterproductive for Blacks to believe that they can build real progress on myths."[37]

Malcolm X, a leader of the Nation of Islam who made a number of anti-semitic remarks before his April 1964 journey to Mecca reoriented his perspective on Jews, expressed appreciation for Jewish nationalism in a May, 1964, article in the *New York Times*. "The American Jews," he wrote, "have raised their own status in this country through their philosophical, cultural, and psychological migration to Israel." With that as inspiration, Malcolm X thought that African Americans "in the same way" could "raise their own status by becoming deeply involved philosophically, culturally, and psychologically with the new African nations."[38]

In his essay "Power and Racism," Stokely Carmichael reflected on his own upbringing in Jewish terms. Recounting his experience watching Tarzan movies as a child, Carmichael remembered cheering for the movie hero by yelling at the screen, "Kill the beasts, kill the savages, kill 'em" until he realized that watching a "white Tarzan . . . beat up the black natives" meant that he was really screaming, "Kill *me*." At that moment, the Black Power leader drew an immediate parallel to Jews. "It was as if a Jewish boy," he opined, "watched Nazis taking Jews off to concentration camps and cheered them on." Carmichael's parallel of the Shoah to the challenges of black life in America drew him closer to an ethno-religious group he otherwise found troubling in many political ways.[39]

To punctate that consciousness, Carmichael pressed his followers to emulate Jews in speeches he delivered in 1966 and 1967. Paraphrasing an oft-quoted admonition from the Jewish sage Hillel, Carmichael reminded young African Americans: "If I am not for myself, who will be? If I am only for myself alone, who am I? If not know, when? If not you, who?" Reflecting on the number of American Jews who traveled to Israel after the Six-Day War, Carmichael also urged African Americans to find Jewish parallels in their own nationalist aspirations. "People who didn't have any rights in that country," the SNCC leader explained in reference to American Jews, "were flying in from all over the world to fight. There's nothing wrong with our doing the same thing."[40]

Black leaders journeyed to Israel as well, learning about how the Jewish state engaged its own social challenges. In some cases, they returned with ideas to help the African American community at home. After Andrew J. Young, then head of the SCLC, returned from an AJC Israel study mission for African American leaders, he wondered whether theories from the kibbutz movement could be applied to the challenges of blacks in urban America. "Most of all," he summarized in a letter to the AJC following his trip, "there is a spirit in Israel which we saw in Mr. Ben-Gurion, in the mayor of Be'er Sheba, in our guide as well as in the kibbutz which I think is most relevant to the challenging time in which we live." William Robinson, a welfare consultant for the Chicago-area federation of churches, suggested to the AJC that it bring African American social workers and educators to one of Israel's youth absorption villages (*aliyat ha'noar*) so that they could learn techniques that might help "educate Negro youngsters who leave the South and go north to the big cities such as New York so that they will be more useful to themselves and to the American society."[41]

Black Power Goes to Israel

Finally, American Zionists imported their Black Power–inspired politics to the State of Israel, launching efforts to protect the citizenship rights of Israeli Arabs, press for religious pluralism among the non-Orthodox Jewish population, and even introduce countercultural attitudes toward drug use and sexuality. With these efforts, American Jews internationalized their embrace of Black Power, applying its lessons to an entirely different political system, and one that, by definition, is supposed to guarantee the rights of its Jews.

During a 1968 meeting of the World Union of Progressive Judaism in Jerusalem, for example, a group of American Reform movement Jews brought U.S.-based religious pluralism ideals to Israel, challenging Orthodoxy's control of prayer at the Western Wall. After the group sought the right for men and women to pray together, the Israeli newspaper *Yediot Ahronot* pushed back. "Is this the right time," the paper asked, "to anger [the Orthodox] simply because a Reform convention decided to demonstrate equality of the sexes in no other way than by mixed prayers at the Wall?" Playing on other aspects of the 1960s American scene, the Israeli editors asked, perhaps rhetorically, "And what if tomorrow an organization of hippies should decide to hold a religious orgy at the Wall with LSD and psychedelic music?" Threats of physical violence against participants in what was called a "pray-in" convinced World Union president Rabbi Maurice Eisendrath to cancel the protest action, though only after affirming that his protestors, many of whom had endured attacks as civil rights demonstrators, feared for the safety of innocent bystanders.[42]

Sometimes the introduction of American Jewish culture didn't play so well in the Jewish homeland, as young Jews confused their American identity markers with their Jewish ones. Only in Israel, it seems, could they have seen the difference. Reflecting on the cultural influences of visiting American Jewish students, the journalist Helen Epstein observed, "The group often sticks out like a colorful thumb in the halls and libraries of the universities." She noted their "bell-bottoms, granny glasses, extravagant sportswear, maxis, or stringy cut-down jeans" as well as their "extensive use of Arab and Israeli handicrafts so that the effect is colorful—to put it mildly." The experience of the overseas student, Epstein explained, centered on three symbols: sexual freedom, drugs and the drug culture, and political activism.[43]

The writer recalled the experience of an Israeli sociology student who, critical of the political immaturity of the American Jewish students, offered with a laugh: "From Vietnam they run away, but to start demonstrations here they're ready." The Israeli, in a searing critique, noted, "They can't even argue with me in Hebrew and yet they think they can analyze the situation here better than I can." By translating "the Israeli reality into New Left terminology," the local student explained, Americans "don't understand that the situation here cannot be judged by the criteria of another country. The overseas student is terribly naive about security needs here." In her estimation, "It's better not to talk about it at all with him."[44]

Finally, oppressed Israeli Jews leveraged the Black Power movement to advance their own efforts for equality in the Jewish homeland. As was the case in a number of domestic political movements in 1960s America, the rise of identity politics in the United States reached beyond the nation's borders. Dissidents throughout Eastern Europe, for example, called on the American youth protests of the 1960s as an inspiration in their own campaign for freedom. When oppressed Jews in Israel learned of the strategy and tactics of the Black Panther movement in the United States, they went to work.[45]

In 1971, a group of Israelis formed their own Black Panthers to protest Ashkenazi discrimination against Mizrahi Jews. As the group's founder Charlie Bitton reflected, "A wave of revolt was washing over the West in those days; the anti-war movement and the struggle of blacks in America."

In response, the Black Panthers issued a manifesto demanding free public education from elementary school through the university as well as reform in wages to challenge the economic divide between the more affluent Ashkenazi workers and those from poorer Sephardi and Mizrahi backgrounds. The group, which existed from March 1971 until October 1973, demanded equal partnership in Israeli society. "We refuse to accept our condition as a 'fact of life' and we won't be satisfied with a small sliver of the national pie," Bitton affirmed. "We demand to be equal partners in deciding how to divide that pie."[46]

The anti-Zionist proclamations of many in the Black Power movement as well as the critique those positions inspired among American Jewish leaders masked a deeper symmetry between black and Jewish nationalist identities in the United States. On the surface, Black Power's critique of the Zionist project as a colonialist exercise pit onetime allies against each other. The consensus-era approach of Dr. King and others gave way to a new era of grassroots activism that paralleled the experiences of Palestinian Arabs with the systemic racism suffered by African Americans in the United States. In the reformulation of leftist politics in the era of Black Power and the New Left, American Jews crafted new ways of expressing an old alliance.

Epilogue

On August 1, 2015, the Union of Reform Judaism (URJ) joined the NAACP on a six-week, 860-mile march from Selma, Alabama, to the nation's capital in Washington, D.C. Alarmed by the growing federal government's accelerating retreat on the issue of voting rights, protestors structured their civil rights action to recall the famed Selma to Montgomery march that helped pressure Congress to pass the Voting Rights Act of 1965. As Rabbi Jonah Dov Pesner, director of the Reform movement's Religious Action Center, explained, the march sought to demonstrate "to our nation's leaders that Americans from a diverse array of faiths and backgrounds share a commitment to racial justice and that it is past time for passage of legislation that will help bring the United States closer to its founding ideals of equality of all."[1]

In the half century since the first Selma march, Reform-movement Jewish leaders could cite an impressive record of activism. Kivie Kaplan, a national vice president in the Reform movement, served as president of the NAACP from 1966 until his death in 1975. Both the Civil Rights Act of 1964 and the Voting Rights Act of 1965 were written in the conference room of the Reform movement's Religious Action Center (RAC) in Washington, D.C. In the 1980s and 1990s, activists in the RAC convened gatherings that led to drafts of the Americans with Disabilities Act, an extension of the Voting Rights Act, the Japanese American Redress Act, the Civil Rights Restoration Act, amendments to the Fair Housing Act, and the Civil Rights Act of 1991.[2]

The prophetic Jewish mandate for social justice emerged as well when the Southern Poverty Law Center dedicated its Civil Rights Memorial in 1989. Its architect and designer, Maya Lin, creator of the Vietnam Veterans

Memorial in Washington, D.C., anchored her new project by paraphrasing one of Dr. King's favorite biblical passages: "We will not be satisfied until justice rolls down like waters and righteousness like a mighty stream." This quotation, originally from the book of Amos, signaled a continuing recognition of Judaism's contribution to civil rights work. Whether citing the book of Deuteronomy's mandate "justice, justice you shall pursue" or invoking the increasingly popular twenty-first-century formulation of the phrase "tikkun olam" to signify the Jewish mandate to repair a broken world, congregational rabbis have continued to call on their sacred texts to honor a generations-old legacy of Jewish support for African American racial equality.

More than two hundred rabbis and congregational leaders answered the call to march again from Selma, enduring the hot and humid August weather of the American South to demonstrate their collective commitment to racial justice. They packed up Torah scrolls from their home congregations, ready to relive Rabbi Abraham Joshua Heschel's well-known description of the 1965 Selma march: "I felt my feet were praying." By celebrating the conclusion of their social justice action in Washington, D.C., these two historic national groups brought back memories of the August 1963 March on Washington for Jobs and Freedom, where Rabbi Joachim Prinz, president of the American Jewish Congress and a refugee from Nazi persecution, offered his reflections just before Dr. King delivered his "I Have a Dream" speech. On this twenty-first-century march from Selma, "America's Journey for Justice," Jewish religious leaders could affirm their community's historic support for racial justice causes.

On Facebook, Instagram, and other social media outlets, the contemporary marchers posted iconic photos of African Americans side by side with Jews, joined together by the Torah. Friends, colleagues, and congregants could "like" the images, share them on their own social networks, and live vicariously through the passion and dedication of their religious leaders. For at least one fleeting moment, twenty-first-century rabbis acted out their own version of Heschel, proclaiming in their photo captions that they, like the venerated rabbi, prayed with their feet. Just as an earlier generation of rabbis left their home congregations in the North in order to bring national attention to racial injustice in the South, they marched too, bringing home powerful memories, stories to tell, and certainly a High Holiday sermon or two for their congregants' reflection.

The impressive grassroots Jewish support for America's Journey for Justice aligned with an early American Jewish civil rights–era historiography that celebrated Jewish political activism on behalf of the black community. It followed a popular narrative that tended to emphasize the golden age of black-Jewish cooperation in the 1950s and early 1960s just as it skirted the high-profile Black Power–inspired confrontations of the mid-1960s. The Selma to D.C. march offered an opportunity for a new generation of Jewish social activists to walk in the shoes of their predecessors and publicly accept the ongoing mandate of that historic experience.

Many of the rabbi participants in the recent Selma march studied at the Cincinnati campus of the Reform movement's seminary, HUC. On a January 1991 research trip to the nearby American Jewish Archives, it is possible I may have joined a few of them attending a Friday evening interfaith Shabbat service at the city's Temple Sholom honoring the legacy of Dr. Martin Luther King Jr. Congregation leaders invited a local African American preacher, Reverend Edward L. Wheeler, to deliver the sermon that evening to offer inspirational words in memory of the slain civil rights leader. Reverend Wheeler's oratory, delivered in an impressive and charismatic style, celebrated King, his dream for a better America, and the legacy of the black-Jewish alliance that helped end Jim Crow. The African American parishioners in attendance registered support for their religious leader with frequent "halleluyahs" from the pews. The many young rabbinic students, in training to deliver their own sermons, marveled at the pastor's ability to speak, inspire, and transform the sanctuary into a high-energy Dr. King–style oratorical revival.

After the service, the rabbinic students gathered at the oneg Shabbat, reflecting on Reverend Wheeler's words, style, and hope. "I wish we could preach like that," one aspiring rabbi proclaimed, while another hoped her Jewish congregants would show rabbis the same sort of spontaneous vocal support that African American parishioners did for their religious leader. In a narrative constructed from the historiographic self-congratulation of early Jewish civil rights narratives, the Jewish attendees recalled the murders of Jewish civil rights workers Mickey Schwerner and Andrew Goodman even as they forgot to include the name of slain African American activist James Cheney. All too often, Jewish public storytelling about the civil rights movement focused too much on Jewish participation at the expense of grassroots African American leadership and activism. To that end, the rabbinic students boasted of Rabbi Heschel in Selma and Rabbi Prinz at the March on Washington. Most of all, they dreamed of all they could do in their future rabbinates to further King's legacy and count themselves among the Jewish heroes of social justice. In spirit if not literally, America's Journey for Justice offered that opportunity.

Immersed that very day in archival documents that told a very different story of black-Jewish relations than that espoused by Reverend Wheeler and the HUC students, I challenged the soon-to-be rabbis on alternative perspectives of Jewish social justice work. It did not go well. I asked what caused the growth of non-Orthodox Jewish community day schools in the 1970s. The consensus response: an impressive and inspiring Jewish return to tradition. Jewish "white flight" from integrating schools did not enter their equation, nor did the challenges of complex education dynamics precipitated by the northward trajectory of the civil rights movement. Fresh from their year-long study in Jerusalem, a few of the students celebrated their affinity for Jewish nationalism, their kinship with the founding pioneers of the early Zionist movement, and their excitement for a strengthened American Zionism in the post-1967 era. My parallels to the rise of black nationalism in the 1960s failed to garner much support. Suggesting a link between the rise of the Soviet Jewry movement and the end of Jewish civil rights work seemed an affront to the very essence of Jewish social justice values.

Reverend Wheeler entered a Jewish social justice time machine that evening. For him, perhaps, a return to an early 1960s version of the black-Jewish relationship aligned with the goal of an evening celebrating Martin Luther King Jr. He, like my UC Berkeley classmate from Harlem years earlier, certainly knew of the alliance's unraveling. An interfaith and interracial service on Dr. King's birthday weekend would not be the appropriate time or place to speak directly about its demise. Reverend Wheeler navigated a careful path, celebrating a hopeful past while keeping his words centered on the possibility of a hopeful future.

As I engaged my peers that evening, I could only reflect on how their understanding of Jews and social justice reflected my upbringing as well. Their sense of historical memory around Jews and civil rights matched my own understandings growing up in the suburbs of Los Angeles. Even though we engaged in a rather frank conversation that revealed very different understandings of the black-Jewish relationship, I harbored no ill will toward, or disappointment in, their historical memory. In a way, I played the role of the African Student Union member to my rabbinic school peers, challenging accepted narratives and forcing a critical reinterpretation of the black-Jewish relationship. At its most basic, that King commemoration proved an evening of nostalgia . . . though my Jewish brethren didn't realize it.

Although the optics of the Selma to D.C. march tipped toward a reinvention of 1950s social justice activism, the contemporary rabbis bore little resemblance to their rabbinic mentors of an earlier era. Jewish civil rights activists fighting Jim Crow in the 1950s and early 1960s risked power, privilege, and, in some cases, their own physical safety in order to advance the cause of racial equality. For them, confronting segregation brought the real fear of white southern reprisals, whether with fire hoses or cattle prods, or in the case of the Freedom Riders, physical assault and firebombing. Southern-venturing rabbis took their safety into their own hands. Several, including Rabbi Heschel himself, suffered marginalization from peers for their decision to devote so much time and energy to an issue many did not view as central to Jewish life. Southern rabbis, fearful of harming their congregants should their white neighbors take offense, limited their support. Even those northern rabbis who protested in the South understood the dangers of moral absolutism. As University of Chicago interim Hillel director Rabbi Richard Winograd reflected after a Birmingham, Alabama, protest, the moral scale between northern Jewish civil rights supporters and southern Jewish segregationists seemed "very even."[3]

As Rabbi Charles Briskin of Temple Beth-El in San Pedro, California, reflected, "They risked their lives. I risked getting sunburned. They had nobody to protect them. We had a police escort. They were beaten or arrested. We were met by many who honked their horns in support." Briskin understood the temporal nature of his activism. "The moment was fleeting," he explained. "I marched on Monday and was at a board meeting [back home] on Wednesday." Other rabbinic participants left the march with a sense of humility as well, even more aware of the depth of institutional racism and the ways in which their own white privilege insulated them from understanding it. For Briskin, the march inspired him "to look inward before attempting to do more external relationship building, especially with communities of color."[4]

Despite the wide range of rabbinic responses to the march, only the NAACP, as the African American community's longest-standing and most centrist civil rights group, and the URJ, as American Judaism's largest progressive Jewish voice, could make such a civil rights action work. In a time when both Jewish and African American communities had long gone their separate ways, these two historic groups remembered, and in large measure, romanticized, a bygone era. For many of the 2015 march's Jewish participants, the Torah acted as a consensus builder, connecting their own religious authority to the common Judeo-Christian bonds they shared with their African American peers. For some of the march's African American participants, though, the story proved more complex.

Even as a continuing black-Jewish alliance, as expressed in the Selma to D.C. march, brought needed attention to voting rights, it also reflected a flagship civil rights organization struggling with a grassroots push for more activist and less hierarchical leadership. Just twenty-one months after the Selma to D.C. march, the NAACP opted not to renew the contract of its president and CEO, Cornell Brooks. Interracial marches, among other more traditional approaches to civil rights work, did not capture a broad enough segment of the African American community. More and more, populist black resistance to white oppression marginalized organizations such as the NAACP, which appeared increasingly out of touch with the everyday lives of its own constituents. In a statement that reflected its desire to speak more directly to the needs of African Americans in the twenty-first century, the NAACP board announced a "strategic re-envisioning to determine how best to position the organization to confront head-on the many challenges of today's volatile political, media and social climates."[5]

A reframing of the Selma to Washington, D.C., march through the lens of contemporary black-Jewish relations illuminates a much more complex dynamic between the two communities and within American Jewry itself. In the most direct and perhaps humbling reflection, the 2015 rabbinic march through the American South resembled my own walk down Sproul Plaza in 1982. In both instances, hopeful and optimistic Jewish social justice activists sought an alliance across racial lines. Each of us called on Judaism's religious mandate as well as our own sense of justice to inform a hopeful next step in the centuries-long struggle for racial equality. Even though a young black Harlem-educated activist responded differently in twentieth-century Berkeley than older associates of the NAACP did in twenty-first-century Selma, both moments played on a Jewish memory that celebrated the role of white allies and the Jewish community's disproportionate representation among them.

Three different historical events dramatize the changing nature of black-Jewish relations in the contemporary period. In each case, an individual or a group active in an early phase of the black-Jewish alliance reappeared, though with different approaches to civil rights reform, race relations, and the black-Jewish alliance. In one case, a former Martin Luther King Jr. associate, Reverend Jesse Jackson, prompted charges of antisemitism during the 1984 presidential election. In another, the Nation of Islam reemerged on the American Jewish scene. Finally, civil rights activist Andrew Young typified growing African American animus toward Israel and Zionism during his tenure as U.S. ambassador to the United Nations. Collectively, these examples complete an historical arc from the early postwar period described in chapter 1 of this book to the state of black-Jewish relations in the early twenty-first century.

The Reverend Jesse Jackson emerged in the early civil rights movement as one of Dr. Martin Luther King's closest associates. A native of South Carolina, Jackson graduated from Greensboro's North Carolina Agricultural and Technical College in 1964 and soon joined the civil rights movement, participating in the 1965 Selma march. King later picked Jackson to head the Chicago office of the SCLC. Just two years later, he emerged as the SCLC's national leader. After a falling-out with SCLC leaders, Jackson joined with the Reverend Al Sharpton in 1971 to form Operation PUSH (People United to Save/Serve Humanity) before continuing a career that would lead to the national political scene.

In 1983, Jackson declared himself a Democratic candidate for the 1984 presidential election. With surprising popularity, Jackson campaigned through the various state primaries, eventually earning a respectful third-place finish after Gary Hart and Walter Mondale. In a January 1984 interview with the *Washington Post*, though, Jackson referred to Jews as "Hymies" and to New York City as "Hymietown." Jewish leaders demanded an apology, especially after supportive comments from Nation of Islam leader Louis Farrakhan stoked an already raging public relations fire. For American Jews, Jackson's antisemitic comments and his reluctance to disavow Farrakhan only reaffirmed the continuing fissures between blacks and Jews, marking an even more distant relationship between Jews and their onetime allies. Public pressure mounted and in February 1984, Jackson appeared at a Manchester, New Hampshire, synagogue to apologize and seek forgiveness from a group of Jewish leaders gathered to hear him.[6]

The rise and fall of Jesse Jackson in the eyes of American Jews reflected the larger historical trends at play in the 1980s and beyond. Envisioned by many African American civil rights leaders as the heir apparent to Dr. King, Jackson lost credibility among Jews with his antisemitic statements. Jewish allies, critical to his early work in the movement, morphed into stereotypical caricatures for the civil rights leader who once occupied a hallowed place among Jewish social justice activists. Black-Jewish relations in the late twentieth century reflected two communities at odds with one another on a number of social issues, many of which Jackson championed in his various initiatives. In some ways, the fallout over the Hymie and Hymietown comments served as a trailing indicator of an already strained intra-communal relationship.

In similar fashion, relations between the organized Jewish community and the Nation of Islam continued to deteriorate. With the death of Elijah Muhammad in 1975, Wallace Deen Muhammad, Elijah's son, led the organization for a short time before rival Louis Farrakhan took control. Under Farrakhan's leadership, the Nation of Islam stepped up its antisemitism, earning firm rebuke from Jewish organizations that a generation earlier had minimized the negative impact of the NOI's rhetoric. In a consensus era such as the 1950s, Jewish leaders chose to look the other way when the NOI espoused hate speech. In that era, publicizing NOI antisemitism offered an unwanted platform to a group that Jewish leaders sought to marginalize.

By the 1980s, though, Farrakhan's continuing campaign against Jews evinced strong pushback. In 1984, Farrakhan remarked, "The Jews don't like Farrakhan, so they call me Hitler. Well, that's a good name. Hitler was a very great man." At a 1985 meeting of the Nation of Islam at Madison Square Garden in New York City, Farrakhan proclaimed, in reference to Jews, "And don't you forget, when it's God who puts you in the ovens, it's forever." In 1991, the NOI's Research Group published *The Secret Relationship Between Blacks and Jews*, accusing Jews of disproportionate participation in the slave trade. Four years later, Farrakhan called for a Million Man March in Washington, D.C. Although the march attracted only about half the intended number, it included participation by such civil rights luminaries as Rosa Parks and Jesse Jackson. Dr. King's son Martin Luther King III attended, as did Professor Cornel West.[7]

The Jewish communal reaction to the Nation of Islam could not have been more different at the turn of the twenty-first century than it had been in the early postwar period. While Jewish leaders fought to protect the religious freedom of black Muslim inmates in the 1950s and marginalized NOI antisemitic rhetoric in the 1960s, they placed Farrakhan at the center of their anti-defamation work in the 1980s and beyond. For a time, the Anti-Defamation League's homepage included a section tracking the real-time activity of the NOI leader. In an era when the larger climate between blacks and Jews remained fraught, the NOI, with its anti-white and anti-Jewish stance, emerged as the very antithesis of the organized Jewish community's own work for tolerance and intergroup understanding. Rather than modeling a form of black nationalism that Jews could emulate, Jewish leaders argued that the NOI represented the worst rejection of pluralism and inclusion.

Finally, the pressured resignation of UN Ambassador Andrew Young in 1979 surfaced long-simmering tensions between blacks and Jews on questions of Israel, Zionism, and Palestinian self-determination. In some instances, old-line civil rights leaders rallied in defense of the Jewish state at a time when many African American activists equated Zionism with racism. Civil rights activist Bayard Rustin, for example, helped form BASIC, Black Americans to Support Israel Committee, in 1975. In a full-page *New York Times* ad, the African American–led Zionist group, which counted famed African American leader A. Philip Randolph among its leaders, took a public stand against the Arab boycott of Israel, reaffirmed American Jews as "the most staunch allies in the struggle for racial justice," and lauded the State of Israel as its region's only nation where "all religions are free and secure in their observance." While BASIC also affirmed the right of Palestinians to self-determination, it rejected "the command of economic blackmailers or of terrorists who would force their own 'solution' at the point of a gun."[8]

The U.S. government shared the fundamental premise of BASIC's statement, supporting the State of Israel as the region's only democracy and rejecting the ideology of the Palestine Liberation Organization, a group formed by Yasser Arafat in 1964 and soon recognized by much of the world as the "sole legitimate representative of the Palestinian people." After a series of terrorist attacks, including airplane hijackings, the massacre of Israeli athletes at the 1972 Munich Olympic Games, and several infiltrations of Israeli towns that led to the deaths of civilians, the U.S. government ordered the diplomatic isolation of the PLO, forbidding envoys from any contact with the group it would officially label a terrorist organization.

The narrative arcs of the early black-Jewish alliance, the question of Palestinian national independence, and the role of the federal government collided in 1977, when former civil rights activist and U.S. Congressman from the state of Georgia, Andrew Young, was appointed by President Jimmy Carter as ambassador to the United Nations. Young, the first African American to serve in that prestigious diplomatic role, represented the golden era of black-Jewish cooperation. In 1964, Young took over leadership of the SCLC, serving as a principal strategist for some of the most important civil rights actions of the movement.

In July 1979, though, Young angered Jewish leaders when he broke diplomatic protocol and met with representatives of the PLO. In what later would be described as the "Andrew Young Affair," the UN ambassador, concerned that the UN would soon issue a formal statement calling for the creation of a Palestinian state, appealed to Arab state leaders to squash the proposal. Deferring to the PLO as the lead organization on the matter, Arab diplomats asked Young to secure the backing of Zehdi Terzi, the PLO's UN representative. Traveling to the home of the Kuwaiti UN ambassador, Young met the PLO leader in violation of his own government's protocol.

Jewish leaders pushed back after Israeli intelligence leaked transcripts of the meeting, which Young did not fully disclose to the State Department. A foreign policy tussle ensued, drawing in larger segments of both the African American and the Jewish American communities. Under pressure, Young resigned his post on August 14, 1979, leading some in the African American community to charge that President Carter in fact had fired the UN ambassador under pressure from Jewish groups.

For some blacks, Young's actions amounted to a brave expression of an African American–inspired foreign policy that valued the rights and needs of persecuted minorities around the world. In a comment that would anticipate the later import of intersectional identity, NAACP head Benjamin L. Hooks said at a special meeting called in the wake of Young's resignation: "Because of our background, heritage, and tradition, there is a natural tendency for many black Americans, historically, to have tremendous sympathy with people who are deprived wherever they are." At the meeting, the NAACP issued a statement "holding up to light the double standard by which Mr. Young has been judged," expressed support for continued African American influence in the development of U.S. foreign policy, and called for continued dialogue with Jewish groups "to lessen the deep polarization which has been worsening between them and African Americans."[9]

For Jews, the affair served as a reminder that the two communities did not share as common a bond nor did they view Jewish nationalism through the same benevolent lens as they did in the Black Power era. According to American Jewish Committee leader Hyman Bookbinder, "The Young Affair has been a painful experience for many of us." He feared it carried "the potential for the emergence of rampant black anti-Semitism because of some of the outrageous things that some blacks have been saying. Some of it is out-and-out anti-Semitism." With those deepening divisions, Bookbinder feared Jews in turn would use the Young Affair as a pretense to walk away from their support of civil rights organizations.[10]

These episodes frame a three-phase historical arc in postwar black-Jewish relations. In the first period of black-Jewish relations, from the mid-1950s until the mid-1960s, leaders from both sides of the racial line presented a public image of intergroup cooperation. Dr. Martin Luther King Jr. welcomed Jews and other white liberals to learn and strategize together. In the second era, timed to coincide with the rise and popularity of the Black Power movement from the mid-1960s until the mid-1970s, both blacks and Jews respected each side's desire to go it alone as Black Power and identity politics reigned. Leaders such as Stokely Carmichael lauded Jewish communal accomplishments to African American audiences while American Zionists borrowed from black nationalists to bolster support of a Jewish state. American Jews now have entered a third phase in their postwar relationship with African American communities. In this most current era that began in the late twentieth century, African Americans realized a critical goal of the Black Power movement: the ability to enter into coalition with whites on a more equal basis. In several high-profile moments, a new generation of black leaders have pushed back against Jewish allies as part of a larger grassroots effort to shake up their own old-line civil rights groups.

In the African American community, organizations such as the NAACP face increasing pressure from a younger generation of blacks unimpressed with both the legal approach of their anchor civil rights organization and its reliance on an interracial strategy that centered on leveraging white allies. Rejecting much of the old-school approach typified by the Selma to D.C. march, African American protestors now confront racism-tinged power structures directly, whether in the form of protesting police brutality in a more sustained grassroots national effort or rallying against offending political figures at all levels of government.

In the contemporary period, white allies face increased scrutiny and at times outright rejection as obstacles to the goal of racial equality. While Dr. King and those of his generation deployed sympathetic whites as a tool to leverage support from mass media as well as from northern liberals, some current-day black activists perceive white participation in their struggle as an invitation to gradualism and paternalism. In earlier years, interracial dialogue and education helped white civil rights workers gain a better understanding of the black experience. Today, the notion that African Americans bear the obligation of teaching whites about their own racism offends a generation of post–Black Power youth who demand that Jews educate themselves about their white privilege before attempting to enter into relationships with people of color. Black activists in this third phase of black-Jewish relations reject outright the Cold War emphasis on cross-cultural education as a social panacea.

Intersectionality

Contemporary black activists also embraced an entirely new approach to intergroup relations based upon the concept of intersectionality. First articulated by Kimberlé Crenshaw in 1989 to describe the complex interaction of racial and gender identity, intersectionality affirms that all people, and especially people of color, possess multiple, overlapping, and sometimes conflicting identities simultaneously. A black woman, for example, faces stereotyping as an African American yet also experiences the social dynamics of her gender. Class differences also can play on the lived experience of an individual, as can one's sexual orientation, age, or any other marker that evinces assumptions about a person.

In the political arena, intersectionality serves as a bonding agent for communities of color. Once a person has explored her or his own intersectional identity, then it becomes easier to understand and empathize with other marginalized people. Oppression of one, to paraphrase King's earlier edict, is oppression of all. In this spirit, African Americans understood the experience of Latino Americans because both suffered, though in different ways, from the same systems of oppression. Intersectionality gifted ethnic and racial minorities kinship bonds that brought them together in a common fight for justice and equality.

While the civil rights movement in the American South sought to bring a regional issue of racial discrimination to the national stage in the early postwar era, intersectional consciousness brings American racism and other forms of discrimination to the international arena in the twenty-first century. In this larger application of intersectional thinking, the forces of capitalism, imperialism, and colonialism act in similar ways on indigenous populations, regardless of country of residence. Communities of color in the United States can understand the experience of marginalized groups around the world because they experience similar treatment at home. In a turnabout from the first phase of the postwar black-Jewish relationship, African American activists now take cause with persecuted minority groups around the world rather than with white Jewish civil rights supporters at home.

Applied to a flashpoint in contemporary black-Jewish relations, intersectional thinking motivates African Americans to rally for the Palestinian cause. In this inversion of interracial alliance of the 1950s and early 1960s, Jews morph from socially conscious progressive advocates for civil rights in the United States to oppressive Zionists depriving the local indigenous population of its right to self-determination in Israel and its occupied territories. In the twenty-first century, black activists experience kinship with Palestinians in the West Bank or Gaza, in contrast to their forebears who made common cause with Jewish civil rights workers in Mississippi or Alabama. In this expression of intersectionality, Palestinians and African Americans join together as the "other," while white America earns rebuke along with the State of Israel and Zionism, who are seen as oppressors.

Cultural Appropriation

Heightened concerns over the appropriation by whites of black (and other communities of color) culture have further complicated black-Jewish relations in the contemporary period. In this affirmation of their own unique contributions to American society, African American activists take offense at those outside their community who leverage black culture for their own benefit. By employing elements of black culture in their lives, whites engage in a form of institutional racism by stealing the cultural property of African Americans and repurposing it for their own use. According to this understanding of cultural interaction, white Americans who employ aspects of a marginalized group's native culture in their own lives disrespect and even weaken that minority's heritage. Sometimes called "cultural misappropriation," this sort of intergroup exchange serves as just another example of racial dominance. To respect African American culture, the argument goes, whites must not usurp it as their own.

Even worse, white-centered reconstruction of black culture moves it so far from its source that it compromises its original meaning. Whites imitating blackness may think they are cool and hip when in fact they are just pretenders who are projecting racial stereotypes for their own perceived social status. At San Francisco State University, for example, a white Jewish man in 2016 who wore his hair in an Afro faced rebuke from an African American woman upset at his usurpation of African American identity. At Pitzer College, a request for white women to abstain from wearing hoop earrings in 2017 started a national conversation about the limits of ethnic exchange. In the twenty-first century, imitation does not always offer the sincerest form of flattery.

The civil rights strategy of Dr. Martin Luther King Jr., if not Stokely Carmichael and Malcolm X, could face scrutiny today from those who interpret these sorts of historic interracial alliances as offensive and racist. In twenty-first-century America, Jews cannot as easily borrow a page from the African American activist handbook. If blacks and Jews played in the same social justice sandbox during the first phase of their alliance, and in separate sandboxes during the second, then those concerned about cultural appropriation would argue that contemporary Jews would have to exit their Black Power–inspired sandbox entirely. If the rise of Black Power proved good for the Jews because it paved the road to heightened

Jewish identity, then contemporary African American activism moved in the opposite direction.

This study celebrates the early postwar years when blacks and Jews boasted of their work together and approaches the Black Power era as one in which Jewish emulation of African American political culture proved not only "good for the Jews" but also a model for other ethnic groups to follow. Jews refashioned their interracial alliance with blacks on an identity-politics model, offering public acknowledgment for the African American activists who inspired it. In this rendition of cultural exchange, I reject the pejorative claim of cultural appropriation, preferring instead to view Jewish emulation of Black Power thinking as a new and mutually beneficial consensus in black-Jewish relations.

Even as the two communities split in several high-profile confrontations during the late 1960s, Jews honored the debt they owed to Black Power–inspired thinking. In their public pronouncements, Jewish leaders credited black nationalists for the gifts they offered American Jews. Similarly, even as blacks pushed back against Zionist ideology as expressed in Israeli policies after the 1967 Six-Day War, African American nationalists still spoke of their respect for the organized Jewish community's ability to thrive in the diaspora and then recreate a national homeland. To apply the contemporary disdain for cultural appropriation to the historical actors in this study would be tantamount to presentism, the historian's sin of inserting current norms into our understanding of the past. Blacks and Jews in the earlier phases of their alliance did not articulate concerns about cultural appropriation. Instead, they rallied around each other according to the political rules of the time.

Black Lives Matter

The rise of the Black Lives Matter (BLM) movement typifies the complex new relationship between African Americans and Jews. At its most basic level, BLM represents a grassroots movement impatient with old-line civil rights organizations. Instead of a formal hierarchical structure, BLM emerged as a loose constellation of activists across the country joined together by a desire to bring the most pressing issues of race and racism to national attention. Created in 2012 after the acquittal of George Zimmerman for the murder of African American Trayvon Martin, BLM proclaims it is "rooted in the experiences of Black people in this country who actively resist our dehumanization" as its leaders demand "a call to action and a response to the virulent anti-Black racism that permeates our society." Rejecting the nationalist calls of an earlier generation of Black Power supporters, BLM affirms it "goes beyond the narrow nationalism that can be prevalent within Black communities," criticizing earlier generations of black civil rights activists who "merely call[ed] on Black people to love Black, live Black and buy Black."[11]

BLM pressed American Jews, once again, into conflict between their support for the fight against racism on the domestic front and their support for the State of Israel on the international scene, reactivating a fifty-year old conflict between the two communities on the question of Jewish nationalism. Tensions with organized Jewish community leaders reached a peak when BLM included anti-Israel positions as a small part of its multi-subject "Vision for Black Lives" platform. Taking aim at both American imperialism and the Zionist movement, BLM authors blasted that "the U.S. justifies and advances the global war on terror via its alliance with Israel and is complicit in the genocide taking place against the Palestinian people."[12]

Immediately, Jewish groups from across the political spectrum condemned the charge of Israeli genocide even as they took care to reaffirm their larger support for black equality. "While we are deeply concerned about the ongoing violence and the human rights violations directed at both Israelis and Palestinians, we believe the terms genocide and apartheid are inaccurate and inappropriate to describe the situation," the National Council of Jewish Women wrote. The Jewish Community Relations Council, the ADL, the URJ, Hillel International, and even T'ruah, a rabbinic organization dedicated to ending Israel's occupation of the West Bank, issued similar critiques. For American Jews, who live in the sometimes-awkward ambivalent space between love of Israel and dedication to racial equality, the BLM pressure test forced them to stake claim. And, in a reflection of the contemporary era's black-Jewish complexity, Jewish leaders struggled to bridge the gap. In large measure, they failed as BLM's accusations of Zionism as a colonial and imperial exercise reigned.[13]

The BLM platform also generated Jewish communal conversation because one of its principal authors, Rachel Dilmer, was born and raised a Jew (though she no longer identifies as Jewish). Dilmer's background focused communal discourse on a Jewish demographic reality largely ignored by communal leaders: the presence as well as marginalization of ethnically diverse Jews in organized Jewish life. Jews of Color (JOC) challenge the black-Jewish dichotomy at its most basic level. What if black is also Jewish? What if Jews are, in fact, black? According to data provided by the San Francisco–based Be'chol Lashon, some 20 percent of American Jews identify in some way as ethnically diverse, even as the overwhelming majority of organized Jewish communal leaders claim white Eastern European origins. According to both the 2002 San Francisco Institute for Jewish and Community Research study and the 2000 National Jewish Population Survey, more than 7 percent of American Jews, totaling some 435,000 people, identify as African American, Asian, Latino, Native American, or mixed race.[14]

To view black-Jewish relations through the lens of African American Jews advances difficult if not painful questions about what constitutes "Jewishness." If Jews during the civil rights movement reached out to blacks in order to benefit "the other," then what does it mean when "the other" is also Jewish? As Ilana Kaufman explained in an Eli Talk viewed more than 12,000 times, "Racism in the Jewish Community: The Uncomfortable Truth," Jews of Color face instant marginalization from their white brethren. Reflecting on the experiences of Tova, a JOC pained by the automatic assumption that she could not be Jewish, Kaufman recounted: "I go to synagogue. My mother is even Jewish. What more can I possibly do to be seen and to be counted and to matter to these people. . . . Not all Jews are white."[15]

In the historiography of black-Jewish relations, scholars, including myself, write with an implicit bias that "others" communities of color as objects, or at best beneficiaries, of (white) Jewish benevolence. We've deprived Jews of Color a platform for articulating the complex intersectional identities that combine one's status as both a Jew and a member of a racial minority. Jews of Color challenge us to ask to what extent Jewish social justice imperatives reflect Jewish whiteness and privilege. How, then, would Jews of Color interpret the recent rabbinic march from Selma? Would those photos of a rabbi, a black, and a Torah need to be rethought? Ilana Kaufman put that very question to the test in the original Selma march. "Have you ever wondered if there were black Jews on the Pettis bridge?" she asked her Eli Talk audience. The question proved rhetorical because, as Kaufman concluded, "the North American Jewish narrative reflects clear distinction between blacks and Jews." For Kaufman, "it is this idea of white as integral to Jewish that deeply informs who and what we imagine when we think about the organized Jewish world."[16]

Fortunately, scholars are devoting increasing attention to a racialized view of American Jewish history. In 2007, Melanie Kaye/Kantrowitz published *The Colors of Jews: Racial Politics and Radical Diasporism*. In 2016, Michael Scott Alexander and Bruce D. Haynes edited a special edition of *American Jewish History* titled "The Color Issue" that included articles on the experiences of Indian Jews in Toronto, Sammy Davis Jr., black and Jewish language, the rise of Jewish "ethnoburbs" in twentieth-century Los Angeles, and Jews of Color in North America. Tabletmag.com has reported as well on Jews of Color. The website for Be'chol Lashon includes links to numerous books, articles, and surveys about Jews of Color in the United States and around the world.[17]

At the grassroots level, Jews of Color organized a national convention in New York City in May 2016 and spoke about historical and systemic racism in Jewish communal life, learned how to build "a powerful racial justice movement as JOCs," and offered a special roundtable for JOC rabbis and rabbinic students. In a session related to the themes of this book and its epilogue, participants learned about "creating lasting diversity in American synagogues" that went "beyond the MLK Shabbat & Freedom Seder." The future of the black-Jewish relationship, then, demands both a fundamental reevaluation of its past as well as a self-reflective and critical examination of its current demographics.[18]

If Jewishness is understood in its racial as well as its religious complexity, then an historiographic school can emerge that will upend even our most basic prevailing assumptions. In the first phase of the postwar black-Jewish relationship, the two differing racial communities integrated in a common fight for racial equality. In the second era of black-Jewish relations, the groups desegregated under the banner of identity politics, each advocating its own distinct agenda. In the third and most current period, deeper awareness of intersectional identities recognizes that blacks and Jews can in fact be one and the same. A new formulation of black-Jewish consensus, understood through the lens of Jews of Color, would undermine the whole notion of reaching across a racial divide.

When black Jews are acknowledged, it forces scholars to reinterpret historical causation at its most basic level. When viewed through the lens of a Jew of Color, how much of Jewish support for civil rights in the 1950s proved a reflection of Jews as whites? How much did Jewish affinity for Black Power demonstrate an affirmation of African American political culture more than a Jewish ethnic revival? How can a new intersectional understanding of Jews of Color inspire scholars to rethink an alliance typically understood as interracial? In the Selma to D.C. march, then, what story would those social media images have told if there had been only one person, an African American Jew, holding a Torah and marching for voters' rights? To reinterpret a word that has come to define the civil rights movement, how would that sort of "integration" force a retelling of the black-Jewish relationship and a reappraisal of what "good for the Jews" means?

ADL	Anti-Defamation League
AIM	American Indian Movement
AJC	American Jewish Committee
AJCongress	American Jewish Congress
AJCSJ	American Jewish Conference on Soviet Jewry
ASU	African Student Union
BASIC	Black Americans to Support Israel Committee
BLM	Black Lives Matter
BPP	Black Panther Party
CCAR	Central Conference of American Rabbis
CCSA	Cleveland Committee on Soviet Anti-Semitism
CJFWF	Council of Jewish Federations and Welfare Funds
CORE	Congress of Racial Equality
HLP	House of Love and Prayer
HUC	Hebrew Union College-Jewish Institute of Religion
JCRC	Jewish Community Relations Council
JDL	Jewish Defense League
JEC	Jewish Education Coalition
JLC	Jewish Labor Committee
JLP	Jewish Liberation Project
JOC	Jew of Color
JTS	Jewish Theological Seminary
JUJ	Jews for Urban Justice
NAACP	National Association for the Advancement of Colored People
NCRAC	National Community Relations Advisory Council
NCSY	National Council of Synagogue Youth
NJCRAC	National Jewish Community Relations Advisory Council
NOI	Nation of Islam
PUSH	People United to Save/Serve Humanity
RAC	Religious Action Center
SCA	Synagogue Council of America
SCLC	Southern Christian Leadership Council
SDS	Students for a Democratic Society
SNCC	Student Nonviolent Coordinating Committee (later Student National Coordinating Committee)

SSSJ	Student Struggle for Soviet Jewry
UAHC	Union of American Hebrew Congregations
UJS	Union of Jewish Students
UNIA	United Negro Improvement Association
URJ	Union for Reform Judaism

Preface

1. "'Is It Good for the Jews?' Liberalism and the Challenges of the 1960s," appearing in Marc Lee Raphael, editor, *Jewishness and the World of "Difference" in the United States* (Williamsburg, Va.: William and Mary Press, 2001).

2. "'Until You Can Fight as Generals': American Jews and Black Nationalism, 1958–1964," appearing in Barry Glassner and Hilary Taub Lachoff, *The Jewish Role in American Life: An Annual Review*, vol. 3 (Los Angeles: University of Southern California, 2004); "The Other War: American Jews, Lyndon Johnson, and the Great Society," *American Jewish History* 89:4 (December 2001); *California Jews*, co-editor with Ava Kahn (Waltham, Mass.: Brandeis University Press, 2003).

Introduction: Is It Good for the Jews? Black Power and the 1960s

1. Norman Podhoretz, "Is It Good for the Jews?," *Commentary* 53:2 (February 1972): 7.

2. Ibid.

3. Ibid. See also Norman Podhoretz, *Why Are Jews Liberals?* (New York: Doubleday, 2009).

4. Will Herberg, *Protestant, Catholic, Jew: An Essay in American Religious Sociology* (Garden City, N.Y.: Doubleday, 1955). "Religious Holiday Observances in the Public Schools," National Community Relations Advisory Council, Report of the Eighth Plenary Session, May 25–28, 1950, 24, 32–33, 35. Manuscript Collection 202, Box 51, Folder 3, AJA.

5. See Murray Friedman, *What Went Wrong? The Creation and Collapse of the Black-Jewish Alliance* (New York: Free Press, 1995); Maurianne Adams and John H. Bracey, *Strangers and Neighbors: Relations between Blacks and Jews in the United States* (Amherst: University of Massachusetts Press, 1999); Eric J. Sundquist, *Strangers in the Land: Blacks, Jews, Post-Holocaust America* (Cambridge, Mass.: Belknap Press, 2005); William M. Phillips, *An Unillustrious Alliance: The African American and Jewish American Communities*, Contributions in Afro-American and African Studies (New York: Greenwood Press, 1991); Stuart Svonkin, *Jews against Prejudice: American Jews and the Fight for Civil Liberties*, Columbia Studies in Contemporary American History (New York: Columbia University Press, 1997). For an examination of black-Jewish relations in the early twentieth century, see Hasia R. Diner, *In the Almost Promised Land: American Jews and Blacks, 1915–1935* (Baltimore, Md.: Johns Hopkins University Press, 1995).

6. See Marianne Rachel Sanua, *Let Us Prove Strong: The American Jewish Committee, 1945–2006*, Brandeis Series in American Jewish History, Culture, and Life (Waltham, Mass.: Brandeis University Press, 2007).

7. Friedman, *What Went Wrong?*, 136. See, for example, Seth Forman, *Blacks in the Jewish Mind: A Crisis of Liberalism* (New York: New York University Press, 1998); Jonathan Kaufman, *Broken Alliance: The Turbulent Times between Blacks and Jews in America* (New York: Scribner, 1988); Svonkin, *Jews against Prejudice*.

8. See, for example, Debra Schultz, *Going South: Jewish Women in the Civil Rights Movement* (New York: New York University Press, 2001); Raymond Mohl, *South of the South: Jewish Activists and the Civil Rights Movement in Miami, 1945–1960* (Gainesville: University Press of Florida, 2003); Clive Webb, *Fight against Fear: Southern Jews and Black Civil Rights* (Athens: University of Georgia Press, 2001); Mark K. Bauman and Berkley Kalin, *The Quiet Voices: Southern Rabbis and Black Civil Rights, 1880s to 1990s*, Judaic Studies Series (Tuscaloosa: University of Alabama Press, 1997). See also Michael E. Staub, *Torn at the Roots: The Crisis of Jewish Liberalism in Postwar America*, Religion and American Culture (New York: Columbia University Press, 2002); Jill Jacobs, *There Shall Be No Needy: Pursuing Social Justice through Jewish Law and Tradition* (Woodstock, Vt.: Jewish Lights, 2009); Cheryl Lynn Greenberg, *Troubling the Waters: Black-Jewish Relations in the American Century*, Politics and Society in Twentieth-Century America (Princeton, N.J.: Princeton University Press, 2006); Deborah Dash Moore, *American Jewish Identity Politics* (Ann Arbor: University of Michigan Press, 2008).

9. American Jewish Committee, "Who Is a Jew?," November 1960, Collection 347.4.124, Box 2, Folder "May 1960–Nov. 1960," 7, YIVO Institute for Jewish Research, New York. See Eli Lederhendler, *New York Jews and the Decline of Urban Ethnicity, 1950–1970*, Modern Jewish History (Syracuse, N.Y.: Syracuse University Press, 2001).

10. See Clayborne Carson, *In Struggle: SNCC and the Black Awakening of the 1960s* (Cambridge, Mass.: Harvard University Press, 1981). Friedman, *What Went Wrong?*; Forman, *Blacks in the Jewish Mind*; Phillips, *An Unillustrious Alliance*.

11. Leonard J. Fein, "Liberalism and American Jews," *Midstream*, 19:8 (October 1973): 3; Harold Schulweis, "The New Jewish Right," *Moment* 1:1 (May/June 1975): 58, 57.

12. Gordon Lafter, "Universalism and Particularism," in David Theo Goldberg and Michael Krausz, *Jewish Identity* (Philadelphia: Temple University Press, 1993): 180.

13. Ibid., 34.

14. Earl Raab, "The Black Revolution and the Jewish Question," *Commentary* 42:1 (January 1969): 32. Rabbi Balfour Brickner, "If I Am Not for Myself . . . Particularism and Universalism in American Jewish Life Today," Papers from the Plenary Session of the Union of American Hebrew Congregations, June 28–July 2, 1972, Los Angeles, I-172, Box 12, Folder "Plenary Session, 1972," 9, American Jewish Historical Society, New York.

15. See, for example, Carlos Muñoz, *Youth, Identity, Power: The Chicano Movement*, rev. and exp. ed. (New York: Verso, 2007); Peter Matthiessen, *In the Spirit of Crazy Horse* (New York: Penguin, 1992); Sara M. Evans, *Born for Liberty: A History of Women in America* (New York: Free Press, 1989). For a synthetic treatment, see John David Skrentny, *The Minority Rights Revolution* (Cambridge, Mass.: Belknap Press, 2002); Van Gosse and Richard R. Moser, *The World the Sixties Made: Politics and Culture in Recent America*, Critical Perspectives on the Past (Philadelphia: Temple University Press, 2003). For an overview of the 1960s, see Todd Gitlin, *The Sixties: Years of Hope, Days of Rage* (New York: Bantam, 1987); Edward P. Morgan, *The '60s Experience: Hard Lessons about Modern America* (Philadelphia: Temple University Press, 1991).

16. Leonard Fein, "The Negro Revolution and the Jewish Community," talk given on March 12, 1969, at a Synagogue Council of America–sponsored conference at Columbia University, Manuscript Collection 294, Box 25, Folder 10, American Jewish Archives, Cincinnati: 14.

17. "Commandments for Our Day," delivered Shavuot morning, May 30, 1971, in Dov Peretz Elkins, *A Tradition Reborn: Sermons and Essays on Liberal Judaism* (South Brunswick, N.J.: A. S. Barnes, 1973): 69–70.

18. Gal Beckerman, *When They Come for Us, We'll Be Gone: The Epic Struggle to Save Soviet Jewry* (Boston: Houghton Mifflin Harcourt, 2010), 151; William Novak and Robert Goldman, "The Rise of the Jewish Student Press," *Conservative Judaism* 25:2 (Winter 1970): 5.

19. Forman, *Blacks in the Jewish Mind*, 193. See Paula E. Hyman, "Ezrat Nashim and the Emergence of a New Jewish Feminism," in Robert M. Seltzer and Norman J. Cohen, *The Americanization of the Jews*, Reappraisals in Jewish Social and Intellectual History (New York: New York University Press, 1995). For more on the history of Orthodoxy in the United States, see Jeffrey S. Gurock, *Orthodox Jews in America*, The Modern Jewish Experience (Bloomington: Indiana University Press, 2009).

20. See, for example, Mark A. Raider, *The Emergence of American Zionism* (New York: New York University Press, 1998).

21. See Beckerman, *When They Come for Us, We'll Be Gone*.

22. Meir Kahane, *The Story of the Jewish Defense League*, 2nd ed. (New York: Institute for Publication of the Writings of Rabbi Meir Kahane, 2000).

23. Raab, "The Black Revolution and the Jewish Question." Fein, "The New Jewish Politics," 35. Schulweis, "The New Jewish Right," 59. Bernard G. Richards, "Is It Good for Jews?," *Congress Bi-Weekly* (February 6, 1970): 15.

24. Papers of Robert Perlzweig, Collection 70/10, Western States Jewish History Archives, Berkeley, California. Jerry Hochbaum, "The Orthodox Community and the Urban Crisis," *Tradition* 10:3 (Spring 1969): 43. Podhoretz, "Is It Good for the Jews?," 7. As late as the contested 2000 presidential election between George W. Bush and Al Gore, the *Jewish Journal* of Los Angeles posted the self-interested question on its cover.

25. See, as well, Hillel Levine and Lawrence Harmon, *The Death of an American Jewish Community: A Tragedy of Good Intentions* (New York: Free Press, 1992). Edward S. Shapiro, *Crown Heights: Blacks, Jews, and the 1991 Brooklyn Riot*, Brandeis Series in American Jewish History, Culture, and Life (Waltham, Mass.: Brandeis University Press, 2006). Jane Anna Gordon, *Why They Couldn't Wait: A Critique of the Black-Jewish Conflict over Community Control in Ocean Hill-Brownsville, 1967-1971* (New York: RoutledgeFalmer, 2001). Sanua, *Let Us Prove Strong*, 169–171.

26. Sundquist, *Strangers in the Land*, 312, 316.

27. Forman, *Blacks in the Jewish Mind*, 136. Jonathan Krasner includes the topic of Black Power and the Jews in his larger treatment of Brandeis University president Morris Abram, in Jonathan Krasner, "Seventeen Months in the President's Chair: Morris Abram, Black-Jewish Relations and the Anatomy of a Failed Presidency," *American Jewish History* 99:1 (January 2015): 27–78.

28. C. L. Greenberg, *Troubling the Waters*, 221–222.

29. Phillips, *An Unillustrious Alliance*, 100, 101, 103, 106.

30. Waldo E. Martin Jr., "Nation Time!," in Jack Salzman and Cornel West, *Struggles in the Promised Land: Toward a History of Black-Jewish Relations in the United States* (New York: Oxford University Press, 1997), 352, 351, 344. Joshua M. Zeitz, *White Ethnic New York: Jews, Catholics and the Shaping of Postwar Politics* (Chapel Hill: University of North Carolina Press, 2007). Matthew Frye Jacobson, *Roots Too: White Ethnic Revival in Post-Civil Rights America* (Cambridge, Mass.: Harvard University Press, 2006). Clayborne Carson, "Black-Jewish Universalism in the Era of Identity Politics," in Salzman and West, *Struggles in the Promised Land*, 183.

31. Harold Isaacs has made a similar argument for the black revival in a 1962 *Commentary* article, asserting, "American Negroes have been rediscovering Africa. In doing so, they are not regaining their identity as long-lost Africans but reshaping their identity as Americans." Harold R. Isaacs, "Integration and the Negro Mood," *Commentary* 34:6 (December 1962). Isaacs is affiliated with the Center for International Studies at MIT.

32. Muñoz, *Youth, Identity, Power*. Kenneth S. Stern, *Loud Hawk: The United States versus the American Indian Movement* (Norman: University of Oklahoma Press, 2002).

33. Matusow, *The Unraveling of America*. Theodore J. Lowi, *The End of Liberalism: The Second Republic of the United States*, 2nd ed. (New York: W.W. Norton, 2010). Bruce J. Schulman, *Lyndon B. Johnson and American Liberalism: A Brief Biography with Documents*, 2nd ed., The Bedford Series in History and Culture (New York: Palgrave Macmillan, 2007). Robert Self, *All in the Family: The Realignment of American Democracy Since the 1960s* (New York: Farrar, Straus and Giroux, 2013).

34. See, for example, Nancy Cott, *The Grounding of Modern Feminism* (New Haven, Conn.: Yale University Press, 1989); Andrew Aoki and Okiyoshi Takeda, *Asian American Politics* (Malden, Mass.: Wiley, 2009); Carolyn Wong, *Voting Together:*

Intergenerational Politics and Civic Engagement Among Hmong Americans (Stanford, Calif.: Stanford University Press, 2017).

35. Carson, "Black-Jewish Universalism," 186–187.

36. Malcolm X as told to Alex Haley, *The Autobiography of Malcolm X* (New York: Random House, 1987), 433.

Chapter 1: Jews and Black Nationalism in the 1950s

1. Friedman, *What Went Wrong?*, 56.

2. For more on the civil rights movement, see William H. Chafe, *Civilities and Civil Rights: Greensboro, North Carolina and the Black Struggle for Freedom* (New York: Oxford University Press, 1981); Henry Hampton and Steven Fayer, *Voices of Freedom: An Oral History of the Civil Rights Movement from the 1950s through the 1980s* (New York: Bantam, 1990); Harvard Sitkoff, *The Struggle for Black Equality: 1954–1980* (New York: Hill and Wang, 1981).

3. Gerald Sorin, *Tradition Transformed: The Jewish Experience in America*, The American Moment (Baltimore, Md.: Johns Hopkins University Press, 1997), 211; M. Friedman, *What Went Wrong*, 192.

4. Editorial, *The Crisis*, February 1958, 105.

5. "Religious Holiday Observances in the Public Schools, National Community Relations Advisory Council, Report of the Eighth Plenary Session," May 25–28, 1950, MS 202, Box 50, Folder 4, 24, 32–33, 35, American Jewish Archives, Cincinnati.

6. American Jewish Committee, Collection 347.4107.118, Box 2, Folder "Community Relations," 1, YIVO Institute for Jewish Research, New York.

7. Ibid., 1, 2.

8. Ibid., 2.

9. Minutes, Executive Committee Meeting, January 19, 1960, American Jewish Congress, Collection I-77, Box 6, "Executive Committee Minutes, 1960," 2, American Jewish Historical Society, New York.

10. Ibid.

11. Nathan Edelstein, "Jewish Relationship with the Emerging Negro Community in the North," presented to the National Community Relations Advisory Council, June 23, 1960, Collection I-77, Box 45, Folder "Jewish Relationship with the Emerging Negro Community in the North," 11, 6, 2, American Jewish Historical Society, New York.

12. Press Release, American Jewish Committee Institute of Human Relations, March 20, 1961, Collection 347.4.124, Box 3, Folder "Dec 1960–May 1961," 2–3, YIVO Institute for Jewish Research, New York.

13. American Jewish Congress and the NAACP, *Civil Rights in the United States in 1951: A Balance Sheet of Group Relations* (New York: American Jewish Congress and the

NAACP, 1951), 11. Herman Kaplow, "Jewish Federations, Their Agencies and the Integration Struggle," 3, Special Collections Box A-89 247, Klau Library, Hebrew Union College, Cincinnati.

14. Marc Dollinger, *Quest for Inclusion: Jews and Liberalism in Modern America* (Princeton, N.J.: Princeton University Press, 2000), 184. Edelstein, "Jewish Relationship with the Emerging Negro Community in the North," 5, 7.

15. Isaacs, "Integration and the Negro Mood."

16. Address of Dr. Joachim Prinz, at the National Biennial Convention of the American Jewish Congress, May 26, 1960, New York City, Collection I-77, Box 9, 1, American Jewish Historical Society, New York.

17. Statement of Dr. Kenneth B. Clark, at the National Biennial Convention of the American Jewish Congress, May 27, 1960, New York City, Collection I-77, Box 9, "Dr. Kenneth B. Clark Speech," 3, 2, American Jewish Historical Society, New York.

18. Ibid., 2.

19. Ibid., 3.

20. "Relations Between Jews and other Minority Groups in Big Cities," Proceedings of the Fifty-Third Annual Meeting, April 22–24, 1960," American Jewish Committee, New York, Institute of Human Relations, 14. Julian Mayfield, "Challenge to Negro Leadership: The Case of Robert Williams," *Commentary* 31:4 (April 1961): 297.

21. Tom Brooks, Associate Editor, *Current*, "Negro Militants, Jewish Liberals, and the Unions," *Commentary* 32:3 (September 1961): 215, 209, 216. Isaacs, "Integration and the Negro Mood."

22. Memo from Charles F. Wittenstein to Dr. S. Andhil Fineberg, "Southern Interagency Conference: Student Nonviolent Coordinating Committee; ADL," November 14, 1962, 3, Collection CSD 25–26, Box 4, Folder "Negroes—Misc.," YIVO Institute for Jewish Research, New York.

23. Tynetta Muhammad, "Nation of Islam in America: A Nation of Beauty and Peace," Nation of Islam website, March 28, 1996, www.noi.org/noi-history.

24. Forman, *Blacks in the Jewish Mind*, 71. Nation of Islam, *The Secret Relationship between Blacks and Jews*, vol. 1 (New York: Latimer Associates, 1991).

25. Friedman, *What Went Wrong?*, 77. Forman, *Blacks in the Jewish Mind*, 70.

26. Memo from Sam Kaminsky to David Danzig, American Jewish Committee, YIVO Institute for Jewish Research, New York, 1. Sam Kaminsky noted, for example, "a possible growth of anti-Semitism among Negroes under the impact of increased promotion of 'black supremacy' movements, such as the Temple of Islam" as well as "rising tensions over desegregation and worsening slum conditions suffered by Negro communities in urban centers." Forman, *Blacks in the Jewish Mind*, 74.

27. Memo from Arnold Forster to ADL Regional Offices, August 25, 1959, 1, American Jewish Archives, Cincinnati.

28. Edelstein, "Jewish Relationship with the Emerging Negro Community in the North," 3, 6, 1–2.

29. Shad Polier, "July 7, 1961, Newsletter," Center for Jewish History, I-77, 3, Box 195, American Jewish Historical Society, New York.

30. Samuel Kaminsky, "Elijah Muhammad and the Muslim in Newark," 2, Collection 347.4107.88, Folder "Anti-Semitism, Muslims, Elijah Muhammad," YIVO Institute for Jewish Research, New York.

31. Memo from Samuel Kaminsky to Dave Danzig, 1.

32. Ibid.

33. Ibid.

34. Ibid.

35. Walter D. Chambers, "Confidential Report, Muslim Meeting-September 8, 1959," 2. Memo from Samuel Kaminsky to Dave Danzig, 1.

36. Isaacs, "Integration and the Negro Mood," 490. William Brink and Louis Harris, "Negroes Assess Negro Organizations," in *The Negro Revolution in America* (New York: Simon and Schuster, 1963), 117. The data were based on a nationwide survey by *Newsweek*.

37. Editorial Staff, *Midstream*, Spring 1962, 26. American Jewish Committee, "Report of the New York Chapter for the Period March 1, 1962, to May 31, 1962," Collection 347.4.124, Box 3, Folder "Apr–Aug '62," YIVO Institute for Jewish Research, New York.

38. American Jewish Congress, "Newsletter 1962," Collection I-77, Box 195, 3, American Jewish History Society, New York.

Chapter 2: Jews, Group Status, and the Great Society

1. Lyndon B. Johnson, "To Fulfill These Rights," Commencement Address at Howard University, June 4, 1965, Washington, D.C., in *Public Papers of the Presidents of the United States: Lyndon B. Johnson, 1965*, vol. 1 (Washington, D.C.: Government Printing Office, 1965).

2. Louis Sandy Maisel et al., *Jews in American Politics: Essays* (Lanham, Md.: Rowman and Littlefield, 2004), 153.

3. Johnson, "To Fulfill These Rights."

4. Matusow, *The Unraveling of America*, 220.

5. George Gallup, *The Gallup Poll: Public Opinion, 1935–1971*, vol. 3 (New York, 1972), 1885, in Steve Goodman, "Jews and American Public Opinion as Reflected in the Gallup Poll, 1935–1971," 32, unpublished paper, May 24, 1974, Small Collection, SC-2419, Box 1127, American Jewish Archives, Cincinnati. American Jewish Congress Resolution on War on Poverty, Adopted at Its Biennial Convention, April 14–19, 1964, 1, I-77, Box 11, American Jewish Historical Society, New York. Among white Protestants, 23.4 percent considered civil rights reform "too slow." Allen S. Maller, "Notes on California Jews' Political Attitudes, 1968," *Jewish Social Studies* 33 (1971): 161–163.

6. Harold I. Saperstein and Marc Saperstein, *Witness from the Pulpit: Topical*

Sermons, 1933–1980 (Lanham, Md.: Lexington Books, 2000), 238; Rabbi Richard G. Hirsch, "The Eradication of Poverty: A Moral Imperative," March 2, 1965, 3–4, Collection I-69, Box 542, Folder "Rabbi Richard Hirsch," American Jewish Historical Society, New York.

7. Henry Cohen, *Justice, Justice: A Jewish View of the Black Revolution*, rev. ed., Union Graded Series, Commission on Jewish Education of the Union of American Hebrew Congregations and Central Conference of American Rabbis (New York: Union of American Hebrew Congregations, 1969), 87, 82, 21.

8. J. Hochbaum, "The Orthodox Community and the Urban Crisis," 43–44.

9. Ibid.

10. Council of Jewish Federations and Welfare Funds, Inc., Memo, October 17, 1966, 1–2, Collection I-69, Box 386, "CJFWF-GA-1966—Resolutions," American Jewish Historical Society, New York. "Joint Program Plan for Jewish Community Relations, 1980–1981" (New York, 1980), 47, 52, quoted in Philip Bernstein, *To Dwell in Unity: The Jewish Federation Movement in America since 1960* (Philadelphia: Jewish Publication Society of America, 1983), 212. Benjamin R. Epstein, quoted in Naomi Levine and Martin Hochbaum, "The Jewish Poor and the Anti-Poverty Program: A Study of the Economic Opportunity Act, Its Failure to Help the Jewish Poor, and Recommendations for Its Revision So That All of This Nation's Poor May Share More Equitably in Its Program and Assistance," 6, Commission on Urban Affairs, November 1971, American Jewish Congress, New York. Resolution Adopted by 36th General Assembly of the Council of Jewish Federations and Welfare Funds, November 15–19, 1967, "Crisis in the Cities," 1, I-69, Box 389, Folder "CJFWF," American Jewish Historical Society, New York.

11. Gallup, *The Gallup Poll*, 1885, in Goodman, "Jews and American Public Opinion," 32.

12. Theodore Ellenoff, "Memorandum to Members of the Executive Board and Urban Affairs Committee," New York Chapter, American Jewish Committee, March 13, 1968, 2, Collection 347.4.124, Box 4, Folder "Sept. 67–March 68," YIVO.

13. The American Jewish Committee Statement on Poverty, April 29, 1964, American Jewish Committee Archives, CSD 185–190, Box 3, Folder "Poverty," YIVO.

14. H. Cohen, *Justice, Justice*, 68; Newsletter of Shad Polier, August 1, 1963, 2, Folder "Shad Polier Newsletter 1963," I-77, Box 196, American Jewish Historical Society, New York.

15. See Daniel Patrick Moynihan, "The Negro Family: The Case for National Action" (1965), University of Texas website, http://liberalarts.utexas.edu/coretexts/_files/resources/texts/1965%20Moynihan%20Report.pdf. Accessed June 7, 2017.

16. H. Cohen, *Justice, Justice*, 68; Newsletter of Shad Polier, August 1, 1963, 2.

17. Ibid., 77–78.

18. For more on affirmative action, see especially Forman, *Blacks in the Jewish Mind*. See as well Philip F. Rubio, *A History of Affirmative Action, 1619–2000* (Jackson:

University Press of Mississippi, 2001); Ira Katznelson, *When Affirmative Action Was White: An Untold History of Racial Inequality in Twentieth-Century America* (New York: W.W. Norton, 2005); and Jerome A. Chanes, "Affirmative Action: Jewish Ideals, Jewish Interests," and Theodore M. Shaw, "Affirmative Action: African-American and Jewish Perspectives," both in Salzman and West, *Struggles in the Promised Land*.

19. David Danzig, "In Defense of 'Black Power,'" *Commentary* (September 1966): 42.

20. Editorial, "An End to Gradualism," *Congress Bi-Weekly: A Review of Jewish Interests* 30:11 (June 24, 1963): 4.

21. Will Maslow, "Report of the Executive Director to the Biennial National Convention of the American Jewish Congress, May 14–May 19, 1968," Doral Country Club, Miami, Florida, I-77, Box 12, Folder "1968 Report of the Exec. Director," 6, American Jewish Historical Society, New York. "American Jewish Congress Resolution on Human Rights, Adopted at its Biennial Convention, Miami, Florida, May 14–19, 1968," SC Box A-93 116, American Jewish Archives, Cincinnati.

22. H. Cohen, *Justice, Justice*, 87, 82, 81.

23. "Equality NOW!," delivered Yom Kippur morning, October 14, 1967, in Elkins, *A Tradition Reborn*, 96, 97.

24. Ibid., 97.

25. Forman, *Blacks in the Jewish Mind*, 2.

26. William Zebina Ripley, *The Races of Europe: A Sociological Study*, Lowell Institute Lectures (New York: D. Appleton Johnson Reprint Corp., 1899); Madison Grant, *The Passing of the Great Race; or, the Racial Basis of European History* (New York: C. Scribner, 1916), 91. While race and racism had most often been used as a tool to marginalize Jews, historians such as Eric Goldstein have discovered ways in which American Jews have capitalized on the social construction of race to advance Jewish communal interests. See Eric Goldstein, "'Different Blood Flows in Our Veins': Race and Jewish Self-Definition in Late Nineteenth Century America," *American Jewish History* 85 (March 1997): 29–55.

27. For more on Jews and whiteness, see Eric Goldstein, *The Price of Whiteness: Jews, Race, and American Identity* (Princeton, N.J.: Princeton University Press, 2007).

28. Karen Brodkin, *How Jews Became White Folks and What That Says about Race in America* (New Brunswick, N.J.: Rutgers University Press, 1998), 2, 175. David Biale, "The Melting Pot and Beyond: Jews and the Politics of American Identity," in David Biale, Michael Galchinsky, and Susannah Heschel, *Insider/Outsider: American Jews and Multiculturalism* (Berkeley: University of California Press, 1998), 28; George Lipsitz, *The Possessive Investment in Whiteness: How White People Profit from Identity Politics*, rev. and exp. ed. (Philadelphia: Temple University Press, 2006).

29. Levine and Hochbaum, "The Jewish Poor and the Anti-Poverty Program," 33.

30. Ibid., 1, 6, 7, 8, 10, 11, 12, 30, 33, 34, 38, 40–42.

31. Ibid., 1, 7, 8, 10, 11, 12.

32. Minutes of the Meeting of the Executive Board, New York Chapter, the American Jewish Committee, March 7, 1968, 3–4, Archives of the American Jewish Committee, Collection RG 347.4.124, Box 4, Folder "Sept. '67–March '68," YIVO Institute for Jewish Research, New York; "Charge Poverty Program Ignores Whites," *New York Post*, January 31, 1968.

33. Sorin, *Tradition Transformed*, 106. Bernard Rosenberg and Irving Howe, "Are American Jews Turning to the Right?" *Dissent* 21 (Winter 1974): 42. Leonard Dinnerstein, "The President and the Jews," *Reform Judaism* 29:2 (Winter 2000): 20.

34. Michael Levin, "Affirmative Action vs. Jewish Men," Josh Henkin, "The Meretriciousness of Merit: Or, Why Jewish Males Oughtn't Be So Smug," and Alan Freeman and Betty Mensch, "The Misplaced Self-Delusion of Some Jewish Males," *Tikkun* 4:1.

35. Gary Phillip Zola and Marc Dollinger, *American Jewish History: A Primary Source Reader*, Brandeis Series in American Jewish History, Culture, and Life (Waltham, Mass.: Brandeis University Press, 2014), 219–220.

36. Leo Pfeffer, Information Bulletin #26, September 1, 1963, 1, 2, "Quotas, Compensation and Unlawful Demonstrations, Part II," CLSA Reports, American Jewish Congress, I-77, Box 31, Folder "CLSA Report," 1963, American Jewish Historical Society, New York.

37. "Policy Statement of the American Jewish Committee," *Jewish Currents* 24 (1970): 5; Arnold Forster and B'nai B'rith, Anti-Defamation League, *A Measure of Freedom: An Anti-Defamation League Report* (Garden City, N.Y.: Doubleday, 1950), 119; Albert Chernin, quoted in Naomi Levine, "Affirmative Action, Preferential Treatments and Quotas, Papers from the Plenary Session, NJCRAC, June 28–July 2, 1972, Los Angeles," 21, 24; Klau Library, Hebrew Union College, Cincinnati; Bernard Fryshman, *Affirmative Action and Equal Opportunity: An Overview* (New York: Commission on Legislation and Civic Action, Agudath Israel of America, 1976), 6, 9, 14, 26; Letter to the Editor, *New York Times*, quoted in David Petegorsky, *CLSA Reports*, American Jewish Congress, New York.

38. See, for example, Mark Gerson, *The Essential Neoconservative Reader* (Reading, Mass.: Addison Wesley, 1996); Murray Friedman, *The Neoconservative Revolution: Jewish Intellectuals and the Shaping of Public Policy* (Cambridge: Cambridge University Press, 2005); Jonathan Rieder, *Canarsie: The Jews and Italians of Brooklyn against Liberalism* (Cambridge, Mass.: Harvard University Press, 1985); Ruth R. Wisse, *If I Am Not for Myself: The Liberal Betrayal of the Jews* (New York: Free Press, 1992); Irving Kristol, *Neoconservatism: The Autobiography of an Idea* (Chicago: Elephant Paperbacks, 1999); Gerald H. Gamm, *Urban Exodus: Why the Jews Left Boston and the Catholics Stayed* (Cambridge, Mass.: Harvard University Press, 1999).

39. Nathan Glazer, "The Crisis in American Jewry," *Midstream* 16:9 (November 1970): 9. As quoted by Clayborne Carson, "The Politics of Relations between African Americans and Jews," appearing in Paul Berman, *Blacks and Jews: Alliances and*

Arguments (New York: Delacorte Press, 1994), 140. Rieder, *Canarsie: The Jews and Italians of Brooklyn against Liberalism*, 124.

40. Louis Harris and Bert E. Swanson, *Black-Jewish Relations in New York City*, Praeger Special Studies in U.S. Economic and Social Development (New York: Praeger, 1970), Table 9, "Worry about Violence and Safety on Streets: National, 1964–1968," 13, 14.

41. Seventy-four percent of New York City Jews thought the pressures and tensions of living in the city worsened between mid-1968 and mid-1969, compared to 59 percent of non-Jewish whites and 72 percent of "blacklash" non-Jewish whites. Harris and Swanson, *Black-Jewish Relations*, 17, Table 11, "Fear of Racial Violence: National, 1968," 15. In New York City in mid-1969, 68 percent of Jews ages 21–34 felt "uneasy" but it grew to 82 percent for ages 35–49, and 81 percent for ages 50 and over. Harris and Swanson, *Black-Jewish Relations*, Table 13, "Opinion by Age and Education: Fear of Racial Violence Makes You Uneasy," 16. Fein, "The New Jewish Politics," 38.

42. Norman Podhoretz, "Liberalism and the Negro: A Round-Table Discussion," *Commentary* 37:3 (March 1964): 25–26.

43. Ibid.

44. Richard Cohen, "Why We Challenge the Federal Aid to Education Law," 3, American Jewish Congress News, 1, I-77, Box 37, Folder "Church/State 1965 Jan–April," American Jewish Historical Society, New York.

45. Against Federal Aid to Education Bill, AJC Collection, CSD 185–190, Box 2, Folder "Education (Fed. Aid)," YIVO Institute for Jewish Research, New York. R. Cohen, "Why We Challenge the Federal Aid to Education Law," 3. Resolution Adopted by 36th General Assembly of the Council of Jewish Federations and Welfare Funds, November 15–19, 1967, Separation of Church and State, 1, CJFWF, I-69, Box 389, Folder "CJF," American Jewish Historical Society, New York. Statement of Anti-Defamation League of B'nai B'rith on the Elementary and Secondary Education Act of 1965, HR 2362 and S. 370, I-77, Box 37, Folder "Church/State 1965," American Jewish Historical Society, New York. Synagogue Council of America Archives, Box 2, Folder "SCA Plenum Minutes, 1960–1965," Plenum Minutes, 4/14/65, 3, I-68, American Jewish Historical Society, New York. Draft Statement on the Economic Opportunity Act of 1964 from Minutes of Executive Committee Meeting 1/13/65, Synagogue Council of America Archives, Box 2, Folder "SCA Executive Committee Minutes," 1963, American Jewish Historical Society, New York.

46. Statement of Howard M. Squadron on behalf of the American Jewish Congress on HR 2362 Elementary and Secondary Education Act of 1965, submitted to the Subcommittee on Education of the House Committee on Education and Labor, February 1, 1965, 1–4, I-77, American Jewish Congress Records, Box 28, Folder "Congressional Testimony, 1956–1976," American Jewish Historical Society, New York; American Jewish Congress Resolution on Religious Freedom and Separation of

Church and State, adopted at its Biennial Convention, April 14–19, 1964, 1, I-77, Box 11, American Jewish Historical Society, New York.

47. Memo from Mrs. Martin L. Steinberg to Mr. R. Sargent Shriver, March 9, 1965, 1–2, Box 110, Folder "NWD Convention 1965," I-77, American Jewish Historical Society, New York.

48. Statement of Morris B. Abram to the Subcommittee on General Education, February 3, 1965, 3, AJC Collection, RG347.4124, Box 3, Folder "Jan '65–Mar '65," YIVO Institute for Jewish Research, New York; Memo to Members of the Monday Discussion Group, New York Chapter, American Jewish Committee, March 22, 1965, 1, AJC Collection, 3474.124, Box 3, Folder "Jan '65–Mar '65," YIVO Institute for Jewish Research, New York. Statement of Anti-Defamation League, of B'nai B'rith; Resolution Adopted by 36th General Assembly of the Council of Jewish Federations and Welfare Funds.

49. For Federal Aid to Education Bill, AJC Collection, CSD 185–190, Box 2, Folder "Education (Fed. Aid)," YIVO Institute for Jewish Research, New York.

50. Excerpts from the remarks of Rabbi Israel Klavan, American Jewish Congress News, April 29, 1966, I-77, Box 12, Folder "Convention Speeches," American Jewish Historical Society, New York.

51. Ben Halpern, "How and Why the American Jewish Community Developed Its Normative Position on Church-State Separation," in *Jewish Education in a Secular Society: A Symposium on Public Aid to Non-Public Education*, Institute for Jewish Policy Planning and Research of the Synagogue Council of America, 1971, 12, 15. I-68, Box 49, Folder "Synagogue Council of America Publications 1960–1969, a–f," American Jewish Historical Society, New York.

52. Seymour Siegel, "A Conservative View," *Congress Bi-Weekly* 39:3 (February 11, 1972): 8.

53. Herbert Weiner, "The Case for the Timorous Jew: Reflections on Church and State in America," *Midstream* 8:4 (December 1962): 6.

54. Ibid., 7, 10.

Chapter 3: American Jews and the Rise of Black Power

1. Recording of Malcolm X, Message to the Grassroots, December 10, 1963, in possession of the author.

2. Arthur Hertzberg, "Negro-Jewish Relations in America: A Symposium," *Midstream* 12:10 (December 1966): 49.

3. C. Eric Lincoln, "Extremist Attitudes in the Black Muslim Movement," 6, presented at the annual meeting of the Society for the Psychological Study of Social Issues, St. Louis, September 1962. Lincoln is author of C. Eric Lincoln, *The Black Muslims in America* (Boston: Beacon Press, 1961). MS COL 202, Box 16, Folder 7, American Jewish Archives, Cincinnati.

4. See, for example, Stokely Carmichael and Charles V. Hamilton, *Black Power: The Politics of Liberation in America* (New York: Random House, 1967); Kathleen Cleaver and George N. Katsiaficas, *Liberation, Imagination, and the Black Panther Party: A New Look at the Panthers and Their Legacy* (New York: Routledge, 2001); Devin Fergus, *Liberalism, Black Power, and the Making of American Politics, 1965–1980*, Politics and Culture in the Twentieth-Century South (Athens: University of Georgia Press, 2009); William L. Van Deburg, *Modern Black Nationalism: From Marcus Garvey to Louis Farrakhan* (New York: New York University Press, 1997). William Brink and Louis Harris, *Black and White: A Study of U.S. Racial Attitudes Today* (New York: Simon and Schuster, 1967), 66.

5. "Position Paper on Black Power," *New York Times*, August 5, 1966; Van Deburg, *Modern Black Nationalism*, 123; Brink and Harris, *Black and White*, 66.

6. *FACTS* 19:2 (July 1970): 510, 515.

7. From Brink and Harris, *The Negro Revolution in America*, 119. Among Americans at large, the same 1966 Louis Harris poll revealed that only 5 percent of respondents approved of black nationalism while 63 percent disapproved. Ibid., 260.

8. Brink and Harris, *Black and White*, 62, 56. Bayard Rustin, "'Black Power' and Coalition Politics," *Commentary* 3:42 (September 1966): 35.

9. Bayard Rustin, Address to the American Jewish Congress Convention, 1966, in *Congress Bi-Weekly* 33:10 (May 23, 1966): 11.

10. Ibid.; Rustin, "'Black Power' and Coalition Politics," 40.

11. Roy Wilkins, *Congress Bi-Weekly* 33:15 (November 21, 1966): 12. Martin Luther King, "In Peace and in Dignity: A Memorable Address to the American Jewish Congress," *Congress Bi-Weekly* 35:8 (May 6, 1968): 17.

12. David Danzig, "To Fulfill These Rights," *Commentary* 3:42 (September 1966): 41–42.

13. Memo from Monroe Schlactus to Arnold Forster, May 15, 1964, 2, Nearprint File, "Negro-Jewish Relationships," American Jewish Archives, Cincinnati.

14. Charles F. Wittenstein, "A White Liberal Looks at Georgia: An Address to the Hungry Club," November 16, 1966, 4, CSD 25–26, Box 4, Folder "Speeches," YIVO Institute for Jewish Research, New York.

15. Memo from Jason R. Silverman to Arnold Forster, May 22, 1964, 1–2, Nearprint File, "Negro-Jewish Relationships," American Jewish Archives, Cincinnati.

16. Memo from Kass to Forster, June 11, 1964, 4, Nearprint File, "Negro-Jewish Relationships," American Jewish Archives, Cincinnati, Ohio. Memo from Sol Kolack to Arnold Forster, May 15, 1964, 1, Nearprint File, "Negro-Jewish Relationships," American Jewish Archives, Cincinnati.

17. Memo from Kass to Forster, June 11, 1964, 1, 6, 8. Ibid., 3–4, 6. The ADL's Mortimer Kass described "no cooperation between us at all" as he lamented the end of any working relationship between black nationalist organizations and his ADL office.

18. David Danzig, "Rightists, Racists, and Separatists: A White Bloc in the Making?" *Commentary* 38:2 (August 1964): 32.

19. C. Bezalel Sherman, "In the American Jewish Community," *Jewish Frontier* 31:6 (July 1964): 18. "Editorial comment," *Jewish Frontier* 31:3 (April 1964): 3. Labor Zionist writer and later Brandeis University professor Marie Syrkin worried that black nationalism would rally the historic opponents of civil rights by inspiring a white backlash against its more aggressive platform. African American leaders, she understood, were "aware that in the last analysis the Negro cause will depend on the effective sympathy of the white majority and that further alienation of white sympathizers may result in a segregationist victory in November." Marie Syrkin, "Can Minorities Oppose 'De Facto' Segregation," *Jewish Frontier* 31: 8 (September 1964): 1.

20. Newsletter of Shad Polier, July 10, 1963, 1, Folder "Shad Polier Newsletter 1963," Collection I-77, Box 196, American Jewish Historical Society, New York. Leo Pfeffer, Information Bulletin #25, August 15, 1963, *CLSA Reports*, American Jewish Congress, 1, Collection I-77, Box 31, Folder "CLSA Report 1963," American Jewish Historical Society, New York.

21. Leon A. Jick, "'De Facto' Segregation: A Discussion," *Jewish Frontier* 31:10 (November 1964): 8. Seven months before Jick published his article, Irving Kane, who chaired the American Jewish Congress's April 1964 Biennial Convention, called out the gap between Jewish "principles and practices." Kane held "great concern" over the profound differences between the rhetorical support offered by national Jewish leaders and the lack of civil rights action among rank-and-file constituents at the local level. The "burning issue of civil rights" failed to gain the traction it needed. Address of Irving Kane, at the American Jewish Congress National Biennial Convention, April 14, 1964, Miami Beach, FL, 4, Collection I-77, Box 11, Folder "Convention Speeches—Carillon Hotel, Miami Beach, April 14–19, 1964," American Jewish Historical Society, New York.

22. Memo from Melvin I. Cooperman to Arnold Forster, May 21, 1964, 1, Nearprint File, American Jewish Archives, Cincinnati.

23. Memo from Sol I. Littman to Arnold Forster, May 25, 1964, 1–2, Nearprint File, American Jewish Archives, Cincinnati.

24. Memo from Kass to Forster, June 11, 1964, 4. Memo from Saul Sorrin to Arnold Forster, May 15, 1964, 1, Nearprint File, American Jewish Archives, Cincinnati, Ohio. Memo from Irwin Schulman to Arnold Forster, May 13, 1964, 1, Nearprint File, American Jewish Archives, Cincinnati. Minneapolis's Michael Gaines reported that some Jewish leaders in his community had started to advocate for a "Jewish withdrawal and/or a Jewish slow-down" from the civil rights movement. Memo from Kass to Forster, June 11, 1964, 4, 8. Memo from Schulman to Forster, 1.

25. Fein, "The Negro Revolution and the Jewish Question," 12.

26. Memo from Littman to Forster, 1. Memo from Jerry Bakst to Arnold Forster,

June 11, 1964, 3, Nearprint File, American Jewish Archives, Cincinnati. Memo from Schlactus to Forster, 2.

27. "Editorial comment," *Jewish Frontier* 31:3 (April 1964): 3. Shad Polier, *Congress Bi-Weekly* 31:11 (September 14, 1964): 5, 6.

28. African American frustration toward Jews in this period was evidenced by a precipitous rise in black antisemitism as young African American nationalists joined leading African American intellectuals, black preachers, and large portions of the greater African American community to express their anger toward Jews. A 1964 analysis of black antisemitism revealed that nearly half of the African Americans surveyed scored high on antisemitic beliefs, compared to about a third of white Americans. Leonard Dinnerstein, *Antisemitism in the United States*, American Problem Studies (New York: Holt, 1971), 209. Polier, *Congress Bi-Weekly* 31:11 (September 14, 1964): 5–6.

29. Maslow, "Report of the Executive Director," May 14–May 19, 1968. Fein, "The Negro Revolution and the Jewish Question," 15.

30. Dr. Seymour Lachman, "Communities in Perplexity," February 17, 1969, 8.

31. Memo from Kass to Forster, June 11, 1964, 7, 4. Also found in a memo from Sorrin to Forster, May 15, 1964, 1. Memo from A. Abbot Rosen to Arnold Foster, May 18, 1964, 1, Nearprint File, American Jewish Archives, Cincinnati.

32. Lawrence I. Jackofsky, "Negro-Jewish Relations of the Contemporary American Scene," Master's Thesis, HUC-JIR, Cincinnati, June 1969, 65–66, Negro-Jewish Relations Collection, Box 1849, American Jewish Archives, Cincinnati.

33. Cohen, *Justice, Justice*, 121.

34. Dresner, "Communities in Perplexity," 21, 4.

35. David Caplovitz, "The Merchant and the Low-Income Consumer," *Jewish Social Studies* 27:1 (1965): 45–53 quoted in Marc Lee Raphael, *Jews and Judaism in the United States: A Documentary History*, Library of Jewish Studies (New York: Behrman House, 1983), 304. Bertram H. Gold, Text of Address at the National Conference of Jewish Communal Service, June 10, 1968, Detroit, Michigan, 7, as quoted in Bertram H. Gold, *Jews and the Urban Crisis*, Klau Library, HUC-JIR, Cincinnati.

36. Arthur J. Lelyveld, "Negro and Jewish Relationships," *Congress Bi-Weekly* 33 (November 21, 1966): 2.

37. Leonard J. Fein, "The Summer of Our Discontent," *Congress Bi-Weekly* 34:16 (December 4, 1967): 9–10.

38. "American Jewish Congress Resolution on the Urban Crisis, adopted at its Biennial Convention, Miami, May 14–19, 1968, SC Box A-93, 116, American Jewish Archives, Cincinnati.

39. Danzig, "To Fulfill These Rights," 41.

40. Gold, *Jews and the Urban Crisis*, 5–6.

41. Ben Halpern, "Negro-Jewish Relations In America: A Symposium," *Midstream* 12:10 (December 1966): 45–46, 44.

42. Hertzberg, "Negro-Jewish Relations in America," 50, 49. The complete transcripts of participants at the symposium can be found in Shlomo Katz, *Negro and Jew: An Encounter in America* (New York: Macmillan, 1967).

43. Dov Peretz Elkins, "Jews and Blacks—Past, Present, Future," delivered at Adult Studies Institute, Har Zion Temple, March 4, 1968, in Elkins, *A Tradition Reborn*, 104.

44. Arnold J. Wolf, Rabbi of Congregation Solel, Chicago, delivered at the March 12, 1969, meeting of the Synagogue Council of America held at Columbia University on the theme "The Negro Revolution and the Jewish Community," 23, MS COL 294, Box 25, Folder 10, American Jewish Archives, Cincinnati.

45. Ibid., 24.

46. "Black Power—A Positive Force," 1, AJC, 347.4.124, Box 4, Folder "Sept '67–March '68," YIVO Institute for Jewish Research, New York. Roland Bertram Gittelsohn, *Fire in My Bones: Essays on Judaism in a Time of Crisis* (New York: Bloch, 1969), 53.

47. Gittelsohn, *Fire in My Bones*, 50, 55.

48. Transcript from "Communities in Perplexity," 2–3.

49. Newspaper article by Rabbi Jacob Chinitz, appearing in a memo from Sanford Weinreb to Will Maslow, Richard Cohen, and Joseph Robison, July 3, 1969, I-77, Box 40, Folder "Jewish Defense League," American Jewish Historical Society, New York.

50. J. Hochbaum, "The Orthodox Community and the Urban Crisis," 43.

Chapter 4: Turning Inward: Black Power and Jewish Youth Movements

1. Rabbi Myron Fenster, "Negro-Jewish Relations in America: A Symposium," *Midstream* 12:10 (December 1966): 21.

2. Brickner, "'If I Am Not for Myself,'" 12.

3. Dresner, "Communities in Perplexity," 21.

4. Fein, "The Negro Revolution and the Jewish Question," 14.

5. Jonathan Sarna, "The Great American Jewish Awakening," *Midstream* 28:8 (October 1982): 33. Harold R. Isaacs, "The New Pluralists," *Commentary* 53:3 (March 1972): 76.

6. Memo from Shad Polier to division and chapter presidents of the Commission on Law and Social Action, October 22, 1957, 1–2, I-77, Box 24, Folder "CLSA memorandum," American Jewish Historical Society, New York.

7. See for example, Darren Kleinberg, *Hybrid Judaism: Irving Greenberg, Encounter, and the Changing Nature of American Jewish Identity* (Boston: Academic Studies Press, 2016), especially 35–48; Dollinger, *Quest for Inclusion*, chapter 2.

8. See Jacobson, *Roots Too*.

9. Lachman, "Communities in Perplexity," 25.

10. Raab, "The Black Revolution and the Negro Question," 32. Lachman,

"Communities in Perplexity," 25. Arthur A. Goren, *The Politics and Public Culture of American Jews*, The Modern Jewish Experience (Bloomington: Indiana University Press, 1999), 222, 205.

11. Perry L. Weed, *The White Ethnic Movement and Ethnic Politics*, Praeger Special Studies in U.S. Economic, Social, and Political Issues (New York: Praeger, 1973), 16, 20. Goren, *The Politics and Public Culture of American Jews*, 213.

12. Goren, *The Politics and Public Culture of American Jews*, 211, 212. Weed, *The White Ethnic Movement and Ethnic Politics*, 19, 22, 213.

13. Goren, *The Politics and Public Culture of American Jews*, 206, 213–214, 222.

14. Donald Feldstein, "Campus Jews," *Midstream* 16:4 (April 1970): 61. American Jewish Congress, "Keep the Faith," 2, I-77, Box 12, Folder "Delegates Kit National Biennial Convention, May 20–24, 1970," American Jewish Historical Society, New York.

15. Daniel Elazar, "The Institutional Life of American Jewry," *Midstream* 17:6 (June/July 1971): 47. Fein, "The Negro Revolution and the Jewish Question," 15. Murray Herbert Danzger, *Returning to Tradition: The Contemporary Revival of Orthodox Judaism* (New Haven, Conn.: Yale University Press, 1989), 65.

16. See, for example, Philip Q. Yang, *Ethnic Studies: Issues and Approaches* (Albany: State University of New York Press, 2000); Denise M. Sandoval, Anthony J. Ratcliff, Tracy L. Buenavista, and James R. Marin, eds., *"White" Washing American Education: The New Culture Wars in Ethnic Studies*, vol. 1 (Santa Barbara, Calif.: ABC-Clio, 2016).

17. Kristin Loveland, "The Association for Jewish Studies: A Brief History," Association for Jewish Studies 40th Annual Conference, Washington, D.C., December 21–23, 2008, 2.

18. David Glanz, "After the Jewish Student Movement—Where Do They Go?," *Congress Bi-Weekly* 40:10 (1973): 15. Loveland, "The Association for Jewish Studies," 3.

19. Ibid., 4–5.

20. Ibid., 7. Novak and Goldman, "The Rise of the Jewish Student Press," 6.

21. Loveland, "The Association for Jewish Studies," 7.

22. Western States Jewish History Archives, Collection 70/10, Folder "Hillel, UCB," Magnes Archives, Berkeley, California. Novak and Goldman, "The Rise of the Jewish Student Press," 5–6.

23. Matthew Maibaum, "The Berkeley Hillel and the Union of Jewish Students: The History of a Conflict," *Jewish Journal of Sociology* 13:2 (December 1971): 163.

24. Ronald I. Rubin, "The New Jewish Ethnic," *Tradition* 13: 3 (Winter 1973): 12.

25. Neil Reisner, "Welcome to Jewish Los Angeles," *Moment* 3:3 (January/February 1978): 34. Hillel Levine, "To Share a Vision," talk delivered to the Council of Federations and Jewish Welfare Funds, November 1969, appearing in *Response* (Winter 1969), reprinted in Jack Nusan Porter and Peter Dreier, *Jewish Radicalism: A Selected Anthology* (New York: Grove Press, 1973), 189.

26. Jewish Education Coalition Press Release, April 30, 1971, 3, 4, WJHS, Collection 74/2, Folder "Jewish Radical," Student Paper, UC Berkeley, 1969–1973, Magnes Archives, Berkeley, California.

27. Western States Jewish History Archive, Collection 74/2, Folder "Jewish Radical Education," Student Paper, UC Berkeley, 1969–1973, Magnes Archives, Berkeley, California. Jewish Education Coalition Press Release, April 30, 1971, 1–2. Sherman Rosenfeld, "Jews Liberate Federation," *The Jewish Radical* 2:4 (Spring 1971).

28. Tsvi Bisk, "A Radical-Zionist Strategy for the 1970s," originally published in *The Jewish Liberation Journal* (November–December 1969), reprinted in Porter and Dreier, *Jewish Radicalism*, 95. See as well Meir Kahane, *Listen World/Listen Jew* (New York: Institute of the Publication of the Writings of Meir Kahane, 1995), 214.

29. Tsvi Bisk, "A Radical-Zionist Strategy for the 1970s," in Porter and Dreier, *Jewish Radicalism*, 95, 97.

30. Jason Porth, "Left Out: A Jewish Response to the New Left and the Rise of a Jewish Student Movement," senior thesis, Department of Sociology, Brandeis University, 1996, 93–94. Originally published in the *Jewish Morning Journal*, January 9, 1969, as well as in J. Kaufman, *Broken Alliance*, 202–203.

31. American Jewish Congress Resolution on Jewish Commitment Adopted at its Biennial Convention, Miami, FL, May 14–19, 1968, 1–2, I-77, Box 12, Folder "1968 Report of the Executive Director," American Jewish Historical Society, New York.

32. Danzger, *Returning to Tradition*, 59, 64. Richard H. Greenberg, *Pathways: Jews Who Return* (Northvale, N.J.: Jason Aronson, 1997), 15. Nathan Glazer, "The Jewish Revival in America II," *Commentary* 21:1 (January 1956): 17–24.

33. From the Proceedings, XV Biennial Convention of the National Federation of Temple Brotherhoods and the Jewish Chautauqua Society, November 8–10, 1953, St. Louis, Missouri, quoted in Jacob Rader Marcus, *United States Jewry, 1776–1985*, vol. 4 (Detroit: Wayne State University Press, 1989), 779. Milton Himmelfarb, "In the Community," *Commentary* 30:2 (August 1960): 160.

34. Richard Cohen, Press Release, April 15, 1962, I-77, Box 10, "Convention 1962," American Jewish Historical Society, New York. Milton Himmelfarb, "Reflections on the Jewish Day School," *Commentary* 30:1 (July 1960): 31.

35. Samuel G. Freedman, *Jew vs. Jew: The Struggle for the Soul of American Jewry* (New York: Simon and Schuster, 2000), 220–221. Egon Mayer and Chaim I. Waxman, "Modern Jewish Orthodoxy in America: Toward the Year 2000," *Tradition* 16:3 (Spring 1977): 9, quoted in Chaim I. Waxman, *American Aliya: Portrait of an Innovative Migration Movement* (Detroit: Wayne State University Press, 1989), 122. A 1967 census conducted by the American Association for Jewish Education revealed that one-third of Jewish children between the ages of three and seventeen were receiving some form of Jewish education. Of those enrolled, 42.2 percent of the students attended once-a-week schools (typically Sunday school), 44.4 percent attended supplemental schools with instruction between two and five days a week, and

13.4 percent matriculated in a Jewish day school. Eugene Rothman, "Whither the Hebrew Day School," *Midstream* 17:6 (June/July 1971): 19.

36. Rothman, "Whither the Hebrew Day School," 20. Chinitz, memo from Sanford Weinreb. Elazar, "The Institutional Life of American Jewry," 47.

37. Bisk, "A Radical-Zionist Strategy for the 1970s," in Porter and Dreier, *Jewish Radicalism*, 95.

38. Ibid.

39. Hindy L. Schacter, "Government and the Parochial School," *Ideas* 2:2–3 (Winter-Spring 1970): 84–85.

40. Rothman, "Whither the Hebrew Day School," 20. Elazar, "The Institutional Life of American Jewry," 47.

41. Morris U. Schappes, "Remarks by Morris U. Schappes," in *Negro-Jewish Relations in the United States: A Symposium* (New York: The Citadel Press, 1966), 62. Originally from "Conference on Negro-Jewish Relations in the United States," May 3, 1964, by the Conference on Jewish Social Studies in New York City, published in *Jewish Social Studies* 27:1 (January 1965). *The Militant: Published in the Interests of the Working People* 28:21, (May 25, 1964): 4.

42. "Jews for Urban Justice: Statement of Purpose," March 1969, 2, I-159, Box 1, American Jewish Historical Society, New York. Porter and Dreier, *Jewish Radicalism*, xxx.

43. Sharon Rose, "The Radical Jewish Movement Wants You: An Abbreviated History of Jews for Urban Justice (1966–1969)," 2, 4, Collection I-159, Box 1, Folder "History of Organization," American Jewish Historical Society, New York.

44. Tsvi Bisk, "A Radical-Zionist Strategy for the 1970s," in Porter and Dreier, *Jewish Radicalism*, 97.

45. Thomas Piazza, "Jewish Identity and the Counterculture," in Charles Y. Glock, Robert N. Bellah, and Randy Alfred, *The New Religious Consciousness* (Berkeley: University of California Press, 1976), 245. Charles Selengut, "American Jewish Converts to New Religious Movements," *The Jewish Journal of Sociology* 30:2 (December 1988): 95. *The Hillel Fortnighter*, January 1968, 3, Collection 70/10, Magnes Archives, Berkeley, California. See also Mark Oppenheimer, *Knocking on Heaven's Door: American Religion in the Age of Counterculture* (New Haven, Conn.: Yale University Press, 2003); Shaul Magid, *American Post-Judaism: Identity and Renewal in a Postethnic Society*, Religion in North America (Bloomington: Indiana University Press, 2013).

46. Irving Solomon, "A New Kind of Yeshivah, House of Love and Prayer," Jewish Radical Student Paper, UC Berkeley, 1969–1973, Collection 74/2, Magnes Archives, Berkeley, California.

47. Ibid. Also see Porter and Dreier, *Jewish Radicalism*, xliii.

48. Dresner, "Communities in Perplexity," 21. Marcus, *United States Jewry, 1776–1985*, 779.

49. Arthur I. Waskow, "Judaism and Revolution Today: Malkhut Zadon M'herah

T'aker," originally appeared in *Judaism* 20:4 (Fall 1971), reprinted in Porter and Dreier, *Jewish Radicalism*, 25, xliii.

50. *Response* 11 (Fall 1971), reprinted in Porter and Dreier, *Jewish Radicalism*, 211. Daniel Elazar, "The Institutional Life of American Jewry," *Midstream* 17:6 (June/July 1971): 44.

51. Danzger, *Returning to Tradition*, 52. See, for example, Riv-Ellen Prell, *Prayer and Community: The Havurah in American Judaism* (Detroit: Wayne State University Press, 1989); Porter and Dreier, *Jewish Radicalism*, xxx.

52. "Aquarian Minyan," Collection 86/6, Box 1, Folder "Newsletters, Originals, Dec. 1976–Sept. 1977," Magnes Archives, Berkeley, California.

53. Reuven Goldfarb, "A history of the Aquarian Minyan, Where It's Been, Where It Is Now," February 9, 1981, Collection 86/6, Box 1, Magnes Archives, Berkeley, California.

54. Danzger, *Returning to Tradition*, 50, 51. Marshall Sklare, "Recent Developments in Conservative Judaism," *Midstream* 18:1 (January 1972): 6.

55. Sklare, "Recent Developments in Conservative Judaism," 6, 17.

56. William Novak, "The Last Word on the Jewish Catalog," *Moment* 1:1 (May/June 1975): 81, 82–83.

57. Gloria Steinem, "After Black Power, Women's Liberation," *New York Magazine*, April 7, 1969, 8. Sylvia Barack Fishman, *A Breath of Life: Feminism in the American Jewish Community*, Brandeis Series in American Jewish History, Culture, and Life (Waltham, Mass.: Brandeis University Press, 1995), 2, 6.

58. Steinem, "After Black Power, Women's Liberation," 13. Letty Cottin Pogrebin, "Anti-Semitism in the Women's Movement: A Jewish Feminist's Disturbing Account," *Moment* 7:7 (July/August 1982): 48. Fishman, *A Breath of Life*, 11–12.

59. Steinem, "After Black Power, Women's Liberation," 9. See also Debra R. Kaufman, *Rachel's Daughters: Newly Orthodox Jewish Women* (New Brunswick, N.J.: Rutgers University Press, 1991).

60. Fishman, *A Breath of Life*, 7. Gurock, *Orthodox Jews in America*, 274.

61. Gurock, *Orthodox Jews in America*, 274.

62. See Simon Greenberg and Jewish Theological Seminary of America, *The Ordination of Women as Rabbis: Studies and Responsa*, Moreshet Series (New York: The Jewish Theological Seminary of America, 1988).

Chapter 5: Black Power, American Jews, and the Soviet Jewry Movement

1. See, for example, Frederick A. Lazin, *We Are Not One: American Jews, Israel, and the Struggle for Soviet Jewry*, David W. Belin Lecture in American Jewish Affairs (Ann Arbor: Jean and Samuel Frankel Center for Judaic Studies, University of Michigan, 2009).

2. Nehemiah Levanon, "Israel's Role in the Campaign," 71, appearing in Murray Friedman and Albert D. Chernin, *A Second Exodus: The American Movement to Free Soviet Jews*, Brandeis Series in American Jewish History, Culture, and Life (Waltham, Mass.: Brandeis University Press, 1999). See Fred A. Lazin, *The Struggle for Soviet Jewry in American Politics: Israel versus the American Jewish Establishment* (Lanham, Md.: Lexington Books, 2005), 23–28.

3. William W. Orbach, *The American Movement to Aid Soviet Jews* (Amherst: University of Massachusetts Press, 1979), 46, 23–4, 4–5.

4. Declaration of Purpose, American Jewish Conference on Soviet Jewry Proposals for National Follow-up, 1, Collection I-77, Box 48, Folder "Conference on the Status of Soviet Jews, 1963–1964," American Jewish Historical Society, New York.

5. The relationship between Soviet Jewry activism and the larger American struggle for racial equality played out in reciprocal ways as well. Congress of Racial Equality leader Roy Innis drew parallels between the shared "long history of oppression" of both blacks and Jews. Invoking the motto of the Soviet Jewry movement, Innis struck a political deal: CORE would back "Let My People Go in the Soviet Union," if American Jews joined African Americans in their cry, "Let my people go in America." Amaryah Orenstein, "Let My People Go!: The Student Struggle for Soviet Jewry and the Rise of American Jewish Identity Politics," Ph.D. dissertation, Brandeis University, February 2014, 125–6.

6. See, for example, Arthur D. Morse, *While Six Million Died: A Chronicle of American Apathy* (New York: Random House, 1968); Ellen Eisenberg, *The First to Cry Down Injustice: Western Jews and Japanese Removal During WWII* (Lanham, Md.: Lexington Books, 2008).

7. "College Students' Struggle for Soviet Jewry," April 1964, Box 1, Folder 1, SSSJ Records, as quoted in Orenstein, "Let My People Go!," 50. Orbach, *The American Movement to Aid Soviet Jews*, 5.

8. Orbach, *The American Movement to Aid Soviet Jews*, 8–9. Jewish Student Organization Collection I-61, Box 67, Folder "Student Struggle for Soviet Jewry Bumper Stickers, Buttons, Stamps," American Jewish Historical Society, New York.

9. Orbach, *The American Movement to Aid Soviet Jews*, 19. Jerry Goodman, "American Response to Soviet Anti-Jewish Politics," *American Jewish Year Book* 66 (1965): 312.

10. Letter from Levine to Ben-Gurion, SC-10176, 1–2, American Jewish Archives, Cincinnati.

11. Ibid.

12. Orbach, *The American Movement to Aid Soviet Jews*, 19–20. For more on the Soviet Jewry movement, see Stuart Altshuler, *From Exodus to Freedom: A History of the Soviet Jewry Movement* (Lanham, Md.: Rowman and Littlefield, 2005).

13. Orbach, *The American Movement to Aid Soviet Jews*, 19–20.

14. Ibid. Rabbi Abraham Joshua Heschel, "The Jews in the Soviet Union," paper presented to the Conference on the Moral Implications of the Rabbinate, The Jewish

Theological Seminary of American, New York, September 4, 1963, reprinted in Abraham Joshua Heschel, *The Insecurity of Freedom: Essays on Human Existence* (New York: Farrar, 1966), 269. Lewis Weinstein, "Soviet Jewry and the American Jewish Community, 1963–1987," *American Jewish History* 77:4 (June 1988): 602.

15. *Congress Bi-Weekly*, December 5, 1966, 45.

16. Orbach, *The American Movement to Aid Soviet Jews*, 27, 5, 28.

17. Ibid., 28. From Shaul Kelner, "Freedom Seder: Ritual Transformation in the American Movement for Soviet Jewry," paper presented at Association for Jewish Studies, Cincinnati, December 22, 2003, Boston.

18. Friedman and Chernin, *A Second Exodus*, 34.

19. Orbach, *The American Movement to Aid Soviet Jews*, 28. Orenstein, "Let My People Go," 58, 61.

20. "Operation Jericho" (undated), 1, SSSJ Records (1:11). Quoted in Orenstein, "Let My People Go," 93–4.

21. Orenstein, "Let My People Go," 93, 95–96. Memo from Jacob Birnbaum to Mrs. Reich, March 12, 1965, SSSJ Records (1:10). Memo from Jacob Birnbaum to Theodore Bikel, March 8, 1965, SSSJ Records (1:10). Orbach, *The American Movement to Aid Soviet Jews*, 28.

22. Orbach, *The American Movement to Aid Soviet Jews*, 25, 26–7. Orenstein, "Let My People Go," 109.

23. Orbach, *The American Movement to Aid Soviet Jews*, 41.

24. Ibid., 40, 27.

25. Ibid., 46. MSS #202, Freedom Bus, 1970, Box 63, Folder 5, American Jewish Archives, Cincinnati. Student Struggle for Soviet Jewry, "The Soviet Jewry Freedom Bus Is Coming to Town" (undated), SSSJ Records (49:1); "Soviet Jewry Freedom Bus Begins Trip," *Jewish Telegraphic Agency*, October 15, 1971; "Petitions with 75,000 Signatures Demanding Freedom for Soviet Jews Given to State Department," *Jewish Telegraphic Agency*, December 15, 1971, archive.jta.org.

26. "Soviet Jewry Freedom Bus Begins Trip"; "Freedom Bus for Soviet Jewry to Visit 33 Cities in 2 Months," *Jewish Telegraphic Agency*, October 6, 1971, archive.jta.org. National Jewish Community Relations Advisory Council, "The POWs Are Coming Home," Collection I-72, Box 75, Folder "Activities—Soviet Jews, 1971," American Jewish Historical Society, New York.

27. National Jewish Community Relations Advisory Council, "Program Exchange Bulletin: Community Activities for Soviet Jewry, May 1–October 31, 1971," Collection I-72, Box 75, Folder "Activities—Soviet Jews, 1971," American Jewish Historical Society, New York.

28. Collection I-61, Box 67, Folder "Student Struggle for Soviet Jewry Bumper Stickers, Buttons, Stamps," American Jewish Historical Society, New York. Collection I-61, Box 68, Folder SSSJ Miscellaneous, American Jewish Historical Society, New York.

29. Collection I-77, Box 40, Folder "Jewish Defense League," American Jewish Historical Society, New York.

30. For an exploration of Brooklyn schools, the JDL, and Black Power, see Jacob S. Dorman, "Dreams Defended and Deferred: The Brooklyn Schools Crisis of 1968 and Black Power's Influence on Rabbi Meir Kahane," *American Jewish History* 100:3 (July 2016): 411–438; Porter and Dreier, *Jewish Radicalism*, 276; Kenneth Braiterman, "The Jewish Defense League: What Safety in Karate?" *Midstream* 16:4 (April 1970): 6. See as well Shaul Magid, "Anti-Semitism as Colonialism: Meir Kahane's Ethics of Violence," *Journal of Jewish Ethics* 1:2 (2015).

31. Orenstein, "Let My People Go," 129–30. Kahane's reference to lettuce referred to popular support of Cesar Chavez's United Farm Workers union.

32. Orenstein, "Let My People Go," 137, 133, 142, quoting from M. Kahane, *Story of the Jewish Defense League*, 3. Meir Kahane, Jewish Defense League: Movement Handbook, 6–7. See also Porter and Dreier, *Jewish Radicalism*; Ron Landsman, "Rabbi Kahane Says Part of Pride Is a Willingness to Use Violence," *Southfield Eccentric*, April 22, 1971, Jewish Defense League Nearprint file, American Jewish Archives, Cincinnati.

33. Haskell L. Lazere, "Dimensions in American Judaism," 10, 347.4.124, Box 4, Folder "Jan–April 1970," YIVO Institute for Jewish Research, New York.

34. Zvi Lowenthal and Jonathan Braun, "Right on Judaism . . . JDL's Meir Kahane Speaks Out: An Interview," in Porter and Dreier, *Jewish Radicalism*, 280. "A Louis Harris poll released on December 2, 1968, found that 'a vast majority of the American people in 1968 clearly [saw] themselves removed from the "liberal" side of politics' —38 percent labeling themselves conservative, 34 percent middle-of-the-road, and only 17 percent liberal (only 2 percent radical). In Will Herberg, "Conservatism, the Working Class, and the Jew," *Ideas* 2–2–3 (Winter-Spring 1970): 25.

35. Orenstein, "Let My People Go," 137, 131; Braiterman, "The Jewish Defense League," 6–7; Janet L. Dolgin, *Jewish Identity and the JDL*, Princeton Legacy Library, rep. ed. (Princeton, N.J.: Princeton University Press, 2014), 26; Robert I. Friedman, *The False Prophet: Rabbi Meir Kahane: From FBI Informant to Knesset Member* (New York: Lawrence Hill, 1992), 83–84.

36. Braiterman, "The Jewish Defense League," 6.

37. Philip Horn, "New Trends on the Campus," *Jewish Frontier* 38:8 (September 1971): 11. Orenstein, "Let My People Go," 148–9. Meir Kahane, quoted in "JDL Offers to Buy Plane Tickets for Two Soviet Jews Sentenced to Death," *Jewish Telegraphic Agency*, December 30, 1970, archives.jta.org.

38. Braiterman, "The Jewish Defense League," 14, 12.

39. Memo from Will Maslow to division and chapter presidents, "Professional Staff re: Jewish Defense League, 3/17/1971," I-77, American Jewish Congress records, Box 24, Folder "CLSA memorandum," American Jewish Historical Society, New York.

40. Beckerman, *When They Come for Us, We'll Be Gone*, 158. Carson, *In Struggle*, 295. Braiterman, "The Jewish Defense League," 9.

Chapter 6: Black Power and American Zionism

1. Arthur Hertzberg, "The Changing American Rabbinate," *Midstream* 12:1 (January 1966): 23–24, 25. For more on American Jews, Zionism, and Israel, see Liel Leibovitz, *Aliya: Three Generations of American-Jewish Immigration to Israel* (New York: St. Martin's Press, 2006).

2. Shlomo Avineri, "The New Left and Israel," 2, Israel Academic Committee on the Middle East, Jerusalem, Klau Library, Cincinnati.

3. Forman, *Blacks in the Jewish Mind*, 180.

4. Zola and Dollinger, *American Jewish History*, 166. Waxman, *American Aliya*, 61.

5. Zola and Dollinger, *American Jewish History*, 167.

6. Waxman, *American Aliya*, 81.

7. Zola and Dollinger, *American Jewish History*, 322–326. The American Jewish Committee, "The American Jewish Committee Background and Emphases for AJC's 1955 Domestic Program, January 1955," 28–29, Collection CJFWF, Box 7, American Jewish Historical Society, New York.

8. Alan M. Stroock, "American Jewish Committee Israel Program," Proceedings of the Fifty-Third Annual Meeting, April 22–24, 1960, 40, Institute of Human Relations, New York, American Jewish Archives, Cincinnati.

9. Danielle Ziri, "The Untold Story of a Jewish Freedom Rider," *Jerusalem Post* website, January 31, 2016, www.jpost.com/Diaspora/The-untold-story-of-a-Jewish-Freedom-Rider-443318.

10. Ibid. Letter from Allan Levine to David Ben-Gurion, 1, SC-10176, American Jewish Archives, Cincinnati.

11. Ibid.

12. Shad Polier, "The Jew and the Racial Crisis," presented at the American Jewish Congress National Biennial Convention, April 16, 1964, Miami Beach, FL, 1, I-77, Box 11, American Jewish Historical Society, New York. Shad Polier, *Congress Bi-Weekly* 31 (September 14, 1964): 5–6.

13. Ibid. Invoking a similar argument, Marie Syrkin of the *Jewish Frontier* held that the rise of Black Power emulated the historic journey of European Jews, who eventually embraced Zionism, contending that "the long Jewish struggle for legal emancipation in various countries—the right to vote, to hold office, and to equal status as a citizen—was the counterpart of the current Negro struggle." Syrkin, "Can Minorities Oppose 'De Facto' Segregation," 7.

14. Katz, *Negro and Jew*, 72–73.

15. Ibid. During a 1966 symposium on blacks and Jews later published by *Midstream* magazine, Shlomo Katz reflected, "When the slogan of Black Power was raised recently, with its primary aim of placing the Negro struggle for equality in Negro hands, even avowed Zionists failed to perceive that such too were the beginnings of the Jewish national liberation movement in Europe." In Katz, *Negro and Jew*,

xiv. During the 1968 National Conference of Jewish Communal Service, AJC executive vice president Bertram H. Gold affirmed, "As one reads the growing black power literature — not the daily rhetoric but the more theoretically based literature — one is reminded of Chaim Zhitlovsky's writings on Jewish nationalism, Ahad Ha'am's emphasis on spiritual Zionism, the many articles on Jewish self-hate and the like." In Gold, "Jews and the Urban Crisis," 5.

16. Freedman, *Jew vs. Jew*, 163. Carson, "Black-Jewish Universalism," 192. Murray Friedman, "Is White Racism the Problem?," *Commentary* 47:1 (January 1969): 61.

17. For more on the American Jewish Committee's response to the 1967 Six-Day War, see Lawrence Grossman, "Transformation Through Crisis: The American Jewish Committee and the Six-Day War," *American Jewish History* 86:1 (March 1998): 27–54.

18. Mainline Protestant churches, once a bedrock of ecumenical support for Jewish liberal causes, retreated as well. In a dispatch to the *New York Times*, Dr. Henry P. Van Dusen, a liberal Christian leader and past president of the Union Theological Seminary, evinced shock and outrage from Jewish leaders when he drew parallels between Israel's victory in 1967 and Nazi militarism in World War II. Describing the Jewish state's campaign as "the most violent, ruthless (and successful) aggression since Hitler's blitzkrieg across western Europe in the summer of 1940," Van Dusen charged Israel's leadership with "aiming not at victory but at annihilation." In Carl Hermann Voss and David A. Rausch, "American Christians and Israel, 1948–1988," *American Jewish Archives* 40:1 (April 1988): 68. Nathan Glazer, "Jewish Interests and the New Left," *Midstream* 17:1 (January 1971): 34.

19. M. Friedman, *What Went Wrong?*, 230. Seymour Siegel, "Danger on the Left, II," *Ideas* 2:2–3 (Winter-Spring 1970): 30.

20. Siegel, "Danger on the Left, II," 31, 30.

21. Porter and Dreier, *Jewish Radicalism*, xxv. Letter from Martin Luther King Jr. to Rabbi Joachim Prinz, October 4, 1967, 4, CSD 25–26, Box 2, Folder "SCLC," YIVO Institute for Jewish Research, New York. Not all African American civil rights groups turned against Israel. Old-line alliances remained within the Congressional Black Caucus, which backed measures to support Israel. Bayard Rustin created Black Americans to Support Israel Committee (BASIC) comprised of over 200 leading African Americans committed to continuing the interracial alliance championed in the early civil rights movement. "We believe Blacks and Jews have common interests in democracy and justice," Rustin argued. "In the fight against discrimination, Black Americans and American Jews have shared profound and enduring common interests that far transcend any differences between us." Carl Gershman, "Blacks and Jews," *Midstream* 22:9 (February 1976): 9.

22. Editorial, "Civil Liberties for Black Panthers," *Jewish Currents* 24:2 (February 1970): 3. Maslow, "Report of the Executive Director, May 14–May 19, 1968," 9. Arthur Hertzberg, *The Jews in America: Four Centuries of an Uneasy Encounter: A History* (New York: Columbia University Press, 1997), 371.

23. Itzhak Epstein, "Open Letter to the Black Panther Party," originally published in *Jewish Liberation Journal*, September 1969, reprinted in Porter and Dreier, *Jewish Radicalism*, 69, 70–71.

24. M. J. Rosenberg, originally appearing in *Village Voice*, February 13, 1969, reprinted in Porter and Dreier, *Jewish Radicalism*, 10, 9. M. J. Rosenberg, "My Evolution as a Jew," originally appearing in *Midstream* (August/September 1970), reprinted in ibid., xlviii.

25. Steven M. Cohen, "American Jewish Feminism: A Study in Conflicts and Compromises," *American Behavioral Scientist* 23:4 (March/April 1980): 524.

26. Simon N. Herman, *American Students in Israel* (Ithaca, N.Y.: Cornell University Press, 1970), 136–137. Menahem Kaufman, "The Case of the United Jewish Appeal," in Allon Gal, *Envisioning Israel: The Changing Ideals and Images of North American Jews*, American Jewish Civilization Series (Detroit: Wayne State University Press, 1996), 232, 233. Hertzberg, *The Jews in America*, 373. For reactions of Jewish communities around the world to the Six-Day War, see Eli Lederhendler, *The Six-Day War and World Jewry*, Studies and Texts in Jewish History and Culture (Bethesda: University Press of Maryland, 2000).

27. Freedman, *Jew vs. Jew*, 164. Porter and Dreier, *Jewish Radicalism*, lii. Waxman, *American Aliya*, 88. Avi Kay, "Making Themselves Heard: The Impact of North American Olim on Israel Protest Politics," the Institute on American Jewish-Israeli Relations of the American Jewish Committee, October 1995, 3.

28. "American Jewish Congress Resolution on Aliyah," adopted at its Biennial Convention, Miami, Florida, May 14–19, 1968, SC Box A-93, 116, American Jewish Archives, Cincinnati. Maslow, "Report of the Executive Director, May 14–May 19, 1968," 34–35. As SNCC historian Clayborne Carson observed, "Jewish support for black advancement efforts declined after 1967 not only because blacks moved toward racial separatism but also because Jews moved toward increasingly group consciousness after the 1967 Arab-Israeli war." Carson, "The Politics of Relations," 140.

29. Forman, *Blacks in the Jewish Mind*, 193.

30. See Dollinger, *Quest for Inclusion*, chapter 7.

31. Roland B. Gittelsohn, "American Jews and Israel: Two Views," *Midstream* 18:2 (February 1972): 58, 59.

32. Gittelsohn, *Fire in My Bones*, 55, 56.

33. "Communities in Perplexity," 3. Gold, *Jews and the Urban Crisis*, 5.

34. Rosenberg, in Porter and Dreier, *Jewish Radicalism*, 8, 10.

35. Aquarian Minyan, Collection 86/6, Box 1, Folder "Newsletters, originals, Dec 1976–Sept. 1977," July 1977, 4, Magnes Archives, Berkeley, California.

36. Benyamin Neuberger, "W.E.B. Du Bois on Black Nationalism and Zionism," *The Jewish Journal of Sociology* 28:2 (December 1986): 142, 139. Originally quoted in NAACP, *The Crisis*, February 1919, 166. Also quoted in W.E.B. Du Bois, "The Negro's Fatherland," *Survey*, November 10, 1917, quoted in Robert A. Hill, "Black Zionism:

Marcus Garvey and the Jewish Question," appearing in V. P. Franklin, *African Americans and Jews in the Twentieth Century: Studies in Convergence and Conflict* (Columbia: University of Missouri Press, 1998), 48, 41. Friedman, *What Went Wrong?*, 78. Rev. J. W. H. Eason, at first UNIA convention in Madison Square Garden, New York, August 1920. Robert G. Weisbord and Richard Kazarian, *Israel in the Black American Perspective*, Contributions in Afro-American and African Studies (Westport, Conn.: Greenwood Press, 1985), 231. Diner, *In the Almost Promised Land*, 54–55, 76.

37. Van Deburg, *Modern Black Nationalism*, 177. Bayard Rustin, "Jews and Blacks: A Relationship Reexamined," *Midstream* 20:1 (January 1974): 11.

38. Malcolm X, "Malcolm Rejects Race Separation," *New York Times*, May 24, 1964, 61.

39. Stokely Carmichael, "Power and Racism," Southern Student Organizing Committee, Nashville, Tennessee, 7. Also quoted in Carson, "Black-Jewish Universalism," 187.

40. Carson, "Black-Jewish Universalism," 187. Theodore Draper, "The Fantasy of Black Nationalism," *Commentary* 48:3 (September 1969): 45. In 1966, Black Power founder Floyd B. McKissick wrote that the same Hillel quote "summarizes in a real sense what Black Power is all about," while Eldridge Cleaver simply affirmed, "The Jews did it. It worked. So now Afro-Americans must do the same thing."

41. Letter from Andrew J. Young to Irving M. Engel, Institute of Human Relations, American Jewish Committee, December 12, 1966, CSD 25–26, Box 4, Folder "Negroes–Misc.," YIVO Institute for Jewish Research, New York. Letter from Maximo Yagupsky to Simon [last name unknown], November 28, 1966, CSD 25–26, Box 4, Folder "Negroes—Misc., YIVO Institute for Jewish Research, New York.

42. Mendel Kohansky, "Reform Judaism Meets in Israel," *Midstream* 14:9 (November 1968): 56.

43. Helen Epstein, "Overseas Students in Israel: Problems and Possibilities," *Midstream* 16:2 (February 1970): 12, 13.

44. Ibid.

45. See Mark Kurlansky, *1968: The Year That Rocked the World* (New York: Random House, 2005).

46. Ina Friedman, "Talking about a Revolution (Again)," *The Jerusalem Report*, November 17, 2003, 45, 46. Erik Cohen, "The Black Panthers and Israeli Society," *Jewish Journal of Sociology* 14:1 (1972): 93–109.

Epilogue

1. Jonah Dov Pesner, "Why We're Marching: America's Journey for Justice," Religious Action Center of Reform Judaism blog, August 18, 2018, http://rac.org /blog/2015/08/18/why-we%E2%80%99re-marching-america%E2%80%99s-journey -justice-0.

2. "The RAC and the Civil Rights Movement," Religious Action Center of Reform Judaism, www.rac.org/rac-and-civil-rights-movement, excerpted from Albert Vorspan and David Saperstein, *Jewish Dimensions of Social Justice: Tough Moral Choices of Our Time* (New York: UAHC Press, 1998).

3. Marc Dollinger, *Quest for Inclusion: Jews and Liberalism in Modern America* (Princeton, N.J.: Princeton University Press, 2000), 164. For more on the complex challenges facing Reform rabbis in the South, see P. Allen Krause, Mark K. Bauman, and Stephen Krause, eds., *To Stand Aside or Stand Alone: Southern Reform Rabbis and the Civil Rights Movement* (Tuscaloosa, Ala.: University of Alabama Press, 2016).

4. Email to the author, June 1, 2017.

5. Melanie Eversley, "NAACP to Dismiss President, CEO Brooks," *USA Today*, May 19, 2017, www.usatoday.com/story/news/2017/05/19/naacp-dismiss-resident-ceo -brooks/101887188.

6. Fay S. Joyce, "Jackson Admits Saying 'Hymie' and Apologizes at a Synagogue," *New York Times*, February 27, 1984, www.nytimes.com/1984/02/27/us/jackson-admits -saying-hymie-and-apologizes-at-a-synagogue.html.

7. "The Nation of Islam," Anti-Defamation League website, www.adl.org /education/resources/profiles/the-nation-of-islam, accessed May 28, 2017.

8. *New York Times*, November 23, 1975, p. 9. "Black Group Supports Israel Denounces Arab Boycott Actions," Jewish Telegraphic Agency archive, September 12, 1975, www.jta.org/1975/09/12/archive/black-group-supports-israel-denounces -arab-boycott-actions.

9. Benjamin L. Hooks, "NAACP Sponsors Black Leadership Meeting," *The Crisis* 86, no. 9 (November 1979): 365.

10. John Herbers, "Aftermath of Andrew Young Affair: Blacks, Jews and Carter All Could Suffer Greatly," *New York Times*, September 6, 1979, p. 18, www.nytimes .com/1979/09/06/archives/aftermath-of-andrew-young-affair-blacks-jews-and -carter-all-could.html.

11. "About the Black Lives Matter Network," Black Lives Matter website, http:// blacklivesmatter.com/about, accessed June 3, 2017.

12. Ben Sales, "Black Lives Matter Platform Author Defends Israel 'Genocide' Claim," *Times of Israel*, August 10, 2016, www.timesofisrael.com/black-lives-matter -platform-author-defends-israel-genocide-claim.

13. Ibid.

14. Debra Nussbaum Cohen, "The Jewish Activist behind the Black Lives Matter Platform Calling Israel's Treatment of Palestinians 'Genocide,'" *Haaretz*, August 10, 2016, www.haaretz.com/world-news/americas/.premium-1.735865. "Counting Jews of Color in the United States," *Be'chol Lashon*, www.bechollashon.org/population /north_america/na_color.php, accessed August 15, 2017.

15. Ilana Kaufman, "Racism in the Jewish Community: The Uncomfortable Truth," ELI talk, August 4, 2015, www.youtube.com/watch?v=QCtBqbsZPLo.

16. Ibid.

17. Melanie Kaye/Kantrowitz, *The Colors of Jews: Racial Politics and Radical Dias-porism* (Bloomington: Indiana University Press, 2007). *American Jewish History* 100, no. 1 (January 2016): Kelly Amanda Train, "'Well, How Can You be Jewish *and* European?': Indian Jewish Experiences in the Toronto Jewish Community and the Creation of Congregation Bina"; Rebecca L. Davis, "'These Are a Swinging Bunch of People': Sammy Davis Jr., Religious Conversion, and the Color of Jewish Ethnic-ity"; Sarah Bunin Benor, "Black and Jewish: Language and Multiple Strategies for Self-Preservation"; Bruce A. Phillips, "Not Quite White: The Emergence of Jewish 'Ethnoburbs' in Los Angeles 1920–2010"; Lewis R. Gordon, "Rarely Kosher: Study-ing Jews of Color in North America." "Jew of Color," *Tablet*, www.tabletmag.com /tag/jews-of-color, accessed August 25, 2017. "Current Research and Projects," *Be'chol Lashon*, www.bechollashon.org/projects/research.php, accessed June 3, 2017.

18. "JOC Convening Schedule," JOC Convening website, May 1–3, 2016, http:// jocconvening.org/schedule.

Adams, Maurianne, and John H. Bracey. *Strangers and Neighbors: Relations between Blacks and Jews in the United States.* Amherst: University of Massachusetts Press, 1999.

Altshuler, Stuart. *From Exodus to Freedom: A History of the Soviet Jewry Movement.* Lanham, Md.: Rowman and Littlefield Publishers, 2005.

Bauman, Mark K., and Berkley Kalin. *The Quiet Voices: Southern Rabbis and Black Civil Rights, 1880s to 1990s.* Judaic Studies Series. Tuscaloosa: University of Alabama Press, 1997.

Beckerman, Gal. *When They Come for Us, We'll Be Gone: The Epic Struggle to Save Soviet Jewry.* Boston: Houghton Mifflin Harcourt, 2010.

Berman, Paul. *Blacks and Jews: Alliances and Arguments.* New York: Delacorte Press, 1994.

Bernstein, Philip. *To Dwell in Unity: The Jewish Federation Movement in America since 1960.* Philadelphia: Jewish Publication Society of America, 1983.

Biale, David, Michael Galchinsky, and Susannah Heschel. *Insider/Outsider: American Jews and Multiculturalism.* Berkeley: University of California Press, 1998.

Brink, William, and Louis Harris. *Black and White; a Study of U.S. Racial Attitudes Today.* New York: Simon and Schuster, 1967.

Brink, William, and Louis Harris. *The Negro Revolution in America; What Negroes Want, Why and How They Are Fighting, Whom They Support, What Whites Think of Them and Their Demands.* New York: Simon and Schuster, 1964.

Brodkin, Karen. *How Jews Became White Folks and What That Says about Race in America.* New Brunswick, N.J.: Rutgers University Press, 1998.

Carmichael, Stokely, and Charles V. Hamilton. *Black Power; the Politics of Liberation in America.* New York: Random House, 1967.

Carson, Clayborne. *In Struggle: SNCC and the Black Awakening of the 1960s.* Cambridge, Mass.: Harvard University Press, 1981.

Chafe, William H. *Civilities and Civil Rights: Greensboro, North Carolina and the Black Struggle for Freedom.* New York: Oxford University Press, 1981.

Chambers, Walter D. "Confidential Report, Muslim Meeting-September 8, 1959."

Cleaver, Kathleen, and George N. Katsiaficas. *Liberation, Imagination, and the Black Panther Party: A New Look at the Panthers and Their Legacy.* New York: Routledge, 2001.

Cohen, Henry. *Justice, Justice: A Jewish View of the Black Revolution.* Union Graded Series, Commission on Jewish Education of the Union of American Hebrew

Congregations and Central Conference of American Rabbis. Rev. ed. New York: Union of American Hebrew Congregations, 1969.

Danzger, Murray Herbert. *Returning to Tradition: The Contemporary Revival of Orthodox Judaism*. New Haven, Conn.: Yale University Press, 1989.

Diner, Hasia R. *In the Almost Promised Land: American Jews and Blacks, 1915–1935*. Baltimore, Md.: Johns Hopkins University Press, 1995.

Dinnerstein, Leonard. *Antisemitism in the United States*. American Problem Studies. New York: Holt, 1971.

Dollinger, Marc. *Quest for Inclusion: Jews and Liberalism in Modern American*. Princeton, N.J.: Princeton University Press, 2000.

Elkins, Dov Peretz. *A Tradition Reborn: Sermons and Essays on Liberal Judaism*. South Brunswick, N.J.: A. S. Barnes, 1973.

Evans, Sara M. *Born for Liberty: A History of Women in America*. New York: Free Press, 1989.

Fergus, Devin. *Liberalism, Black Power, and the Making of American Politics, 1965–1980*. Politics and Culture in the Twentieth-Century South. Athens: University of Georgia Press, 2009.

Fishman, Sylvia Barack. *A Breath of Life: Feminism in the American Jewish Community*. Brandeis Series in American Jewish History, Culture, and Life. Waltham, Mass.: Brandeis University Press, 1995.

Forman, Seth. *Blacks in the Jewish Mind: A Crisis of Liberalism*. New York: New York University Press, 1998.

Forster, Arnold, and B'nai B'rith. Anti-defamation League. *A Measure of Freedom, an Anti-Defamation League Report*. Garden City, N.Y.: Doubleday, 1950.

Franklin, V. P. *African Americans and Jews in the Twentieth Century: Studies in Convergence and Conflict*. Columbia: University of Missouri Press, 1998.

Freedman, Samuel G. *Jew vs. Jew: The Struggle for the Soul of American Jewry*. New York: Simon and Schuster, 2000.

Friedman, Murray, and Albert D. Chernin. *A Second Exodus: The American Movement to Free Soviet Jews*. Brandeis Series in American Jewish History, Culture, and Life. Waltham, Mass.: Brandeis University Press, 1999.

Friedman, Murray. *The Neoconservative Revolution: Jewish Intellectuals and the Shaping of Public Policy*. Cambridge: Cambridge University Press, 2005.

Friedman, Murray. *What Went Wrong? The Creation and Collapse of the Black-Jewish Alliance*. New York: Free Press, 1995.

Gal, Allon. *Envisioning Israel: The Changing Ideals and Images of North American Jews*. American Jewish Civilization Series. Jerusalem: Magnes Press, 1996.

Gamm, Gerald H. *Urban Exodus: Why the Jews Left Boston and the Catholics Stayed*. Cambridge, Mass.: Harvard University Press, 1999.

Gerson, Mark. *The Essential Neoconservative Reader*. Reading, Mass.: Addison Wesley, 1996.

Gitlin, Todd. *The Sixties: Years of Hope, Days of Rage*. Toronto; New York: Bantam, 1987.

Gittelsohn, Roland Bertram. *Fire in My Bones; Essays on Judaism in a Time of Crisis*. New York: Bloch, 1969.

Glock, Charles Y., Robert N. Bellah, and Randy Alfred. *The New Religious Consciousness*. Berkeley: University of California Press, 1976.

Goldberg, David Theo, and Michael Krausz. *Jewish Identity*. Philadelphia: Temple University Press, 1993.

Gordon, Jane Anna. *Why They Couldn't Wait: A Critique of the Black-Jewish Conflict over Community Control in Ocean Hill-Brownsville, 1967–1971*. New York: Routledge-Falmer, 2001.

Goren, Arthur A. *The Politics and Public Culture of American Jews*. The Modern Jewish Experience. Bloomington: Indiana University Press, 1999.

Gosse, Van, and Richard R. Moser. *The World the Sixties Made: Politics and Culture in Recent America*. Critical Perspectives on the Past. Philadelphia: Temple University Press, 2003.

Grant, Madison. *The Passing of the Great Race; or, the Racial Basis of European History*. New York: C. Scribner, 1916.

Greenberg, Cheryl Lynn. *Troubling the Waters: Black-Jewish Relations in the American Century*. Politics and Society in Twentieth-Century America. Princeton, N.J.: Princeton University Press, 2006.

Greenberg, Richard H. *Pathways: Jews Who Return*. Northvale, N.J.: Jason Aronson, 1997.

Greenberg, Simon, and Jewish Theological Seminary of America. *The Ordination of Women as Rabbis: Studies and Responsa*. Moreshet Series. New York: The Jewish Theological Seminary of America, 1988.

Gurock, Jeffrey S. *Orthodox Jews in America*. The Modern Jewish Experience. Bloomington: Indiana University Press, 2009.

Hampton, Henry, and Steven Fayer. *Voices of Freedom: An Oral History of the Civil Rights Movement from the 1950s through the 1980s*. New York: Bantam, 1990.

Harris, Louis, and Bert E. Swanson. *Black-Jewish Relations in New York City*. Praeger Special Studies in U.S. Economic and Social Development. New York: Praeger, 1970.

Herberg, Will. *Protestant, Catholic, Jew: An Essay in American Religious Sociology*. Garden City, N.Y.: Doubleday, 1955.

Herman, Simon N. *American Students in Israel*. Ithaca, N.Y.: Cornell University Press, 1970.

Hertzberg, Arthur. *The Jews in America: Four Centuries of an Uneasy Encounter: A History*. New York: Columbia University Press, 1997.

Heschel, Abraham Joshua. *The Insecurity of Freedom; Essays on Human Existence*. New York: Farrar, 1966.

Isaacs, Harold R. "Integration and the Negro Mood." *Commentary*, December 1962.

Islam, Nation of. *The Secret Relationship between Blacks and Jews*, vol. 1. New York: Latimer Associates, 1991.

Jacobs, Jill. *There Shall Be No Needy: Pursuing Social Justice through Jewish Law and Tradition*. Woodstock, Vt.: Jewish Lights, 2009.

Jacobson, Matthew Frye. *Roots Too: White Ethnic Revival in Post-Civil Rights America*. Cambridge, Mass.: Harvard University Press, 2006.

Kahane, Meir. *The Story of the Jewish Defense League*. 2nd ed. Jerusalem; Brooklyn, N.Y.: Institute for Publication of the Writings of Rabbi Meir Kahane, 2000.

Katz, Shlomo. *Negro and Jew: An Encounter in America*. New York: Macmillan, 1967.

Katznelson, Ira. *When Affirmative Action Was White: An Untold History of Racial Inequality in Twentieth-Century America*. New York: W.W. Norton, 2005.

Kaufman, Debra R. *Rachel's Daughters: Newly Orthodox Jewish Women*. New Brunswick, N.J.: Rutgers University Press, 1991.

Kaufman, Jonathan. *Broken Alliance: The Turbulent Times between Blacks and Jews in America*. New York: Scribner, 1988.

Kristol, Irving. *Neoconservatism: The Autobiography of an Idea*. Chicago: Elephant Paperbacks, 1999.

Lazin, Frederick A. *We Are Not One: American Jews, Israel, and the Struggle for Soviet Jewry*. David W. Belin Lecture in American Jewish Affairs. Ann Arbor: Jean and Samuel Frankel Center for Judaic Studies, University of Michigan, 2009.

Lederhendler, Eli. *New York Jews and the Decline of Urban Ethnicity, 1950–1970*. Modern Jewish History. 1st ed. Syracuse, N.Y.: Syracuse University Press, 2001.

Lederhendler, Eli. *The Six-Day War and World Jewry*. Studies and Texts in Jewish History and Culture. Bethesda: University Press of Maryland, 2000.

Leibovitz, Liel. *Aliya: Three Generations of American-Jewish Immigration to Israel*. New York: St. Martin's Press, 2006.

Levine, Hillel, and Lawrence Harmon. *The Death of an American Jewish Community: A Tragedy of Good Intentions*. New York: Free Press, 1992.

Lincoln, C. Eric. *The Black Muslims in America*. Boston: Beacon Press, 1961.

Lipsitz, George. *The Possessive Investment in Whiteness: How White People Profit from Identity Politics*. Rev. and exp. ed. Philadelphia: Temple University Press, 2006.

Lowi, Theodore J. *The End of Liberalism: The Second Republic of the United States*. 2nd ed. New York: W.W. Norton, 2010.

Magid, Shaul. *American Post-Judaism: Identity and Renewal in a Postethnic Society*. Religion in North America. Bloomington: Indiana University Press, 2013.

Maisel, Louis Sandy, Ira N. Forman, Donald Altschiller, and Charles Walker Bassett. *Jews in American Politics: Essays*. Lanham, Md.: Rowman and Littlefield, 2004.

Marcus, Jacob Rader. *United States Jewry, 1776–1985*. 4 vols. Detroit: Wayne State University Press, 1989.

Matthiessen, Peter. *In the Spirit of Crazy Horse*. New York: Penguin Books, 1992.

Matusow, Allen J. *The Unraveling of America: A History of Liberalism in the 1960s.*
Athens: University of Georgia Press, 2009.

Moore, Deborah Dash. *American Jewish Identity Politics.* Ann Arbor: University of
Michigan Press, 2008.

Morgan, Edward P. *The '60s Experience: Hard Lessons about Modern America.* Philadelphia: Temple University Press, 1991.

Morse, Arthur D. *While Six Million Died: A Chronicle of American Apathy.* New York:
Random House, 1968.

Muñoz, Carlos. *Youth, Identity, Power: The Chicano Movement.* Rev. and exp. ed. New
York: Verso, 2007.

Oppenheimer, Mark. *Knocking on Heaven's Door: American Religion in the Age of Counterculture.* New Haven, Conn.: Yale University Press, 2003.

Orbach, William W. *The American Movement to Aid Soviet Jews.* Amherst: University of
Massachusetts Press, 1979.

Phillips, William M. *An Unillustrious Alliance: The African American and Jewish American Communities.* Contributions in Afro-American and African Studies. New York:
Greenwood Press, 1991.

Podhoretz, Norman. *Why Are Jews Liberals?* New York: Doubleday, 2009.

Porter, Jack Nusan, and Peter Dreier. *Jewish Radicalism: A Selected Anthology.* New
York: Grove Press, 1973.

Prell, Riv-Ellen. *Prayer and Community: The Havurah in American Judaism.* Detroit:
Wayne State University Press, 1989.

Raider, Mark A. *The Emergence of American Zionism.* New York: New York University
Press, 1998.

Raphael, Marc Lee. *Jews and Judaism in the United States: A Documentary History.*
Library of Jewish Studies. New York: Behrman House, 1983.

Rieder, Jonathan. *Canarsie: The Jews and Italians of Brooklyn against Liberalism.* Cambridge, Mass.: Harvard University Press, 1985.

Ripley, William Zebina. *The Races of Europe: A Sociological Study.* Lowell Institute Lectures. New York: D. Appleton Johnson Reprint Corp., 1899.

Rubio, Philip F. *A History of Affirmative Action, 1619-2000.* Jackson: University Press of
Mississippi, 2001.

Salzman, Jack, and Cornel West. *Struggles in the Promised Land: Toward a History of
Black-Jewish Relations in the United States.* New York: Oxford University Press, 1997.

Sanua, Marianne Rachel. *Let Us Prove Strong: The American Jewish Committee, 1945-
2006.* Brandeis Series in American Jewish History, Culture, and Life. Waltham,
Mass.: Brandeis University Press, 2007.

Saperstein, Harold I., and Marc Saperstein. *Witness from the Pulpit: Topical Sermons,
1933-1980.* Lanham, Md.: Lexington Books, 2000.

Schulman, Bruce J. *Lyndon B. Johnson and American Liberalism: A Brief Biography with*

Documents. The Bedford Series in History and Culture. 2nd ed. New York: Palgrave Macmillan, 2007.

Seltzer, Robert M., and Norman J. Cohen. *The Americanization of the Jews.* Reappraisals in Jewish Social and Intellectual History. New York: New York University Press, 1995.

Shapiro, Edward S. *Crown Heights: Blacks, Jews, and the 1991 Brooklyn Riot.* Brandeis Series in American Jewish History, Culture, and Life. Waltham, Mass.: Brandeis University Press, 2006.

Sitkoff, Harvard. *The Struggle for Black Equality: 1954–1980.* New York: Hill and Wang, 1981.

Skrentny, John David. *The Minority Rights Revolution.* Cambridge, Mass.: Belknap Press, 2002.

Sorin, Gerald. *Tradition Transformed: The Jewish Experience in America.* The American Moment. Baltimore, Md.: Johns Hopkins University Press, 1997.

Staub, Michael E. *Torn at the Roots: The Crisis of Jewish Liberalism in Postwar America.* Religion and American Culture. New York: Columbia University Press, 2002.

Sundquist, Eric J. *Strangers in the Land: Blacks, Jews, Post-Holocaust America.* Cambridge, Mass.: Belknap Press, 2005.

Svonkin, Stuart. *Jews against Prejudice: American Jews and the Fight for Civil Liberties.* Columbia Studies in Contemporary American History. New York: Columbia University Press, 1997.

Van Deburg, William L. *Modern Black Nationalism: From Marcus Garvey to Louis Farrakhan.* New York: New York University Press, 1997.

Waxman, Chaim I. *American Aliya: Portrait of an Innovative Migration Movement.* Detroit: Wayne State University Press, 1989.

Weed, Perry L. *The White Ethnic Movement and Ethnic Politics.* Praeger Special Studies in U.S. Economic, Social, and Political Issues. New York: Praeger, 1973.

Weisbord, Robert G., and Richard Kazarian. *Israel in the Black American Perspective.* Contributions in Afro-American and African Studies. Westport, Conn.: Greenwood Press, 1985.

Wisse, Ruth R. *If I Am Not for Myself . . . : The Liberal Betrayal of the Jews.* New York: Free Press, 1992.

Zola, Gary Phillip, and Marc Dollinger. *American Jewish History: A Primary Source Reader.* Brandeis Series in American Jewish History, Culture, and Life. Waltham, Mass.: Brandeis University Press, 2014.

concern, 95; frank assessment of black-Jewish alliance, 92–93, 207n17; on JDL tactics, 148; on Nation of Islam, 41; opposition to public funds for private schools, 76; quota concerns, 69; and Soviet Jewry movement, 143

antisemitism, 7, 52, 64, 68, 130, 137, 160. *See also* black antisemitism

Antler, Joyce, 130

assimilation: collision with Jewish-centered activism, 5; debate over cost for Jewish identity, 3; and freedom of religion environment, 2; vs. identity politics, 102; Jewish adoption of white suburban racial prejudice, 29–30, 93; as Jewish claim of American identity, 4; Jewish move away from, 9, 17; Jewish youths' rejection of, 106–7; public schools as key to, 73; and student challenge to communal leadership, 117–18

Association for Jewish Studies (AJS), 114–15

Avineri, Shlomo, 151

Axelrod, Rabbi Albert, 127

Bakst, Jerry, 93

Bardin, Schlomo, 128

Bauman, Mark, 4

Beckerman, Gil, 8–9

Ben-Gurion, David, 137, 153–54, 155–56

Berrigan, Fr. Daniel, 127

Biale, David, 65

Bikel, Theodore, 124, 161

Birnbaum, Jacob, 135, 140, 141, 142

Bisk, Tsvi, 118, 122, 124

Black Americans to Support Israel Committee (BASIC), 181

black antisemitism: from black nationalists, 12, 200n26, 209n28;

in Black Power's criticism of Israel, 160; and Jesse Jackson, 179–80; and Jewish discrimination against blacks, 35; Jewish Left's criticism of, 162; Jewish minimizing of, 82, 90, 94–96; Nation of Islam, 39, 40, 41, 44–45; overview, 7

black-Arab alliance (1970s), 159

black-Jewish alliance: black nationalists as destroyers of, 12, 15, 89–90; Black Power's transformation of, 7–8, 81–82, 89–91; challenge to filiopietistic accounts of, 29–34, 90, 175–78; characteristics of turn-of-21st-century relationship, 183–84; cultural appropriation issue, 186–87; differences in American experience and, 32–35; Great Society's impact on, 52–56; irony of organizational split leading to greater influence on Jewish community, 151; NAACP's move away from, 88–89; overview, xiv–xv; post-1970s distant relationship, 179–80; power differential and loss of, 100; reframing of Selma march in 2015, 178; reinventing the 1960s alliance in the early 1970s, 18–21; strains on in 1950s, 27–38; tensions with moderate black leadership during rise of Black Power, 85; whiteness status for Jews as threat to, 63. *See also* civil rights movement

Black Lives Matter (BLM), 187–91

black Muslims, views countering them as threat to Jews, 40–41. *See also* Nation of Islam

black nationalism, 27–46; AJCongress's support for, 98; criticism of Jewish gradualism and tokenism, 34–39; early Jewish support for (1950s),

29–34; general American disapproval of, 84, 207n7; Jewish fears of white backlash from, 89, 208n19; and New Pluralism, 110; purge of Jews from leadership in civil rights organizations, 63, 86–87, 95, 98, 99–100, 106, 109; and support for affirmative action, 60; ultimate rejection of, 156–57

Black Panther Party (BPP), 81, 84, 116, 146–47, 160, 161–62

Black Power movement: affinity with Zionism, 82, 101–2, 151, 152, 157, 162–63, 165–70, 218n13, 218–19n15; anti-Zionism after Six-Day War, 157–62; challenge to consensus-based liberalism, 12, 45–46, 86–87; Clark's anticipation of, 37; and cultural pluralism, 109–11; definition of, 5–6; early responses from Jewish community, 40, 41–45, 98–99; embrace of cultural nationalism, 18; emergence of, 80–81; and federal aid to Jewish religious schools, 73–74; and first wave feminism, 129; Gittelson's advocacy for, 165–66; Great Society's common conclusions with, 49; history of, 82–86; and identity politics influence on ethnic activism, 7–12, 15–18, 90, 103, 109, 183; influence on identity politics in Israel, 9–10, 170–72; inspiration for African American studies programs, 112–13; and JDL, 144–47; Jewish opposition to, 86–89; and Jewish retreat from civil rights movement, 92–93, 208n24; and Jewish return to tradition, 107, 119; and Jewish social advocacy, 7–9, 17, 81–82; Jewish support for, 82, 89–103; lack of numerical support from African

Americans, 44–45, 84–85; overall influence on ethnic activism, 17–18, 109; predictions of rise of, 38–39; primary source Jewish support for, 15–16; and promotion of ethnic identity, 82, 98, 105, 125; as rejection of consensus-based approach, 12; transformation of civil rights alliances, 19–20; use of violence issue compared to Zionism, 156. *See also* Nation of Islam

Blaustein, Jacob, 154
Bookbinder, Hyman, 56, 183
Brandeis, Louis, 153
Brickner, Rabbi Balfour, 105
Briskin, Rabbi Charles, 177
Brodkin, Karen, 64–65
Brooks, Cornell, 178
Brooks, Tom, 38
Brown v. Board of Education, 28, 37

Caplovitz, David, 96
Carlebach, Rabbi Shlomo, 125
Carmichael, Stokely, 19, 83, 97, 99, 157, 160, 169
Caron, Herbert S., 139
Carson, Clayborne, 14–15, 158, 220n28
Central Conference of American Rabbis (CCAR), 6, 101–2, 137, 153, 165
Chabad, 120, 141
Chambers, Walter D., 43
Chinitz, Rabbi Jacob, 102
Christian religious leaders: criticism of Israel over Six-Day War, 219n18; support for Soviet Jewry from, 138, 140

church-state separation, 2, 72–79
Civil Rights Act (1964), 53, 173
Civil Rights Memorial, 173–74
civil rights movement: and balkanization of American life, 7; black

Jewish support for Black Power, 48; social mobility as found in access to power, 99; and white status for Jews, 52–53, 63–69; working-class white opposition to, 60–61

Green, Arthur, 127

Greenberg, Cheryl Lynn, 13

Greenberg, Rabbi Irving "Yitz," 114

group-based identity politics. *See* identity politics

group-based liberalism. *See* Great Society

Gurin, David, 123

Gurock, Jeffrey, 131

Halpern, Ben, 77, 99

Hamilton, Charles V., 101

Hansen, Marcus Lee, 106–7

Harel, Isser, 133

Harman, Abraham, 163

Hasidism, 115, 125

Haynes, Bruce D., 190

Hebrew, teaching of, 122, 164

Hebrew University, 163

Herberg, Will, 107

Hertzberg, Rabbi Arthur, 81, 99, 150, 157, 163

Herzl, Theodor, 101

Heschel, Rabbi Abraham Joshua, xiv, 28–29, 89–90, 138–39, 174, 177

Hillel chapter, UC Berkeley, 115–16

Himmelfarb, Milton, 121

Hirsch, Rabbi Richard, 53–54

Hochbaum, Rabbi Jerry, 55, 102

Hochbaum, Martin, 65–66

Holocaust consciousness, xi–xii, 135, 154

Hooks, Benjamin L., 182–83

Horn, Philip, 147

Hottelet, Richard C., 160

House of Love and Prayer (HLP), 125

Howe, Irving, 66–67

identity. *See* ethnic identity; intersectionality in black-Jewish relations

identity politics: vs. assimilation, 102; and balkanization of American life, 7; black nationalists as exemplars of, 7–8; and Black Power's overall influence on ethnic activism, 7–12, 15–18, 90, 103, 109, 183; blurring of religious and secular lines for Jews, 105; as consequence of failure in individual rights equality, 48; and cultural pluralism, 111; emergence of, 5; as energizing influence on liberalism, 18–19; Gittelson's adoption of, 165–66; importance for social justice results, 98–101; in Israel, 9–10, 151, 152, 158, 170–72, 220n28; JDL and Black Power, 147; Jewish embrace of, 7–12, 15–17, 48–49, 59–60, 90, 103, 116, 121; 1960s emergence of, 5–6; in Soviet Jewry support movement, 133–34, 136, 138–39. *See also* Black Power movement

individual rights-based liberalism: vs. affirmative action programs, 52, 60; civil rights organizations' focus on, 47–48; and conservative concern over Great Society, 51; vs. group-based rights in racial reforms, 71–72; JDL's criticism of, 147; Johnson's critique of, 51; Orthodox Jewish support for, 55

Innis, Roy, 168, 215n5

institutional racism: and black activist rejection of Jewish help, 88; as cause for culture of poverty, 57–58; deep-seated nature of, 48; equal opportunity as insufficient to address, 51, 60, 61–62; focus on African Americans, 32–33; Jewish

King, Martin Luther Jr.: vs. Black Power movement, 80, 81, 83; consensus-based approach to social justice, 12; individually based legal equality as goal, 47, 60; and Jackson, 179; on liberalism's failure to enact fundamental change, 86; on Six-Day War, 160–61; on Soviet Jewry, 139; welcome of Jews into civil rights movement, 183

Klavan, Rabbi Israel, 76–77

Kolack, Sol, 88

Lachman, Seymour, 95, 110

Lazere, Haskell L., 147

Lelyveld, Rabbi Arthur J., 97, 161

Levine, Rabbi Allan, 137, 155–56

Levine, Hillel, 117, 142–43

Levine, Irving, 110–11

Levine, Naomi, 65–66

Lewis, Oscar, 57

liberal gradualism: affirmative action as answer to, 59–60, 61; and black activist rejection of Jewish help, 88, 97; current black activist rejection of, 184; and failure to reach racial inequality, 27, 33, 34, 36; Jewish support for, 36; Kahane's criticism of, 145; as leading to paternalism, 37; rise of Black Power in response to, 83

liberalism: challenge to implosion theory for 1960s, 18; complicity in institutional racism, xii; conflict over affirmative action, 60; crime issue and concerns about Johnson's, 71, 205n41; as enemy to African Americans, 100–101; filiopietistic accounts of Jewish activism, 29–34, 90, 175–78; identity politics as energizing influence, 18–19; inability to address systemic racial

inequality, 7, 35–36; Jewish critique and abandonment of (1960s), 6, 70–71; Jewish political activism focus on universalist goals, 3–4; King's critique of Jewish, 86; and Orthodox challenge to church-state separation, 76–77; voter rejection of in late 1960s, 53, 70, 217n34. *See also* consensus-based liberalism; individual rights-based liberalism

liberal paternalism, 22–23, 27, 33, 37–38, 51, 85, 184

Lichtenstein, Rabbi Aharon, 140–41

Lin, Maya, 173–74

Lincoln, C. Eric, 45, 82–83

Lipsitz, George, 65

Littman, Sol, 92, 93

Loveland, Kristin, 114

Lowell, A. Lawrence, 68

Lowi, Theodore, 18

Malcolm X, 20, 39–40, 44, 80, 83, 84, 169

March on Washington (1963), 160–61, 174

Martin, Waldo E. Jr., 14

Maslow, Will, 61–62, 94, 161

Matusow, Allen J., 18, 51

Mayfield, Julian, 38

Miller, Rabbi Judea B., 95–96

Miller, Rabbi Uri, 138

Million Man March (1989), 180–81

Mintz, Alan, 127

Moldover, Edward D., 66

Moore, Cecil, 95

Moynihan, Daniel Patrick, 58–59

Muhammad, Elijah, 39–40, 42, 43–44, 45

Muhammad, Wallace Deen (son of Elijah), 180

Muhammad, Wallace Fard, 39

NAACP, 28, 86, 88–89, 173, 178, 183, 184

Nashim, Ezrat, 9

National Council of Jewish Women, 74–76

National Council of Synagogue Youth (NCSY), 144

nationalism. *See* black nationalism; Jewish nationalism

National Jewish Community Relations Advisory Council (NJCRAC), 69, 148–49

Nation of Islam (NOI): African American perspectives on, 44–45; and American Jews, 39–46; early Jewish support for, 97; Jewish alienation from, 180; Jewish organizational tolerance of, 29, 41–45; as part of Black Power movement, 80, 81, 84

New Left, 18, 157–58, 162

New Pluralism, 72, 109–12

Newton, Huey P., 84

nonviolent vs. violent approach to oppression, 155, 156, 157, 166

Novak, William, 9, 115, 129

Orbach, William, 133

Orenstein, Amaryah, 141, 142, 146

Orthodox Jewish community: criticism of Great Society, 55; emergence as ethnic pressure group, 9, 11; feminist movement in, 131; quota concerns, 69; Reform challenges to Israel's, 170–71; and religious education, 74, 76, 112, 120; response to Six-Day War and Zionist revival, 164; role in religious-ethnic revival, 120; and Soviet Jewry movement, 136, 140–41; support for Black Power from, 102; support for civil rights movement, 28

Palestine Liberation Organization (PLO), 181–82

Palestinians, African American support for, 182–83, 185, 188

parochial schools, federal aid to, 72–74, 75, 108, 121, 122

paternalism, liberal. *See* liberal paternalism

Pawley, James, 31–32, 42

Pesner, Rabbi Jonah Dov, 173

Pfeffer, Leo, 69, 123

Phillips, William M., 13–14

Pinsker, Leon, 101–2

Podhoretz, Norman, 1, 5, 11, 71–72

Polier, Shad, 41–42, 45, 57, 90–91, 94, 156–57

Porth, Jason, 119

poverty alleviation: and culture of poverty, 57–59; War on Poverty, 49–51, 52–54, 65–66, 78

prejudice vs. discrimination, and Jewish response to black antisemitism, 94–95

Priesand, Sally, 131

Prinz, Rabbi Joachim, 36, 120, 160–61, 174

prophetic mandate in Judaism, xi–xii, 6, 28, 96, 173–74

public education, importance for protection of religious liberty, 73, 77, 120–21, 122

quotas, affirmative action, 52, 68–69

Raab, Earl, 7, 11, 110

Rabbinical Council of America, 76–77

racial discrimination: affirmative action as method to root out, 60; Ashkenazi discrimination against Mizrahi Jews, 171–72; and group-based thinking, 52; by Jews against blacks, 30–32, 92, 123–24, 160; Jews as victims of, 2, 64; vs. prejudice, 94–95